EMERGING FINANCIAL MARKETS IN THE GLOBAL ECONOMY

EMERGING FINANCIAL MARKETS IN THE GLOBAL ECONOMY

Editors

Larry Sawers
Daniel Schydlowsky
David Nickerson
American University, Washington, DC

World Scientific
Singapore • New Jersey • London • Hong Kong

Published by

World Scientific Publishing Co. Pte. Ltd.

P O Box 128, Farrer Road, Singapore 912805

USA office: Suite 1B, 1060 Main Street, River Edge, NJ 07661

UK office: 57 Shelton Street, Covent Garden, London WC2H 9HE

British Library Cataloguing-in-Publication Data
A catalogue record for this book is available from the British Library.

EMERGING FINANCIAL MARKETS IN THE GLOBAL ECONOMY

ISBN 981-02-3845-2

Printed in Singapore by Regal Press (S) Pte. Ltd.

ABOUT THE CONTRIBUTORS

Philip Bartholomew was on leave from being the Director of Bank Research, Office of the Comptroller of the Currency when he wrote his chapter and is now Senior Economist, House Banking Committee, U.S. Congress.

Marguerite S. Berger is Chief of the Microenterprise Unit at the Interamerican Development Bank in Washington.

Joel Bergsman is a consultant on foreign direct investment, private sector development, and international trade and industrialization policy. He recently retired from the International Finance Corporation where he was Manager of the Foreign Investment Advisory Service.

Stephen Guisinger is Professor of International Management at the School of Management, University of Texas at Dallas.

Cécile Lapenu is a post-doctoral Research Fellow at the International Food Policy Research Institute in Washington.

José Luque was President of the Lima Stock Exchange and Vice-President of the Association of Stock Exchanges of Spain and Latin America when he wrote the chapter for this book. He is now a lawyer in private practice.

Michael Marrese is now with Global Emerging Markets, Chase Manhattan Bank, London. Prior to that, he was Section Chief and Senior Economist at the International Monetary Fund.

Bart Minten is an Assistant Professor at the University of Leuven, Belgium.

David Nickerson is Associate Professor of Economics at the American University in Washington.

Eliane Ralison is Research Analyst at the Ministère de la Recherche Scientifique, Antananarivo, Madagascar.

Désiré Randrianaivo is Director, Department of Rural Development at the Ministère de la Recherche Scientifique, Antananarivo, Madagascar.

Jean-Claude Randrianaivo is Socio-economist at the Ministère de la Recherche Scientifique, Antananarivo, Madagascar.

Larry Sawers is Professor of Economics at the American University in Washington.

Daniel Schydlowsky is Professor of Economics at the American University in Washington.

Andras Uthoff is with the Comisión Ecónomica para América Latina in Santiago, Chile.

Eric Weaver is founder and Executive Director of Lenders for Community Development, a multi-bank community development corporation in San Jose, California.

Gary Whalen is Senior Economist at the Bank Research Division of the Office of the Comptroller of the Currency.

Manfred Zeller is a Research Fellow at the International Food Policy Research Institute in Washington.

CONTENTS

Part One

Introduction

FINANCIAL MARKETS AND ECONOMIC DEVELOPMENT

Larry Sawers, David Nickerson, and Daniel Schydlowsky

The rapid emergence of active financial markets in a number of developing countries during the 1990s is a momentous phenomenon. Economists and economic policy makers have long been aware that economic development is impossible without adequate financial flows, but most developing countries until recently so manipulated and repressed their financial markets that finance for many worthwhile investments could not be found. The dramatic increase in the influence of neo-liberal thinking and *laissez-faire* governance in developing countries has recently led to reforms of the capital market in dozens of developing countries. Many other countries are anxiously studying their successful neighbors in order to adopt policies, programs, and regulations that have a proven track record. Investors in the industrialized countries have responded by flooding the most flourishing emerging capital markets with hundreds of billions of dollars in the last few years.

Many of the financial market reforms that have received so much attention by policy makers, economists, and investors do not touch the very poor. To make the poor a part of the process of economic development, institutions that are specifically designed to make small loans to microenterprises are required. In the last few years, there has been rapid institutional innovation and a dramatic increase in lending to very small enterprises.

At the same time that capital markets in developing countries have blossomed, the so-called transition economies are seeking to develop their capital markets as well. Indeed, the competition to woo investors among countries traditionally categorized as Third World and the transition economies has been an impetus for capital market liberalization in both groups of countries. Before the collapse of the Soviet Union, capital markets did not exist there nor in the Soviet bloc of Eastern Europe. Developing viable financial markets from scratch, and defining and enforcing property rights in law that would allow those capital markets to function are perhaps the most important challenges facing economies in transition. Until the financing of investment is possible, growth and development in the transition economies will remain strangled. Without property rights that are properly specified and consistently enforced, capital will never be forthcoming. Investors in the industrialized countries have rewarded progress in this direction in the most successful transitional economies, such as those of Poland and the Czech Republic, with billions of dollars over the last few years. Policy makers in lagging economies, such as those of Albania, Bulgaria, and Mongolia, are hoping to learn how to restructure their financial markets and legal codes so as to attract a share of international capital flows.

Thinking about Finance and Development

In the 1950s when policy makers began to turn their attention to the economic development of the poor countries of the world and modern development economics was first jelling as a field, economists were convinced that a large supply of capital was the key to growth. The conventional wisdom of the day was embodied in the famous Harrod–Domar model, which, under certain assumptions, showed that growth was solely dependent upon capital flows. Development strategies were molded around the necessity of raising national saving rates. Many economists, despairing at the possibility for increasing saving in countries that were desperately poor, hoped for foreign aid and foreign direct investment as sources of capital.

Development economists' early fixation on capital weakened by the 1970s. The petroleum price hikes produced an avalanche of financial resources in the petroleum-exporting countries that could not be absorbed there. Global capital markets were soon awash in recycled petrodollars so that real (*ex post*) rates of interest on sovereign debt were very low and, at times, actually negative. Many developing countries found that it was easy to borrow from commercial banks in the industrialized countries, to the extent that finance ministers later complained that they had been pressured to borrow more than was prudent by aggressive loan officers in the Citibanks of the world. Some countries such as Tanzania had enjoyed a flood of foreign aid in the 1960s and 1970s, but were still not able to take off. Hence it was clear that there was something other than the lack of capital standing in these countries' paths to development. In other countries, especially the Asian tigers, growth itself seemed to generate increases in saving rates as a by-product of the development process. The lack of capital no longer appeared to be the binding constraint on economic development that it had ten or 20 years earlier.

Developments in economic modeling and econometrics seemed to confirm this downgrading of capital's importance. Formal growth models produced by economists from the late 1950s showed that increases in physical capital played only a small role in explaining growth. As these models grew increasingly sophisticated and consistent, they became even more convincing. Instead of emphasizing physical capital, economists began to stress the importance of human capital and the quality of labor, technological progress, and increases in capacity utilization. Even later, allocative efficiency arising from reduced transaction costs, clearer definition and firmer enforcement of property rights, and macroeconomic stability came to be considered of central importance.

As capital scarcity moved down in economists' ranking of obstacles to development, developing countries became less desperate for foreign direct investment (FDI). Moreover, hostility toward multinational corporations (MNCs) had been mounting since the 1960s, fueled by the belief that they were the chief agents of the industrialized countries in their efforts to dominate and exploit the poor countries of the world. Economists, especially in Latin America and Africa, other social scientists, and political leaders in the less developed countries (LDCs) excoriated and villanized the MNCs. They were vilified for repatriating excess profits, subverting the local culture, displacing national investors, demanding exorbitant tax breaks, manipulating local politics, overcharging for patents, selling inappropriate goods, and introducing inappropriate technology. If these costs of direct investment were onerous and if FDI's benefits were small because capital was plentiful, then limitations on MNCs appear legitimate. It became standard procedure to impose stringent controls on foreign investment in developing countries: foreigners were excluded from entire industries; companies were required to hire and train local managers and steadily increase the share of local shareholders; restrictions on profit repatriation and royalty payments were commonplace and inputs had to be purchased from domestic suppliers rather than imported. Even the nationalization of MNCs became increasingly frequent. Not surprisingly, the countries with the most onerous restrictions on foreign investment found that they had the most difficulty in attracting foreign capital. Some multinationals actually packed up and left rather than submit to tough restrictions.

During the 1980s, economists began to realize that they had gone too far in dismissing the importance of physical capital in development. In sharp contrast to the 1970s, the 1980s were a decade of capital scarcity for much of the developing world, especially Latin American and Africa. Continued economic growth, high domestic saving rates, and massive import of capital from Japan put the East Asian Tigers and Tiger Cubs into a very different category. Interest rates soared as the United States began absorbing capital from the world's financial markets and banks refused to throw good money after bad as one developing country after another found that they could no longer service their debt. The balance of trade surpluses — and the fiscal and monetary austerity needed to produce these surpluses — which the debt crisis forced on many developing countries was an obvious obstacle to growth. The need to obtain fresh infusions of capital was clear and the inability or unwillingness of global financial markets to supply those funds underlined the need for economic reform.

The dramatic increase in the influence of neo-liberal thinking and *laissez-faire* governance in developing countries toward the end of the 1980s and into the 1990s played a crucial role in the changing attitudes toward capital. In the 1960s and 1970s, governments in the developing countries were expected to take the leading role in the development process. Typically, the government owned and operated all formal financial institutions. Stringent controls on FDI and domestic capital markets did not seem anomalous since most aspects of the economy were highly regulated. In the countries now in transition, the government played an even more dominating role. Neo-liberalism rejected this governmental activism and placed its faith in the market, including the capital market. The spread of liberal political philosophy made intricate controls on capital flows appear increasingly anachronistic.

In addition, successes with trade liberalization encouraged the notion that financial market liberalization might also be beneficial for similar reasons. As economists developed a convincing explanation for why early financial market liberalizations in Chile and Argentina in the late 1970s had failed so spectacularly, confidence in the success of future liberalizations grew. Liberalization of domestic financial markets in the United States and the United Kingdom appeared to spur an investment boom that continues to the present. In the late 1980s and early 1990s, the liberalization of foreign capital flows in Europe was also an apparent success. The collapse of the Soviet Union, where capital markets were not permitted, left the world with a single superpower and a single model of economic development. The inability of the Japanese economy to grow during the 1990s provided further confirmation that rigid control of capital markets was dysfunctional in the new globalized economy.

By the 1980s, and especially the 1990s, there was sufficient data in many developing countries to allow the application of formal growth modeling that previously had been used almost exclusively on data from industrialized countries. These new studies showed that physical capital formation was far more important in explaining growth in the developing economies than in the industrialized countries where production is more capital intensive and the returns to capital are more modest. A widely publicized study in 1986 demonstrated that over half of the growth in *per capita* GDP in developing countries was accounted for by increases in physical capital (Chenery, Robinson, and Syrquin 1986, Table 2–2). Later studies showed that in countries where growth was relatively slow, virtually all of the growth in *per capita* income was accounted for by increases in physical capital. Furthermore, the correlation between economic growth and fixed capital formation among developing countries was widely noted.

This rediscovery by economists that capital was vital to economic development coincided with a remarkable change in attitudes among political leaders in the developing world toward FDI. M NCs came to be viewed as heros rather than villains. Countries that had been openly hostile to foreign investment, such as Argentina, Chile, China, Egypt, India, Jamaica, Mexico, the Philippines, and Turkey actively courted MNCs. Rules that had restricted FDI were quietly repealed in country after country. The effort in the United Nations to draft a code of conduct for multinationals was quietly shelved. Instead, provisions in the Uruguay Round of the General Agreement on Tariffs and Trade (GATT) mandating the phasing out of local content, production, sales, export, and technology controls were negotiated. Expropriations of foreign properties in developing countries, formerly almost a routine, became rare. Many developing countries passed laws or even rewrote their constitutions so as to disallow expropriation of foreign assets.

The debt crisis itself encouraged a preference for FDI instead of debt. Multinationals, after all, could repatriate profit only if and when they were earning any. In contrast, debt had to be serviced whether or not the project financed by that debt generated any income.

Complementing the change in attitudes toward FDI was a revolution in thinking about equity markets. Before the 1990s, trading in developing country equities was extremely limited. Most companies in developing countries were public enterprises, family businesses, or parts of an industrial/financial group whose equity shares were not publicly traded. Many developing countries had a stock exchange, but few companies were listed, trading volume was low, and few if any foreigners were willing and/or permitted to participate. A decade after the debt crisis broke out, equity markets were being established in one developing country after another and existing equity markets experienced decisive transformation and explosive growth. Just as the hostility to the operations of foreign corporations within the LDCs waned, so too did the animosity to foreign ownership of shares in local businesses. Furthermore, as trade regimes were liberalized and local enterprises became increasingly subject to the pressures of global competition, businesses in the developing countries needed more capital than local financial markets could easily satisfy. In some LDCs, most notably Chile and Argentina, government pension reform provided substantial impetus to equity market growth since individuals now had individual retirement accounts that could be invested in equities. Privatization further spurred equity market growth: government enterprises were simply too big to sell to one or a handful of local investors. Some countries were driven by political considerations (reforming pension systems or creating citizen-capitalists) to divest their public enterprises to their own citizens by selling or distributing equity shares.

The increase in foreign capital flowing to the developing countries in the 1990s has been truly dramatic. Between 1989 and 1997, private capital flows grew from $27 billion to $256 billion (World Bank 1998, p. 9; 1991, p. 24). In those nine years, $1.2 trillion in long term private capital flowed into developing countries, and over $500 billion of that flow was in 1996 and 1997 alone. FDI, which averaged $7 billion annually in the late 1970s and $11 billion between 1980 and 1986, topped $120 billion in 1997 (World Bank 1987, p. 33). The share of global FDI going to the developing countries grew from 21 percent in 1990 to 36 percent in 1997 (World Bank 1998, p. 19). The growth of bond and equity markets in emerging economies in the 1990s was truly breathtaking. Sales of bonds issued by developing countries and placed abroad went from $100 million to $54 billion between 1990 and 1997. Portfolio equity flows rose tenfold in that period, from $3.2 billion to $32.5 billion. These figures amount to revolutionary changes in the way investment is financed in the developing countries.

This radical restructuring of global financial markets did not come without serious problems. In the middle of 1997, a financial crisis began in Thailand and quickly spread to Malaysia, Indonesia, and South Korea. Japan's economy had stalled earlier in the decade and the rest of East Asia soon fell into a major depression. In 1998, the crisis spread to Russia and threatened Brazil (and thus the rest of Latin America). The world held its breath, fearing the contagion might spread. The massive capital flows that had so recently been celebrated now appeared to be a mixed blessing. Malaysia reimposed controls on capital movements, and economists, finance ministers, and bankers everywhere debated how to restructure the global financial architecture. Whether the Asian crisis will produce a mere tweaking of the world's financial markets or a major restructuring remains to be seen.

Even before the Asian crisis began, the enormous increase in capital flowing to developing countries as a whole did not produce universal prosperity. Only a handful of countries captured the bulk of the capital flows. For example, throughout the 1990s, ten developing countries received roughly three-quarters of all FDI going to developing countries (World Bank 1998, p. 20). Countries that made it into the top ten recipients in 1991, 1994, and 1997 included Mexico, China, Malaysia, Argentina, Indonesia, and Brazil. Other countries that were among the top ten recipients in at least one of those years were Venezuela, Thailand, Turkey, Hungary, Peru, Nigeria, Poland, Chile, and India. Among these fifteen countries, FDI is farther concentrated. China, Brazil, and Mexico together received over half of all FDI going to developing countries in both 1994 and 1997; China's share alone was 39 percent in 1994 and still 30 percent in 1997. Other than China, most recipients of FDI were middle income countries with fairly successful liberalization programs. By the end of the decade, India had begun to receive substantial amounts of FDI. The only country in Africa to receive a large portion of the FDI was Nigeria — investment there was primarily in petroleum extraction. Other forms of capital flows were also highly concentrated among a few lucky countries.

While global financial markets were being transformed in the 1990s, there were also dramatic changes in informal financial markets in developing countries. Growth rates of microfinance exceeded those in formal financial markets. In Bangladesh, the Grameen Bank grew ever more successful at making micro loans and the Grameen model was replicated in scores of countries in Asia, Latin America, and Africa. By lending small amounts to a member of a small group, each of whose members was jointly responsible for repaying the loan, the Grameen Bank was able to overcome the problems of asymmetric information and lack of collateral that had plagued earlier attempts to extend credit to the very poor. On a theoretical level, economists made great strides in analyzing the problems of informal finance. Numerous empirical studies of informal financial markets have enabled us to gain a better understanding of the credit markets that the poor face in the developing world. In the 1980s, microfinance was the province of aid agencies and concessional lenders. By the 1990s, commercial lenders in many countries had discovered how to profitably lend to very poor entrepreneurs operating in the informal sector.

The Plan of the Book

In May of 1996, a conference entitled "Emerging Capital Markets: Implications for Economic Development," organized by the editors (with the help of our colleague, Professor Maria Floro), was held on the campus of American University in Washington, D.C. The conference drew more than two hundred participants, including representatives from the World Bank, IMF and numerous ministries of finance, as well as academics and finance practitioners. The following chapters in this volume are among the best of the thirty or so papers presented at the conference. Each analyzes an important aspect of capital market development in developing and transition economies. Together, they present a coherent analysis of the important problems in financing the development in emerging economies. While these papers were written in 1996, authors were encouraged to update their work in preparation for the publication of this volume, and several of them undertook major revisions.

In most developing and transition countries, the majority of the resources for economic development come from domestic savers. Perhaps the most important reason why most households save, especially in the more prosperous economies, is to finance consumption after retirement from the active labor force. In most industrialized countries and in many emerging economies, saving for retirement is used to finance the government's budget deficit. In keeping with its free market philosophy, Chile in the early 1980s began to direct retirement savings into private equity markets. This has provided a crucial source of financing for Chile's growth, the highest in Latin America in the last fifteen years. These reforms, are said to have put the pension system on a sound fiscal basis, helped to reduce the fiscal deficit and raised the nation's saving rates to very high levels. Some countries, for example, Argentina, have modeled their pension systems along Chilean lines and still others (including the United States) are considering implementing reforms that utilize a key aspect (individual equity accounts) of the new Chilean system.

The Chilean reforms have attracted the world's attention and received extraordinary praise. Andras Uthoff in "Pension Reform in Chile" shows that much of this praise ignores many very serious shortcomings of the Chilean system. First, the new reforms, by basing pensions on individual savings accounts, turn away from a concern for equity and social solidarity. Second, the reforms were expected to increase, and are said to have increased the nation's saving rate, but this is based on certain assumptions of neo-classical economics that have not and cannot be tested empirically. Moreover, despite optimistic expectations, the population coverage of the pension system has not increased significantly because the very poor do not have the means and the affluent do not have the incentive to join the system. The net increase in national saving must also reflect the fiscal deficit, which has actually been worsened, not improved, by the reforms. Workers contributing to the pension system tend to put their money into the newly authorized accounts while those remaining in the old system are likely to draw on their pensions that are still funded out of the government budget. The impact of the reforms on the fiscal balance and the country's saving rate are thus not as rosy as sometimes portrayed. Furthermore, administrative costs continue to absorb a very large share of pension contributions (although less than before). One of the reasons for this is the lack of competition among the firms that invest the individual equity accounts. Most of the pension funds are invested in government bonds or in the booming stock market. Thus, the reforms have helped to bid up stock prices, but have contributed little to long term investment or infrastructure. The high yields achieved in the early stages of the reforms are therefore unsustainable. As the stock market has slumped in the last few years, yields on individual retirement accounts have become negative. Uthoff finishes his paper with a number of suggestions of how to reform the reforms.

Before the 1980s, equity markets in developing countries played a trivial role in financing economic development. As late as 1990, foreign investors bought only just over $3 billion in developing country equity shares, but three years later, that figure had mushroomed to $45 billion, and has since remained strong despite the Mexican crisis of 1995 and the Asian crisis of 1997–1998 (World Bank 1998, p. 9). Domestic investors also snapped up shares in local companies. Equity markets were often the favored vehicle for the privatization of state-owned enterprises. Scores of developing countries scrambled to put in place the institutions that would permit active trading in publicly held shares. "The Peruvian Capital Market" by José Luque is an account of one country's efforts to create a market in equities. Since 1990, the Lima Stock Exchange has shown enormous growth, its annual trading volume rising from $56 million to more than $5 billion in five years. Correspondingly, daily trading volume has soared from $360 000 in 1990 to $24 million in the first half of 1996.

Luque reviews the macroeconomic background to this impressive development, citing the market-oriented reforms of the Fujimori government and its efforts to reestablish Peru as a responsible international financial entity. In addition, he cites the various specific policy measures that have benefited from the generation of saving, the inflow of foreign funds, and more specifically the formal capital market. Rewriting the nation's tax code was only one of many steps taken by the government to foster an equity market. He then discusses in some detail the different elements of market modernization that have made this market growth possible and that were in turn supported by the increase in trading. These include compensation and settlement procedures, a securities depository and clearing house, the dematerialization of clearing, an electronic trading system, an internationally accepted numbering agency, and international data dissemination. All of these elements combine to bring the Lima market to the cutting edge of modernity and allow it to compete effectively in attracting international funds to the Peruvian economy. Accordingly, Luque concludes that the prospects for market growth in the coming years are highly favorable.

At the same time that a revolution has swept formal sector credit markets in developing countries, many countries have also experienced dramatic new experiments in informal financial markets. Part Three of the book presents three papers that examine innovations in microfinance.

Advances in microfinance in Latin America have allowed lenders to manage the risk and costs of lending to very small borrowers who are dependent on income from self-employment or business ownership, a previously untapped market niche. The data presented in Marguerite S. Berger's paper, "Microfinance: An Emerging Market within the Emerging Markets," shows that microfinance can be profitable. Nevertheless, the size of the loan portfolios and total assets of financial institutions engaged in microfinance remain small by the standards of commercial banks.

Over the past ten years, dramatic changes in the financial sectors of most Latin American countries have increased competition and created new opportunities for the expansion of microfinance. Commercial private sector participation is on the rise, both through the creation of formal lending institutions from the portfolios of nonprofits (often called "upgrading") or by the entrance of commercial banks and finance companies into the microfinance market (called "downscaling"). While microfinance is allowing investors to tap a new emerging market within the emerging markets, there may still be a trade-off between the objectives of investors and the objectives of expanding economic opportunities for the poor. Continued growth of the microfinance industry will depend on further policy reform, standardization, and transparency of information in lending institutions, and the industry's capacity to innovate and increase efficiency in order to serve the lowest end of the market.

While there has been an explosion in microfinance in the 1990s, there is virtually no research on whether or not any of this lending has any effect on economic development or any other variable of interest to development economists. Manfred Zeller and his colleagues at the International Food Policy Research Institute in Washington and the Ministère de la Recherche Scientifique in Antananarivo, Madagascar, have conducted a study on the effectiveness of micro lending using community-level data from 188 villages in rural Madagascar. The country is one of the poorest in the world and its agricultural resources are extremely overused. The situation that Madagascar faces appears to be among the most bleak in the world. Yet, these researchers have been able to establish statistically the importance of providing credit to small farmers.

The study by Zeller *et al.*, "Linkages Between Rural Financial Markets, Poverty Alleviation and Conservation of Soils and Forests: The Case of Madagascar," presents an econometric analysis of the determinants of and interdependencies among the three components of sustainable development: economic growth, environmental sustainability, and poverty alleviation. The authors developed a two-stage, least squares, fixed-effect model in an attempt to explain the endogenous placement of microfinance institutions, rice yields, rural migration and wages, and the change in soil fertility. Explanatory factors are exogenous and policy variables such as the communities' social capital, their exposure to weather risks, and their access to commodity markets and public services.

The emergence of active capital markets in the developing world has profound and widespread implications for the industrialized countries. The financial meltdown of Thailand, Indonesia, Malaysia, and South Korea in 1997–1998, for example, created turmoil in equity markets in the United

States, Europe, and Japan. Far less well known is the effect of innovations in informal lending — many of which were pioneered in Bangladesh and then replicated in scores of developing countries — on financial markets in the industrialized countries. In his article, "Bridging the Gap Between Regulated Financial Institutions and Low-Income Borrowers," Eric Weaver shows that many of the lessons learned in Bangladesh are being applied in the United States.

Weaver argues that microfinance (loans under $50,000 in the U.S. context) by regulated financial institutions is on the upswing in the United States. The reasons for the increase include increases in competition, the rapid pace of bank mergers, advances in technology, changes in strategy that have made it possible to carry out micro-lending profitably for the first time, and changes in the U.S. regulatory framework. Early indications are that the micro-lending business may be even more profitable than anticipated. The principal barriers to making profitable small loans in the past were high transaction costs relative to loan size and excessive risk. Banks and other savings institutions have been able to overcome those barriers through the use of high-technology credit scoring systems to streamline the loan evaluation process, standardized products, and risk-based pricing models.

Smaller financial institutions find that they cannot by themselves sustain this high-technology approach. Hence, they are teaming up with larger institutions to pursue the goal of community economic development in low income neighborhoods. One such institution is the Lenders for Community Development (LCD) owned by 23 financial institutions in Santa Clara County, California. LCD provides small business loans of between $5000 and $50,000 from a pool of funds invested by the member banks. Weaver, the chief executive officer of LCD, argues that his organization can bridge the gap between regulated financial institutions and low-income small business borrowers by relying on existing bank systems for marketing, loan documentation and loan servicing. In addition, LCD receives subsidies through partnerships with nonprofit organizations, the use of consultants funded by charitable contributions, below-market capital from member banks, cross-subsidy between LCD's affordable housing and small business lending programs, and the use of volunteer labor from local bankers. LCD manages risk through risk-sharing among member banks, extensive technical assistance to borrowers, and loan guarantees from outside parties. Weaver concludes that LCD has encouraged the growth of businesses owned by minorities, women, and low-income individuals, thereby stimulating economic development in disadvantaged communities and increasing employment.

Part Four of the book examines the difficult and complex process of creating capital markets in formerly socialist countries without a tradition of markets of any sort. Problems are compounded when macroeconomic instability increases the risk of bank lending throughout the economy. Philip F. Bartholomew, Larry R. Mote, and Gary Whalen in "Systemic Risk: An Overview with Applications to Transitional Economies," analyze system-wide risk. Stability of the private banking system has historically been a major concern in developed economies, leading to extensive and divergent systems of financial regulation across countries. Such stability is an even more pressing concern in transitional economies, where state banking systems are being privatized, existing debt is being carried by private shareholders in such banks, and systems of clearing both domestic and international payments are extremely rudimentary. During recent years, government regulators in developed economies have devoted much attention to precluding *systemic risk*, which is the risk posed to real economic activity by widespread and contagious insolvency among private banks. The policies adopted in these economies will have far reaching implications for the development of nascent financial regulations in the transitional economies of Eastern Europe and the former Soviet Union. Furthermore, an understanding of the problems posed by system risk is especially crucial to an analysis of the causes of and solutions to the Asian economic crisis that began in 1997.

Bartholomew, Mote and Whalen begin their analysis of the regulation of systemic risk in developed economies by examining operational definitions of such risk. Concluding that any operational policy against widespread insolvency in the banking system must take into account potential disruptions to long term borrower-lender relations between firms and banks, the authors argue that the basic market failure underlying notions of systemic risk in the regulatory literature all involve the occurrence of negative externalities, inflicted from capital markets to the manufacturing and agricultural sectors. Using recent episodes from Scandinavia and the United States, the authors then argue that, contrary to advocates of deregulation in financial markets, such banking externalities are of a significant magnitude and are likely to pose a serious risk to macroeconomic stability. The authors then enumerate the reasons why systemic risk is likely to be a cause for concern to regulators in transitional economies, citing the increased flow of intraday credit (without equivalent means of diversification) between banks in a common payments system, the likely concentration of bank loan portfolios in such economies, the homogeneity of newly-privatized banks in terms of management techniques and investment opportunities, and, most importantly, the relative costliness of important informational asymmetries between commercial lenders and borrowers, and between lenders participating in the payments system. The paper concludes with an extensive discussion of policy options, and the value of financial monitoring and regulation by a central government.

Another curse that banking systems in transition economies face is the bad debt that newly privatized banks must carry. Socialist governments typically financed state enterprises with little regard to risk assessment. Since the state owned both borrowing and lending institutions, there was little risk involved. When state enterprises and banks are privatized, the banks end up with an excess burden of nonperforming loans and loans with low yields that threaten their solvency. Such loans inhibit the profitability of the private banking system and may preclude it from financing a large volume of domestic investment. The bad debt may cause banks to lend to failing firms rather than new or restructured firms, cause solvent but illiquid firms that have been privatized to fail owing to an inability to repay old debt, create a politically unacceptable divergence between deposit and lending rates, threaten macroeconomic stability as banks endeavor to recapitalize using retained earnings, and delay the introduction of modern accounting and regulatory procedures in order to conceal fundamental weaknesses in the banking system. For these reasons, restructuring of this stock of bad debt has become an urgent public policy problem for such economies. The overhang of bad debt is not dissimilar to the problems faced by several East Asian countries at the end of the 1990s. Though Michael Marrese does not address the issue directly, the lessons learned in Slovakia may prove useful in the East Asian context.

Marrese in "Addressing the Bad-Debt Problem in the Slovak Economy" uses the recent experience of Slovakia, during 1990–1994, to illustrate these problems and to describe how reforms in both the private and public sectors have successfully addressed the difficulties posed by large stocks of bad debt. He first provides a brief theoretical analysis of the implications of inherited bad debt for the stability and solvency of the banking system, followed by an illuminating institutional description of the recent history of Slovak banking. Building on this introduction and on extensive data concerning the Slovak banking system, Marrese then argues that Slovakia's eclectic approach to the restructuring of bank debt has been successful in mitigating the adverse effects of bad debt, despite its apparent divergence from standard prescriptions for economic policy. The Slovak approach included a combination of public policies such as debt write-offs in exchange for government bonds, the recapitalization and removal or subsidization of nonperforming loans through tax revenues, new accounting and capital-adequacy regulations, and initiatives pursued by newly-privatized banks themselves (such as extensive collateralization, increased reserves and the adoption of Western valuation and management methods). Marrese shows, however, that the success of these reforms has depended in crucial ways upon the general upturn in the Slovak economy during recent years.

The final three articles of this volume address issues related to foreign capital flows. With the debt crisis of the 1980s behind us, global capital markets have experienced renewed interest in investing in the developing world. Because of the high liquidity and volatility of portfolio investment when compared with FDI or even commercial bank loans, developing countries that have received portfolio investment have exposed themselves to a considerable risk. If many investors decide at the same time that they no longer wish to hold these investments, the wave of assets sold on equity and bond markets and the subsequent effort to repatriate the investment funds brings havoc to capital and foreign exchange markets and can produce macroeconomic disasters. The Mexican peso crisis of December 1994, for example, triggered an $8 billion exodus of capital from the country and a deep depression from which the country has not yet fully recovered. Other countries, especially Argentina, that were also dependent on portfolio capital imports were badly hit. Global financial markets were disrupted by a similar crisis that broke out first in Thailand in June 1997.

Andras Uthoff in "Short Term Capital Inflows and Long Term External Equilibrium" first points out that the growth in portfolio investment's share in total capital flows (at the expense of bank lending and FDI) in Latin America is not just a result of changes in domestic policy. It is a global phenomenon that is in part related to the changing supply of capital, low interest rates in the industrialized countries, and the evolution of financial institutions. Furthermore, it is important to note that the level of investment within any particular country depends not only on the national saving rate and the level of capital imports, but also upon the price of investment relative to other prices. This in turn depends upon exchange rates and terms of trade, among other factors. Using this framework, Uthoff examines capital flows into six key Latin American economies. Countries that experienced a sudden release of their foreign exchange constraint due to an influx of portfolio investment produced an excess supply of foreign exchange and an appreciation of the real exchange rate. This increased the domestic demand for tradeables and at the same time produced a wealth effect on consumption due to the sudden and substantial appreciation of financial and real asset prices. Consequently, aggregate demand expanded, imports increased, current account deficits rose, and thus capital imports increased even further. As domestic expenditure rose more than domestic output, the level of national saving fell. Maintaining stable macroeconomic indicators in this environment was extremely difficult. It has hence been demonstrated that market liberalization is insufficient by itself to slow the growth in imports or the decline in saving; active public policy is required. Uthoff closes with a discussion of policy instruments available to the government. He recommends a dirty float, efforts to sterilize the monetary effects of reserve accumulation, as well as controls on short term capital movements.

Given the avalanche of FDI going to developing countries, is it not surely the case that there is plenty of investment funds for any developing country that is ready to welcome foreign capital? The conventional wisdom among students of investment location has long been that governments (whether it be Alabama or Albania) do not need to offer tax concessions or other inducements to attract FDI because tax waivers or direct subsidies are rarely large enough to sway the locational decision. Joel Bergsman in "Is There Competition for Foreign Direct Investment?" however disagrees. There are now many potential sites with a similar 'business climate,' labor supply, access to raw materials, transport, and energy. Most international investors are not seeking a location in a specific country and many are not even seeking a specific region. For these truly footloose investors, differences in the tax-subsidy package offered by different governments can be decisive in determining where the firm decides to locate its new facility. Thus, governments must compete with each other for investment.

As noted above, the negative and positive consequence of FDI, external borrowing, and portfolio investment flows on developing economies has long been debated. In this discussion, however, the macroeconomic effects of capital flows have received little attention. Stephen Guisinger attempts to fill this gap in his article, "The Macroeconomic Consequences of Investment Liberalization for Developing Countries." Investment liberalization should increase the efficiency of the allocation of intermediated funds, but the impact on budget deficits, inflation rates, and growth rates of GDP is unclear. Nevertheless, there is no agreed upon measure of the restrictiveness of investment regimes comparable to the effective rate of protection that can measure the restrictiveness of trade regimes. A number of studies have assessed the benefits and costs of changes in foreign investment flows, but none have explicitly examined the consequences of investment liberalization. Guisinger is forced to resort to a number of indirect measures of the macroeconomic consequences of the liberalization of capital markets in developing countries. First, he draws inferences from the experience of trade policy reform in other countries, drawing the parallels between trade and investment liberalization. A second approach is to simulate investment regime liberalization with large-scale macroeconomic models. The study concludes with what the author describes as optimistic agnosticism. Investment liberalization probably does not have any adverse macroeconomic impact and, under certain conditions, may have very favorable effects.

References

Chenery, H., S. Robinson, and M. Syrquin (1986). *Industrialization and Growth: A Comparative Study*. Oxford University Press, New York.

World Bank (1998). *Global Development Finance 1998: Analysis and Summary Tables*. Washington.

World Bank (1987). *World Development Report* 1987. Oxford University Press, New York.

World Bank (1991). *World Development Report 1991*. Oxford University Press, New York.

Part Two

Capital Markets in Developing Countries

PENSION REFORM IN CHILE

Andras Uthoff[1]

Introduction

Pension reform in Chile was largely motivated by the need to remedy its structural failures that were caused by the use of defined benefits within a pay-as-you-go system. These failures can and did lead to financial imbalances. The reform attacked the disparity between lifetime contributions and benefits at the time of retirement. The philosophy behind the reform was that workers participating in the system must learn to perceive a correspondence between efforts and benefits, and managers must learn to defend pension funds against inflation and political pressures.

Chile's pension reform is characterized by the gradual but complete substitution of the pay-as-you-go system by an individual capitalization system. Participants are all treated equally with respect to their rights and obligations (no preferential benefits). They are free to choose among competing fund management firms in which they want their contributions to be deposited. Their funds are capitalized. Records of transactions are transparent and provided on a monthly basis. The management firm's equity is completely isolated from the pension fund while their business is exclusively that of managing a single pension fund. Entry into the pension fund management industry is free in order to reduce administration costs through competition. These firms charge an administration fee that is deducted from contributions

[1]This paper has not been submitted to editing by CEPAL; responsibility for its content rests solely with the author.

and an insurance premium for disability and dependent survival risks (in the case of death of the contributor). Participants are free to move between management firms. Information on the pension fund portfolio managed by each firm and on its executive staff are also regulated and supervised by government-run institutions. Firms are not free to choose among different investment alternatives, but are strictly regulated.

The Chilean reform is considered an example for the rest of the region and several international institutions advocate that other countries use important components of the Chilean reform. The purpose of this paper is to give some insights into issues raised by this advocacy. The reform should be praised in that, within the social functions of a pension system, it correctly isolates redistributive objectives that are of a fiscal nature from insurance objectives. The reform also highlights the fact that unless the pension system positively contributes to an efficient financial management of its reserve (or pension) funds, the objective of providing good pension benefits will not be achieved in the long run.

This paper analyzes economic and financial functions that are commonly thought to have been improved by the pension reform undertaken in Chile, the increase in national saving and the deepening and strengthening of the financial system. I will argue that the radical increases in national saving cannot be attributed solely or directly to the reform. Furthermore, although the reform provides a source of long term financial saving, the system has been unable to intermediate such funds into long term real investments. Lastly, most of the social improvements, such as the increase in population coverage and the provision of better pension benefits, are yet to be seen as the reformed system matures.

In the next section, I describe the main characteristics of the Chilean pension reform framework and comment on its replication in the region. In the section following, I present some of the main results of the first 15 years of operation of the Chilean reforms. I conclude with policy recommendations and current challenges to the reform.

Main Characteristics of the Chilean Reforms

Two characteristics of the reforms in the Chilean pension system are described below. These are their main participants, and the structure of pension benefits finance. I further discuss their implication for the development of capital markets.

Five main participants can be identified in the Chilean reformed system. These are the *affiliates*, who when actually contributing are called *contributors*, the *private pension fund management firms* (Administradoras de Fondos de Pensiones, AFPs), the *National Risk Commission*, the *insurance companies*, and the *government*.

Affiliates are wage workers, who are obliged to participate in the pension system. If they were employed at the time the reform was put into practice, they could have chosen to stay in the old system. New entrants into the wage labor force must participate in the new system. They contribute 10 percent of their net wages into individual capitalization accounts on a monthly basis, pay a fee to the management firm, and a premium to an insurance company. The fee was originally composed of fixed and proportional components, but later it was left for redistributive reasons with only a proportional component. In total, the workers contribute about 12.7 percent[2] of their net wages. He/she can choose to contribute additional funds into a voluntary account, which are not part of the pension fund. Affiliates are free to move their funds between private pension fund management firms on the basis of public information about current and past performance of their pension funds returns.

Contributors are not the same as the affiliates, as many of the latter have become self-employed and/or are temporary or permanently unemployed or out of the wage labor force. The self-employed can voluntarily participate in the system, but efforts to have them do so have not been very successful. The armed forces have a separate pension system. Affiliates only have access to their pension fund in cases of disability, retirement, and death (for the surviving dependents). The fund cannot be used as collateral or unemployment insurance. By the time of retirement, the affiliate can choose among three alternatives: a programmed retirement with the AFP, life insurance with an insurance company, or a combination of both.

[2]Ten percent is the net addition to the individual fund, and the other 2.7 percent includes administrative costs and insurance premia. Administrative costs are considered high by international standards.

AFPs are open corporations with the exclusive purpose of managing a single pension fund. They must maintain an equity in proportion to the number of affiliates. This equity is completely independent and isolated from the pension fund itself. They must guarantee a minimum return to pension fund investment, which is estimated on the basis of the average return obtained by all AFPs. If the affiliate so chooses at the time of retirement, the AFP must pay pension benefits under the programmed retirement benefit alternative. Otherwise, the AFP must transfer the individual pension to an insurance company selected by the affiliate.

The National Risk Commission is an independent organization composed of the three superintendents from the financial sectors (those from the banking superintendence, securities and insurance superintendence, and pension fund management firms superintendence). They also have four additional member selected from the AFPs' association. This Commission is in charge of evaluating risk of financial instruments and provides very strict regulation with respect to the portfolio composition of the AFPs. The Commission may subcontract with private risk classification firms for the task of evaluating risks and providing the necessary recommendations.

Insurance companies must be able to provide benefits through insurance schemes for disability and widowers and/or child survivors risks, as well as lifetime pension benefits through insurance schemes based on individual actuarial estimates for those affiliates choosing such an alternative. They charge a monthly premium to cover the disability and dependent survival risks, and charge an additional commission whenever the affiliate chooses life insurance at the time of retirement.

The government performs three roles. It prudentially regulates and supervises the pension fund management firms according to D.L. 3500 and additional norms which appeared after 1981. This is performed by the *Pension Fund Management Firms Commission* (Superintendencia de AFPs). It also normalizes the transition period through the *Social Security Normalization Institute* (Instituto de Normalización Previsional), where benefits for all those who chose to remain in the old system are estimated and paid. It also estimates the compensation bonuses for all those who choose to move into the new system. The government is also in charge of supplying assistance pension benefits for people who have not qualified for a pension benefit in either of the two forms, but qualify for assistance according to an income means test. Finally, the fiscal budget covers the fiscal cost of the transition, including recognition bonuses, pensions for those who were already retired or decided to stay in the old system, contributions to those participating and having seniority in the new system but who for several reasons have not reached a pension fund large enough to finance the minimum pension benefit warranted by law. These fiscal costs are not always treated as part of the Chilean pension reform, but it is appropriate to do so.

The pension benefit is funded with an accumulated capital composed of five sources: (i) contributions net of commissions; (ii) pension fund investment returns; (iii) the recognition bond and its fixed real return; (iv) voluntary saving from the affiliates themselves; and (v) the government's contribution in order to achieve a minimum pension fixed by law. In case of disability or payments to survivors when the affiliate has died, these five sources are complemented by additional funding from the insurance company. All premia and benefits are regulated and supervised by the state.

Several implications for the development of capital markets arise from the particular characteristics of the Chilean pension reform. In the first place, since the reform provides long term savings hopefully destined for long maturity real projects, there is a need for an appropriate macroeconomic environment. This should include low and controlled rates of inflation (or otherwise an indexed financial system)[3] and positive but moderate real interest rates.[4] Last but not least, it should also create confidence in the stability of the real exchange rate.[5]

[3]This is needed to avoid risks associated with price changes, as well as encouraging long term horizons for the capitalization of pension funds and the development of domestic investment projects by private agents.

[4]They should reflect the effective real cost of capital and thus contribute to an efficient allocation of the latter. This would help in the estimation of solvency condition of banks and debtors as well as in the promotion of competition among financial instruments denominated in national currency.

[5]The purpose is to create competitiveness within the tradable sector with comparative advantage, as well as to avoid speculative capital movements across the border.

In the second place, the large fiscal costs of the transition period require the strengthening of public sector finances. The transition fiscal costs include provision for payments of recognition bonds, the finance of pensions for those retired by the time the reform took place, and the payment of benefits to those who remained in the old system after the reform and are retiring now. The government must also provide for the additional contributions needed to achieve minimum pension[6] as well as for the finance of assistance pension[7] benefits for those who pass the means test.

Financial intermediation will also improve if the banking system is not repressed by the existence of either large public banks or credit controls (subsidized interest rates and/or quantitative controls). However, reforming the traditionally repressed banking sector does not justify its total liberalization. The transition should include: achieving banks' and debtors' solvency; developing prudential bank regulation in order to limit depositors' insurance; developing solvency control mechanisms and making these transparent public goods for depositors; and developing organizational regulations to limit the commercial banks' role within the financial sector (multibanks and financial complementation).

The most important developments are those needed in the securities and insurance markets. These include:

- A competitive stock market with clear requirements for entry, norms for creating open corporations, publicly standardized transparent accounting practices, transparent stock market pricing to facilitate an accurate and continuous valuing of pension fund investment portfolios based on common stock prices;
- Prudential regulation of the management of institutional savings such as those involved in pension funds and insurance companies, including limits to the diversification of portfolio investment and risks, reserve requirements for management firms, and capital requirements for debtors;

[6]Minimum pension is guaranteed by law and implies a subsidy equal to the difference between the equity needed to pay the pension, and the accumulated fund by the participant. Those who are eligible are those who paid social security taxes for more than twenty years.

[7]Assistance pensions are direct subsidies to all those who have not participated in the system and pass a means test.

- Independent risk classification firms that may assess the relevance of given financial instruments and issuers for investment by institutional investors, especially those managing funds that result from compulsory laws;
- The custody of securities in the Central Bank.

The implications of this reform are straightforward. The rapid accumulation of funds, especially in countries with young age structures of their population, requires the development of financial markets. Incentives to create new open corporations, to promote new financial intermediaries, and to supply new securities are important elements of the reforms. To have a real impact on the domestic economy, there is a permanent need for developing financial instruments representing investment opportunities in infrastructure and in strategic real projects by domestic issuers, instead of allowing increasing shares of long term domestic saving to be invested abroad.

Assessment of the Main Results of Chilean Experience

Two functions of pension systems should kept in mind when assessing pension reforms. *Social functions* include making certain that workers will save to finance their own consumption when retired or disabled, as well as that of their surviving dependents after they die. Governments create mandatory pension systems under the assumption that people are myopic and do not voluntarily save for these purposes. Thus, they have created mechanisms that should assure access to pension benefits in the event of death, survival of dependents and/or disability. These savings should be protected against inflation and hopefully capitalized in real terms to provide for good pension benefits. Social objectives of pension systems also include the reduction of economic inequalities by developing a solidarity scheme to provide resources for those unable to save by themselves. This redistribution can be implemented either within the pension systems themselves, or performed under fiscal policy programs separate from the pension system.

The *economic and financial functions* of modern pension systems include contributions to national saving (assuring that compulsory institutional saving will not substitute for other domestic sources of saving). Furthermore, pension systems should help to develop the nation's capital markets.

The Chilean reform isolates the pension system from political pressures, especially by separating its financial management from that of any other governmental program involving the redistribution of income.

Equality in the reformed Chilean system is limited to a correspondence between each worker's saving efforts and his/her pension benefits. A subsidiary role is played by the government and done within the fiscal budget. Minimum pensions for those affiliated with the system and assistance pensions for those unable to participate in the system are provided under the basis of income mean tests and funded from general taxes. This radical change requires a strong political commitment in favor of the reform.

It is difficult to prove whether the reforms have met the social functions objectives since no standardized comparison can be made (Mujica 1993). Such a proof would require quite complex intergenerational models combined with earnings functions profiles that are estimated in different historical contexts. The statement that pension benefits are larger in an individual capitalization scheme than in a pay-as-you-go scheme are based only on theoretical grounds. It can be proven (Uthoff 1995) that under the first scheme, the average returns to individuals' saving effort is equal to the real rate of return on capital, whereas in the pay-as-you-go system, it is equal to the rate of growth of the wage bill. Neoclassical models show that in countries with scarce capital and abundant labor (as in most economies in Latin America), and under optimal and efficient conditions in the long run, the rate of return on capital would be larger than the rate of growth of output. If in addition we assume no changes in the functional distribution of income, this would justify the statement that pension benefits would be better in the reformed system. However, this remains to be empirically tested.

It was also expected that population coverage in the new system would be better than in the pay-as-you-go system it replaced. This expectation was based on the fact that lower contribution taxes, transparency in the financial management, and the promise of better pension benefits would be sufficient incentives for the self-employed with saving capacity to participate. Nevertheless, population coverage has not significantly increased. (See Table 1.) The continued high incidence of poverty and informal sector activities in Chile, the multiple saving and investment alternatives for high income self-employed, and the fact that pension funds can not be withdrawn as

Table 1. Indicators of Social Function Objectives

	Administrative Costs	Population Coverage		Return to Individual Savings		Fiscal Costs
Year	Share of Contribution	Share of Labor Force		Within the Pension Fund	GNDI Growth Rate	Percentage of GDP
		Affiliates	Contributors			
1981	—	39.0	—	12.6	—	4.1
1982	40.3	39.3	24.8	26.5	–19.6	8.3
1983	60.8	43.0	28.0	22.7	0.4	7.5
1984	64.0	49.6	29.3	2.9	6.1	7.7
1985	49.2	56.8	32.9	13.4	–1.9	6.7
1986	45.1	60.7	35.0	12.0	6.4	6.3
1987	41.0	66.4	38.5	6.4	8.9	5.4
1988	29.6	69.9	38.9	4.8	12.3	5.2
1989	26.8	74.4	41.0	6.7	8.5	4.5
1990	24.4	79.1	41.5	17.7	0.8	4.6
1991	24.0	85.6	51.8	28.6	6.0	4.5
1992	23.7	88.9	54.4	4.0	9.2	4.3
1993	23.7	90.2	53.5	16.7	4.8	4.5
1994	22.3	95.6	54.3	17.8	7.5	4.5
1995	22.6	99.0	56.4	–2.5	15.7	4.3
1996	22.9	—	—	3.5	7.9	—
1997	22.7	—	—	4.8	9.0	—
1998	22.7	—	—	—	—	—

Sources: SAFP (various years) *Boletín Estadístico*; Ministerio de Hacienda, Dirección de Presupuestos, *Boletín de las Finanzas Públicas*, 1987–1995; Banco Central de Chile (various numbers), *Boletín Mensual*.

in a saving account seem to explain the small increase in population coverage in the reformed system (Uthoff 1997).

There are two implications of the reform that affect national saving rates (Diamond 1995), both of which need to be identified and measured. The first involves the government's effort to meet the deficit of the former system plus any additional transitional fiscal costs. This requires an important adjustment of government finances, with implications either for current accounts and/or for public savings. The Chilean reform implied having the size of the social security debt made explicit and the financing of the fiscal cost to pay it, available. The particular manner in which the debt will be paid by transferring resources from the government to families will determine the composition of national saving into its public and private components. The second is the change in the nature of contributions to the system. Contributions in the original system were social security taxes that were paid to be eligible for defined pension benefits under given conditions. The new contributions are mandatory saving paid to accumulated funds in individual accounts to which owners have access at retirement. In this case, what is affected is the saving of families.

Table 2 shows the effects of the reform on national saving as a percentage of GDP. Column (1) shows the size of the transition costs (deficit) needed to implement the reform. Column (2) shows the size of net saving due to the change (from taxes into saving) in the nature of contribution to social security. The net social security saving effect is estimated assuming no substitution takes place for other voluntary sources of saving by families. Throughout the whole period 1980–1994, the size of the deficit was larger than the size of social security saving from families, implying a negative direct effect on national saving.

These same figures can be used for a complementary calculation. This is presented using two alternatives estimates provided by Arrau (1995). Table 3 assumes that the social security deficit (including the transition costs) is already included in the government current expenditures, and hence has substituted for other public saving. In this case, public saving was small at 1.6 percent of GDP in 1980–1984, increased to 4.8 percent of GDP in 1985–1994, and contributed 3.2 percentage points of GDP of the 18.2 percentage point increase in Gross National Saving in Chile.

As shown in Table 4, on the other hand, the social security deficit is added to the government's current surplus, and shows the effective saving effort needed to undertake the reform. To be consistent, this deficit is subtracted from the private social security saving, because it represents transfers for the consumption of older family members. In this case, the public saving was 7.4 percent of GDP in 1980–1984, increased to 9.3 percent GDP in

Table 2. Saving and Fiscal Deficits During the Transition Period (% of GDP)

Year	Government	Families
	Transition Social Security Cost	Reformed Social Security Saving
1980	1.7	0.0
1981	4.1	0.9
1982	8.3	1.8
1983	7.5	1.7
1984	7.7	1.9
1985	6.7	2.0
1986	6.3	2.2
1987	5.4	2.3
1988	5.2	2.7
1989	4.5	2.9
1990	4.6	3.0
1991	4.5	2.8
1992	4.3	3.3
1993	4.5	3.6
1994	4.5	3.9
Avg. 1980–1984	5.9	1.6
Avg. 1985–1989	5.6	2.4
Avg. 1990–1994	4.5	3.3

Sources: For 1980–1984, Arrau (1995); for 1985–1988, Arrau (1992) adjusting the figures with 1986 GDP; after 1989, Dirección de Presupuesto, *Estadísticas de las Finanzas Públicas 1989–1994*.

Table 3. National Saving Disaggregation without Including Social Security Deficit (% of GDP at current prices)

Year	Gross National Saving[1]	Government Saving			Private Saving		
		Current Surplus[2]	CSF[3,*]	Total[2,3]	Social Security[4]	Non Social Security[5]	Total[6]
1980	13.9	8.5	0.0	8.5	0.0	5.4	5.4
1981	8.2	5.8	0.0	5.8	0.9	1.5	2.4
1982	2.1	–2.9	0.0	–2.9	1.8	3.2	5.0
1983	4.4	–2.3	0.0	–2.3	1.7	5.0	6.7
1984	2.9	–1.2	0.0	–1.2	1.9	2.0	4.1
1985	7.8	0.4	0.0	0.4	2.0	5.4	7.4
1986	11.5	1.3	0.0	1.3	2.2	8.0	10.2
1987	17.3	3.0	0.5	3.5	2.3	11.5	13.8
1988	22.3	3.0	3.0	6.0	2.7	13.6	16.3
1989	23.7	3.0	3.7	6.7	2.9	14.1	17.0
1990	24.2	2.5	2.3	4.8	3.0	16.4	19.4
1991	24.1	3.7	0.7	4.4	2.8	16.9	19.7
1992	24.8	4.9	0.3	5.2	3.3	16.3	19.6
1993	23.9	4.8	–0.2	4.6	3.6	15.7	19.3
1994	25.4	4.9	0.2	5.1	3.9	16.4	20.3
Avg. 1980–1984	6.3	1.6	0.0	1.6	1.6	3.5	4.7
Avg. 1985–1989	16.5	2.1	2.4	3.6	2.4	10.5	12.9
Avg. 1990–1994	24.5	4.2	0.7	4.8	3.3	16.3	19.7

Sources: Arrau (1995).

[1]Figures at current prices.

[2,3]Until 1988, Vial y Marfán (1995); from 1989, Dirección de Presupuesto, *Estadísticas de las Finanzas Públicas 1989–1994*.

[4]Until 1988; AFP Hábitat (1992), "Diez Años de Historia del Sistema de AFP," Santiago; from 1989, SAFP *El Sistema Chileno de Pensiones*.

[5]Private Saving – Saving for retirement

[6]Gross National Saving – Public Saving

*CSF: Copper Stabilization Fund

Table 4. National Saving Disaggregation Including Social Security Deficit (% of GDP at current prices)

Year	Gross National Saving[1]	Government Saving				Private Saving		
		Social Security Deficit[2]	Current Surplus[3]	CSF[4,*]	Total	Social Security[5]	Non Social Security[6]	Total[7]
1980	13.9	1.7	8.5	0.0	10.2	–1.7	5.4	3.7
1981	8.2	4.1	5.8	0.0	9.9	–3.2	1.5	–1.7
1982	2.1	8.3	–2.9	0.0	5.4	–6.5	3.2	–3.3
1983	4.4	7.5	–2.3	0.0	5.2	–5.8	5.0	–0.8
1984	2.9	7.7	–1.2	0.0	6.5	–5.8	2.2	–3.6
1985	7.8	6.7	0.4	0.0	7.1	–4.7	5.4	0.7
1986	11.5	6.3	1.3	0.0	7.6	–4.1	8.0	3.9
1987	17.3	5.4	3.0	0.5	8.9	–3.1	11.5	8.4
1988	22.3	5.2	3.0	3.0	11.2	–2.5	13.6	11.1
1989	23.7	4.5	3.0	3.7	11.2	–1.6	14.1	12.5
1990	24.2	4.6	2.5	2.3	9.4	–1.6	16.4	14.8
1991	24.1	4.5	3.7	0.7	8.9	–1.7	16.9	15.2
1992	24.8	4.3	4.9	0.3	9.5	–1.0	16.3	15.3
1993	23.9	4.5	4.8	–0.2	9.0	–0.9	15.7	14.9
1994	25.4	4.5	4.9	0.2	9.6	–0.6	16.4	15.8
Avg. 1980–1984	6.3	5.9	1.6	0.0	7.4	–4.6	3.5	–1.1
Avg. 1985–1989	16.5	5.6	2.1	2.4	9.2	–3.2	10.5	7.3
Avg. 1990–1994	24.5	4.5	4.2	0.7	9.3	–1.1	16.3	15.2

Sources: Arrau (1995).
[1]Until 1984, data based on 1977; since 1985, data based on 1986.
[2]For 1980–1984, Arrau (1992); for 1985–1988, Arrau (1992) adjusting the figures using 1986 GDP; since 1989, Dirección de Presupuesto, *Estadísticas de las Finanzas Públicas*, 1989–1994.
[3,4]Until 1988, Vial y Marfán (1995); since 1989, Dirección de Presupuesto, *Estadísticas de las Finanzas Públicas 1989–1994*.
[5]Private Saving – Business Saving
[6]Table 3, column 5
[7]Gross National Saving – Public Saving
*CSF: Copper Stabilization Fund

1990–1994, and contributed 1.9 percentage points of the 18.2 percentage point increase in Gross National Saving as a percent of GDP.

The implications are straightforward. In order to implement the reform, public saving is important and the private social security saving may not be large enough. In order to explain the increase in saving experienced in Chile between 1980–1984 and 1990–1994, one needs to understand what happened to the non-social-security private saving, which increased as a percent of GDP by 12.8 percentage points between the two periods.

This increase in private saving that was not for retirement could not have materialized had there not been reforms in other areas of the economy. Worth mentioning are those reforms that have created an adequate macroeconomic framework producing realistic and credible prices (low level of inflation, real positive but moderate interest rates, and stable and credible real exchange rates), stable economic growth, the consolidation of democracy, the privatization of public enterprises that in the past were not open corporations, the regulation and supervision of the financial sector, and last but not least the creation of tax incentives to reinvest profits.

An important change in tax incentives was implemented in 1984. Its purpose was to promote the reinvestment of profits by corporations. To that end, the reform reduced the tax rate for undistributed profits in open corporations from 46 to 10 percent. At the same time, the reform created a uniform tax on distributed profits by reducing the rate on open corporations from 43.3 to 31.5 percent and maintaining the tax rate at 31.5 percent for closed corporations. This change in tax rates is seen as a major factor contributing to an increase in non-social-security private saving (mainly corporate saving) in Chile between 1980–1984 and 1990–1994.

Since pension funds are the result of mandatory saving from affiliates, it is the government's role to assure adequate financial management of the affiliates' funds. For this purpose, the state has retained within the new legislation an important regulatory and supervisory role. Pension Fund Management Firms are subject to very strict regulations summarized below:

Prudential Regulations for Investment of Pension Funds
• Pension funds can be only invested in financial instruments authorized by law. • Pension funds are subject to very strict norms concerning their portfolio diversification, both by financial instruments and by issuers. • All financial instruments subject to investment by pension funds must be evaluated and approved by the National Risk Commission. • All instruments of pension funds portfolios are valued daily with prices established by the AFPs supervisory commission. (Eighty-five percent of portfolios are valued at current stock exchange prices). • The financial management of any pension fund is subject to a required minimum return. • This minimum is determined relative to the performance of the other AFPs competing in the market. • At least 90 percent of pension fund securities are in custody at the Central Bank.

There are also some organizational regulations concerning the pension fund management industry. These are as follows:

Organizational Regulations of Pension Fund Management Firms
• Each AFP is an open corporation with its equity completely independent and isolated from the pension fund it manages. • Each AFP can manage a single fund. • The pension management firm is responsible for warranting minimum returns to the fund and will respond, whenever necessary, to reach those minima, with required capital kept in custody at the Central Bank.

Permanent innovations are being performed on the institutional framework and regulation of pension fund financial management. The purpose is to protect the affiliates' savings, as well as ensure that the portfolio allocates resources into long term real investment needs. Despite these regulations, the pension funds accumulated by all AFPs, as shown by the figures in Table 5, represents 40 percent of GDP and are still largely concentrated in short term investment instruments. Approximately half is invested in Central Bank and Treasury bonds and commercial bank deposits.

Table 5. Portfolio Composition of Pension Funds in Chile

Year	Central Bank and Treasury Bonds %	Bank Deposits and Bonds %	Mortgage Securities %	Firm Bonds and Debentures %	Common Stock %	Accumulated Funds (in millions of US$)	As a Share of GDP %
1981	28	62	9	1	0	$219	0.9
1983	44	3	51	2	0	1670	6.4
1985	43	23	32	2	0	3986	10.9
1987	42	28	21	3	6	4883	15.5
1988	35	30	21	6	8	5954	16.5
1989	42	21	18	9	10	7359	19.7
1990	44	17	16	11	12	9758	26.5
1991	38	12	13	13	24	13,811	34.4
1992	40	12	14	10	24	15,400	31.7*
1993	41	9	14	8	28	19,788	34.5*
1994	40	9	13	7	31	23,926	41.0*
1995	39	9	15	6	31	25,433	40.8*
1996	40	7	18	8	25	27,192	40.3*
1997	42	14	17	6	23	29,584	40.8*

Source: AFPs Superintendence monthly bulletins.
*National accounts were revised and these last figures are not comparable with the ones above.

In turn, the high historical yields in portfolio investment have resulted from capital gains due to increasing prices of already existing common stock and do not represent real wealth creation. As a result, during 1995 and the first months of 1996, the funds had negative real returns since stock prices fell during that time (see Table 5).

Finally, in relation to capital market developments, the AFP industry has demonstrated large economies of scale. At present, the three largest firms (out of 18) are managing 54 percent of pension funds corresponding to 69 percent of the affiliates and 67 percent of the contributors. (See Table 6.)

Conclusions

In assessing the first fifteen years of the Chilean pension reform, this paper has reviewed the implications of social as well as economic and financial objectives. The social objectives of the pension system were changed by

Table 6. Concentration of the Pension Fund, Affiliates and Contributors in Chile, 1981–1995

	1981	1987	1991	1993	1995	1997
Number of AFPs	12	12	13	22	18	13
Share of Affiliates within largest three (%)	67	63	67	68	69	69
Share of Contributors within largest three (%)	—	66	69	68	67	65
Share of Funds within largest three (%)	71	67	59	54	54	55
Share of Affiliates within largest six (%)	86	89	87	85	86	88
Share of Contributors within largest six (%)	—	90	87	85	85	89
Share of Funds within largest six (%)	91	89	87	80	79	85
Number of Affiliates (thousands)	1400	2890	4109	4709	5152	5780
Number of Contributors (thousands)	—	2024	2487	2792	2449	2662
Portfolio value (millions of US$)	300	4803	13,811	15,400	25,433	29,584

Source: Monthly bulletins from the AFPs Superintendence.

the reforms. The new system places less emphasis on social solidarity and redistribution. The system is now completely isolated from political pressures, and equality is pursued matching benefits with efforts at the individual worker's level. Other redistributive goals are left within the mandate of fiscal policy.

The reforms have failed to reach other social objectives, such as securing the reduction of administrative costs and an increase in population coverage. The AFP industry has turned out to be oligopolistic, and marketing costs took a large share of the affiliate contributions during the earlier years of operations. Further regulations have helped to correct this problem, but more improvements are needed. Population coverage has not significantly increased over the earlier system when measured on the basis of actual contributors (and not affiliates). Finally, although until now, the new system has generated significantly higher yields than those implicit in the old system (the rate of growth of gross disposable income), these yields have largely resulted from capital gains and are thus unsustainable.

It is likewise uncertain that pension reform has attained its financial economic objectives. National saving in Chile increased mostly because of increases in non-social-security private saving and from public saving efforts. The first resulted from incentives coming from other reforms that were complementary to the pension system reform. (These reforms involve the development of a threefold framework that includes financial saving incentives, macroeconomic and political stability, and development of prudential and organizational regulations within financial markets.) Intermediation of pension funds has failed to finance infrastructure and real investment for long term wealth creation.

Several challenges for the Chilean authorities are suggested by the analysis of this article. These include: (i) to continue increasing population coverage; (ii) to make the pension funds of those close to retirement age less vulnerable to shocks in the financial markets; (iii) to improve the regulation of the AFP industry by strengthening competition among AFPs, reducing administrative costs, and improving information transparency for the education of affiliates; (iv) to regulate the role of financial conglomerates in the AFPs industry and the boards of directors of the pension fund management firms; and (v) to strengthen the increasing allocation of pension funds (formed by long term financial savings) into real investments such as infrastructure and mining.

References

Arrau, P. (1992). El Nuevo Régimen Previsional Chileno. In *Regímenes Pensionales*, Fundación Friedrich Ebert de Colombia, September.

Arrau, P. (1995). *Evolución de la Tasa de Ahorro Nacional en Chile: 1980–1994.* Preliminary draft, Unidad de Financiamiento, CEPAL, Santiago.

Banco Central. *Boletín Mensual.* Various dates.

Diamond, P. (1995). Economic Support in Old Age. Annual Conference on Development Economics, May 1–2, Washington.

Dirección de Presupuestos (1995). *Estadísticas de las Finanzas Públicas, 1989–1994.* Santiago.

Mujica, R. (1993). Sistemas de Seguridad Social: La Experiencia Chilena. Serie de Documentos de Trabajo, No. 149, Interamerican Development Bank, Washington.

Superintendencia de AFP (SAFP) (1994). *El Sistema Chileno de Pensiones.* Santiago.

Uthoff, A. S. (1997). *Baja Cobertura de la Seguridad Social en América Latina: Un Problema de Incentivos o de Exclusión Social? LC/R* 1764, 26 Noviembre.

Uthoff, A. (1995). Reforma a los Sistemas de Pensiones en América Latina y el Caribe. Serie Financiamiento del Desarrollo, No. 29, CEPAL, Santiago, February.

Vial, J., and M. Marfán (1995). Políticas para el Crecimiento Económico en los 90, El Caso de Chile. *Notas Técnicas de CIEPLAN*, No. 157, March.

THE EMERGING PERUVIAN CAPITAL MARKET

José Luque

The Lima Stock Exchange has grown in volume from $55 million in 1990 to over $5 billion in 1995, and is still growing. Along the way, it has helped to finance Peru's structural adjustment. The expansion of this market has resulted from the interaction of national policies and improvements in the stock market operating system. These two elements are analyzed in the first two sections of this paper. A section that looks at prospects for the future concludes the paper.

Economic Panorama

Before 1990, the Peruvian economy was restricted by a structure of laws and policies that significantly distorted the functioning of markets and therefore impeded economic development. These economic policies caused stagnation of the economy, accelerating inflation, and a substantial fall in real income. As a result of the way in which the previous government handled the Peruvian foreign debt, the country was isolated from the international financial community. Table 1 presents summary statistics indicating the substantial progress that the Peruvian economy has enjoyed since 1990.

The government of President Alberto Fujimori instituted an array of liberal and structural reforms. These included the privatization of public companies, trade and financial market liberalization, the elimination of price controls and subsidies, the suppression of controls on capital movements,

Table 1. Some Economic Indicators

	1991	1992	1993	1994	1995	1996[1]
Inflation (%)	139.2	56.7	39.5	15.4	10.2	6.3
Exchange Rate Devaluation (%)	0.97 76.4	1.63 68.0	2.16 32.5	2.13 0.0	2.33 7.9	2.44 5.2
GDP Growth Rate (%)	2.8	–2.9	6.5	12.9	6.9	2.2[2]
International Liquidity (millions of US$)	1304	2001	2701	5696	6641	6993
Foreign Sector (millions of US$) Current Account Balance Commercial Balance	 –814 –139	 –1659 –556	 –1646 –535	 –2101 –1021	 –3748 –2116	 -679[3] -350[3]

[1]As of June 1996.
[2]Growth May 1996 compared to May 1995.
[3]As of first quarter of 1996.

greater incentives for foreign investment, the deregulation of the labor market, and the adoption of a private pension system. In addition, the government moved aggressively to bring peace to the country. This was one of the most important policies leading to the reduction of country risk and the growth in national and foreign investment. The government also acted to establish macroeconomic stability. In 1990, the Fujimori government adopted an economic program whose initial objectives were to control inflation and apply strict fiscal discipline, which would lead to sustained economic recovery, guarantee a sound balance of payments, and initiate the reinsertion of the country into the international financial system. Fiscal policy aimed to reduce the public sector deficit in order to relieve domestic financial pressures. Efforts were made to increase tax revenues as well as to reduce public spending. An effective cash budgeting mechanism was employed to keep spending in check.

Annual inflation fell from 7650 percent in 1990 to 10.2 percent in 1995, the lowest in the previous twenty-three years. The fiscal deficit, which in 1990 represented 3.7 percent of GDP, was converted to a surplus of 2.9 percent of GDP by 1994. This came about as a result of a substantial increase in revenue from the sale of state-owned enterprises and by reductions in recurrent spending. As a result of delays in the privatization program in

1995, the budget surplus as a percentage of GDP declined. Paralleling these improvements, international net reserves increased to US$6.6 billion by the end of 1995. Six months later, reserves reached US$7 billion. In order to achieve sustained growth, economic policy aimed at stimulating domestic saving and mobilizing financial resources was introduced in order to generate an increase in productive investments.

Table 2 shows the growth in the country's investment and how this has been financed. The data show that domestic saving has been insufficient to finance investment. Total investment grew from 16.4 percent of GDP in 1992 to 23.8 percent in 1995, principally due to the dynamic private sector, while domestic saving as a share of GDP increased by only 5 percent during the same period. This increase in domestic saving occurred mostly in the private sector and was caused largely by the development of the private pension system, growing competition in the financial sector, and macroeconomic stability.

Table 2. Saving and Investment (% of GDP)

	1992	1993	1994	1995
Private gap	**–3.0**	**–3.6**	**–4.1**	**–5.6**
Private saving	10.3	11.5	13.5	14.1
Private investment	13.3	15.1	17.6	19.7
Public gap	**–0.9**	**–0.4**	**–0.1**	**–0.7**
Public saving	2.2	3.0	3.7	3.4
Public investment	3.1	3.4	3.8	4.1
Foreign gap	**3.9**	**4.1**	**4.2**	**6.4**
Domestic saving	12.5	14.5	17.2	17.5
Domestic investment	16.4	18.5	21.4	23.8

The increase in domestic saving was smaller than in domestic investment, and this required an increase in foreign saving. Consequently, the deficit in the current account of the balance of payments grew, expanding from 3.9 percent of GDP in 1992 to 6.4 percent in 1995. It should be noted, however, that the current account deficit was financed basically by an inflow of long term private capital, much of it resulting from privatization or investment by foreign companies. Important public companies in the telecommunications, energy, and mining sectors were sold, bringing US$4.6 billion to the government and US$4.7 billion in future investment commitments.

This privatization process has in turn permitted the increased dynamism of the stock market, especially through the Citizens Participation Program, a mechanism used by the government to recruit new investors through the sale on credit of shares of the most profitable companies. The first of these sales occurred in 1995 with the listing on the stock exchange of Cementos Norte Pacasmayo, the first public company in which this privatization mechanism was applied, and through which 18 440 new owners were recruited. More recently, approximately 260 000 new owners were created by this program through the placement of shares held by the government in the Peruvian Telefónica Company.

President Fujimori's administration worked to reestablish relations with Peru's creditors, renegotiating the country's debt with various multilateral organizations and members of the Paris Club. In September 1991, the reintegration of the country into the international financial community was formally initiated. Peru corrected its arrears with the Inter-American Development Bank (IDB), which granted credits in exchange. Moreover, Peru signed an agreement with the International Monetary Fund (IMF) through which Peru entered the Program for the Accumulation of Rights (PAD). In March 1993, Peru successfully fulfilled its PAD — thereby removing the condition of ineligibility imposed on it since 1986 — and could then use the resources of the Fund. This made possible the signing of a three-year Expanded Facility Agreement whose goals were satisfactorily attained. It should be noted that the signing of the agreement with the IMF made possible the elimination of arrears with the World Bank and the IMF, as well as allowed advantageous renegotiation of the country's debt with member countries of the Paris Club. This has contributed to improving the image of the country and reducing Peru's country risk, hence permitting a greater inflow of foreign investment.

To this should be added the beginning of negotiations with the Committee of Creditor Banks for putting in place a Brady Plan for the Peruvian public debt that amounted to US$9 billion (US$4.4 billion in principal and US$4.6 billion in interest arrears). Preliminary agreements resulted in a 45 percent reduction of the principal and a 25 percent reduction of interest.

The deregulation of the financial market involved a series of measures, the most important of which were the liberalization of interest rates and of financial operations, the elimination of all restrictions on the participation of foreign banks and insurance companies in the Peruvian market, the elimination of state monopolies in the financial sector, and the liberalization of the foreign exchange market.

A series of legal provisions such as the General Law on Banking, Financial and Insurance Institutions expanded the operational scope of the capital market and particularly the stock market. This law implemented multiple banking, making it possible for financial institutions to add to their traditional functions, financial leasing operations, mutual funds administration, temporary subscriptions to initial issues of securities, provision of financial consulting services, and brokerage services in subsidiary companies. Moreover, the new banking legislation covers other institutions such as investment banks and consumer credit companies. The latter offer direct credit to households to acquire durable consumer goods, accept time deposits, and issue bonds and negotiable certificates of deposit. The legislation also created the so called mortgage draft, an instrument that permits financing medium and long term purchase of housing through the issue of negotiable drafts in the capital market. As a result of this new legislation, there is greater competition within the financial system, particularly in banking.

Financial institutions that participate in the stock market have an expanded array of financing and investment sources. Financial entities that are now beginning to participate actively in the capital market include clearing houses, mutual funds, investment banks, pension fund administrators, and risk classifiers.

The Lima Stock Exchange

Stabilization and structural reforms aimed to increase Peru's domestic saving and create a favorable climate that would attract foreign capital, principally long term capital. The stock market has played an important role in the saving-investment process, helping to promote productive activity and therefore sustained growth of the economy.

Activity on the Lima Stock Exchange experienced explosive growth during the reform period. In 1990 the total amount traded on the exchange amounted to US$55 million. As can be seen in Table 3, it exceeded $5 billion in 1995 and reached US$3.6 billion during the first half of 1996. Average daily trading rose from US$360,000 in 1990 to US$27 million during the first half of 1996. During 1995 the total volume of equities traded in dollars was 30 percent greater than in 1994; 90 percent of these transactions took place on the trading floor of the stock exchange. By mid 1996, nearly 250 companies were listed on the stock exchange, including some of the most important in the country (see Table 4). A large proportion of these are traded frequently. In a good number of cases, business restructuring via mergers, acquisitions, and increases in capital have been motivated by the desire to increase equity financing.

Table 3. Trading Volume on the Lima Stock Exchange (in US$ millions)

	1991	1992	1993	1994	1995	1996[1]
Exchange Floor	206.16	553.52	1906.10	3691.90	4754.32	2620.32
Cash Transactions	121.66	408.78	1629.30	3071.00	3925.98	2034.11
Report Operations	84.50	144.74	276.80	620.90	828.34	586.21
Over the Counter	384.79	180.63	75.45	362.70	525.40	991.41
Cash Transactions	383.58	147.96	62.45	327.19	507.08	963.30
-Bonds	15.60	24.16	33.03	152.85	204.02	326.02
-Short-Term Instruments	367.98	123.80	29.42	10.83	7.20	9.24
-Central Bank Certs.-C.U.C.T.	0.00	0.00	0.00	158.75	286.66	610.37
-Mortgage Draft	0.00	0.00	0.00	4.76	9.20	17.67
-Cash Term Double Operations	1.21	32.67	13.00	35.51	18.32	28.11
Total Traded L.S.E.	590.95	734.15	1981.55	4054.60	5279.72	3611.73
Daily Average Volume Floor	0.84	2.26	7.72	14.65	19.02	20.80
Daily Average Volume OTC	1.56	0.74	0.31	1.44	2.10	7.86
Daily Average Volume LSE	2.40	3.00	8.03	16.09	21.12	28.66

[1]First half of 1996.

Table 4. Registered Holdings, Securities Depository and Settlement House (in US$ millions)

	As of Dec 31, 1993	As of Dec 31, 1994	As of Dec 31, 1995	As of May 30, 1996
Number of securities registered	182	210	236	241
Number of accounts	49,727	73,923	83,285	77,943
Market Capitalization	5084.44	8162.54	11,701.20	13,123.98
Value of registered holdings	1238.88	2343.54	2593.83	2788.30
Dematerialized (%)	24.37	28.71	22.17	21.25
N° of foreign investors	1342	2643	5451	5293
Value of foreign holdings	688.53	1485.64	1560.08	1798.01
foreign holdings (%)	55.58	63.39	60.15	64.48

The volume of transactions in the Over-the-Counter (OTC) Market has also continued to grow. It should be noted that the initial transactions in this market were basically in short-term instruments. However, the long-term fixed income market is in full development. At the close of 1995, the share of the OTC market in total trading on the stock exchange did not exceed 10 percent, but its share increased to 27 percent in the first half of 1996. Greater volumes were recorded in Central Reserve Bank Certificates and bank certificates, together representing 71 percent of the total traded in the OTC market. Transactions in bonds contributed another 23 percent. In the first half of 1996, fourteen companies issued bonds worth more than US$300 million. In early 1996, the Lima Stock Exchange reduced the margin requirement on fixed-income securities to make this part of the market more dynamic. It also authorized the carrying out of repurchase operations in fixed-income securities.

Equities traded on the Lima Stock Exchange earned attractive returns for the investor in recent years. As can be seen from Table 5, in 1992, the exchange had a return of 124 percent annually in dollars, making it the second most profitable securities exchange in the world. In 1995 the Lima stock market, like other financial markets in Latin America, performed poorly due to a series of external factors, most especially the peso crisis in Mexico, followed by political-economic instability in Argentina and Brazil. In the first half of 1996, the Lima Stock Exchange generated returns of 9.9 percent in the General Index Portfolio and 12.6 percent in the Selective Index Portfolio.

Table 5. Quotation Indices (Base December 30, 1991 = 100)

	1991	1992	1993	1994	1995	1996[1]
Common stocks						
Banks	100.00	482.79	1702.94	2632.12	2656.96	3080.96
Industrial	100.00	252.29	301.75	412.68	359.81	358.94
Mining	100.00	181.94	842.08	1775.69	2276.89	2839.09
Insurance	100.00	183.41	1163.61	1709.84	1668.63	2163.15
Utilities	100.00	633.32	1271.24	1794.05	2809.57	2825.31
Diverse	100.00	270.28	897.16	1434.67	1245.29	1389.65
Worker shares[2]						
Industrial	100.00	339.95	878.24	1023.55	715.50	776.88
Mining	100.00	397.99	926.86	2195.05	1985.96	2410.23
General Index	100.00	372.95	930.47	1414.92	1243.37	1366.15
Nominal Change (%)	288.20	272.95	149.49	52.07	−12.12	9.87
Real Change (%)	62.37	138.00	78.87	31.80	−20.28	3.28
US$ Change (%)	115.00	122.40	88.67	50.46	17.34	4.47
Selective Index	100.00	486.52	985.86	1678.91	1686.32	1898.61
Nominal Change (%)	—	386.52	102.64	70.30	0.44	12.59
Real Change (%)	—	210.48	45.26	47.60	−8.88	5.84
US$ Change (%)	—	190.13	53.24	68.51	−5.53	7.06

[1]As of June 30, 1996.
[2]Worker shares are a special class of stock, preferentially entitled to share in profits but with no say in management.

Table 6. Market Capitalization (in US$ millions)

	1991	1992	1993	1994	1995	1996[1]
Common stocks	—	—	58.6	68.2	164.8	218.3
Private Pension Funds	165.6	385.7	1176.9	2243.7	2099.3	2265.2
Banks & Financial Inst.	373.2	738.8	837.1	1512.8	2001.1	2183.7
Industrial	63.5	82.7	281.8	521.5	765.4	1246.9
Mining	36.0	78.8	337.3	424.4	380.7	344.8
Insurance	172.7	662.2	1344.9	1666.2	3706.5	4126.8
Utilities	58.7	67.5	140.1	211.5	358.7	358.9
Diverse						
Worker shares						
Industrial	177.7	438.0	640.3	894.1	756.5	709.1
Mining	70.5	176.0	267.4	617.5	580.8	741.4
Diverse	—	—	—	2.5	1.7	1.7
Securities Issued Abroad	—	—	—	—	885.8	1448.4
L.S.E. Capitalization	1117.9	2629.7	5084.4	8162.4	11,701.2	13,644.5

[1]As of June 30, 1996.

Stock exchange capitalization representing the value of all the shares inscribed in the Stock Exchange at market prices, also showed a rapid growth. As shown in Table 6, total capitalization reached US$13.7 billion by mid 1996, a figure some 16.7 percent greater than at the end of 1995. Utilities shares represented 30 percent of the total, followed by those of banks and financial institution with 17 percent and industrial firms with 16 percent.

Investment Promotion

The establishment of an attractive legal framework for promoting investment has played an important role in the Peruvian capital market. The norms set on this matter grant clear and transparent rules for investors to participate freely and without restrictions in any activity whatsoever. Similarly, specific standards have been set for promoting foreign investment, providing foreign capital with nondiscriminatory treatment, promoting entry, and freely permitting the remittance of profits abroad. Provision also exists for writing contracts that guarantee tax stability and the establishment of security clauses with the World Bank and with the Overseas Private Investment Corporation (OPIC).

Table 7. Registered Nonresident Investors, Securities Depository and Settlement House

	As of December 31, 1994		As of December 31, 1995		As of May 31, 1996	
Country	Number of Holders	Holdings in Millions of US$	Number of Holders	Holdings in Millions of US$	Number of Holders	Holdings in Millions of US$
USA	956	852.72	1891	883.59	1,830	1032.59
Chile	1036	66.22	1562	44.84	1,387	42.
UK	229	218.40	758	331.82	764	401.52
Panama	76	70.19	340	55.24	351	49.70
Peru	98	4.15	174	2.32	132	1.26
Luxemburg	36	70.89	100	62.95	118	88.18
Virgin Islands	14	54.80	69	43.90	91	39.99
Australia	18	40.53	83	46.80	73	58.50
Switzerland	22	14.22	42	17.27	43	14.04
Others	158	93.52	432	71.35	504	70.33
Total	2643	1485.64	5451	1560.08	5293	1798.01

As shown in Table 7, nonresident investment has exhibited dynamic growth and reached US$1.8 billion in 1996 (as compared to US$1.5 billion in 1994).

Various legal provisions grant tax benefits to income earned in the stock market. For example, capital gains obtained through trading on the exchange floor are exempt from income tax. So too are interest and capital readjustments paid to holders of nominative shares representing debentures and mortgage drafts issued for a period greater than one year. In addition, interest earned by nominative bonds is exempt from paying the General Sales Tax (a form of Value Added Tax).

Compensation and Settlement

In November 1994, the Lima Stock Exchange introduced a new compensation and settlement system. This system permits the financial settlement of operations carried out in cash on the exchange floor, based on the net debit and credit balances (differences between sales and purchases) of the stock brokers and dealers, thereby replacing the issuance of checks for value of securities sold, as well as deconcentrating the deposit of funds from the settlement of operations that had previously been placed in only one bank. Among the most important advantages of the new system are the elimination of the costly and risky use of cash, the more effective management of the trustee function on which clearing houses and stock brokers depend, and the optimal use of material and human resources by both the exchange clearing houses and stock brokers.

One of the participants in the compensation and settlement process is the Compensating Bank, which carries out transfers between special current accounts of the clearing houses or stock brokers and the centralized account of the Lima Stock Exchange. At the request of the creditor clearing houses or stock brokers, the compensating bank can transfer the required amounts to their checking accounts in other banks through interbank transfers via the Peruvian Central Reserve Bank.

Securities Depository and Settlement House

The Securities Depository and Settlement House (CAVALI) is a service of the Lima Stock Exchange, created in 1989, with the purpose of settling operations and registering securities represented by book entry accounts on the basis of dematerialization. In February 1995, the second version of the Securities Depository was initiated. This reform fully incorporated the recommendations made on the matter by the Group of Thirty (G30), principally regarding the application of the delivery versus payment principle.

The CAVALI uses sophisticated technology that permits national and foreign users to be interconnected in real time to obtain information on their stock holdings in a framework permitting extreme security and confidentiality. Interconnection is permitted for stock dealers, custodial banks, and institutional investors in order to carry out electronic transfers of securities between the different account holders, as well as to get on-line information on stock holdings of their clients. Furthermore, CAVALI issues cards that permit the acquisition of information on holdings through terminals located in the offices of stock brokers/dealers, in CAVALI itself, and soon through automatic tellers as well.

CAVALI provides companies that issue securities electronic-mail service through which it provides daily information on transactions in the companies' securities. At the request of the issuer, it makes delivery of the rights in cash and shares to the titleholders through direct credit to their bank accounts or in CAVALI, permitting them to service the holders of their shares and debentures rapidly and at a low cost. Similarly, there is a connection to the Society for Worldwide Interbank Financial Telecommunications (SWIFT) network for the purpose of providing foreign investors direct and safe access to their securities accounts in CAVALI. It is also important to note that the Depository of the Lima Stock Exchange has been recognized by the Ibero-American Federation of Stock Exchanges (FIABV) as one of the few that have achieved total dematerialization of securities and for complying fully with the recommendations of the G30 (see Table 4).

Electronic Trading System

In August 1995, the new ELEX negotiation platform, developed by the Austrian firm Effectinvest Bank of Austria, began operation. This system permits electronic negotiation of shares, bonds, mortgage drafts, repurchase operations, and short term instruments through terminals located in the offices of the stock brokers/dealers. Furthermore, it is important to note that the system has been developed in Windows in a client/server structure that permits easy use and simultaneous visualization of different information tables in real time. ELEX grants stock brokers/dealers the same opportunities and possibilities of access to the system through a work station, as well as coexistence (in the case of operations carried out in the stock market) between negotiations on the floor and remote negotiations through terminals. From the start of electronic trading, there has been a natural migration of the negotiations from the trading floor to the offices of stock brokers.

Also noteworthy is that work has started on a project called DATACAST for the dissemination of stock exchange information through a commercial television signal, a broadcasting process that makes possible the transfer of information jointly at a national and international level to a greater number of users.

Primary Placement of Fixed-Income Securities

One of the segments little exploited by most of the companies is the primary market. This is one area in which the stock exchange is concentrating its efforts in order to increase the consolidation of the market for new issues of either fixed or variable income. In this regard, the Board of Directors of the Lima Stock Exchange agreed in mid 1996 to put at the disposal of the market a special mechanism for the primary placement of fixed-income securities, different from the existing secondary negotiation mechanism. Putting this mechanism into operation responded to the important growth shown in the primary issue of fixed-income securities, presently constituting an important financial alternative for companies.

The Lima Stock Exchange Numbering Agency

It is also important to mention the Lima Stock Exchange's affiliation with the Association of National Numbering Agencies (ANNA), headquartered in Brussels. It is the fourth numbering agency in Latin America and the only entity in Peru authorized to assign ISIN codes to Peruvian securities under internationally recognized standard structure. The ISIN codes are made up of 12 digits, the first two indicating the country of the security, the next nine identifying the issuer and the issue. The last digit is a verifier that permits associating a negotiable security with a unique code at the local and international level.

National and International Dissemination

In order to encourage the diffusion of securities exchange activity throughout the nation, the exchange has eight information offices in principal cities (Cusco, Chiclayo, Huancayo, Ica, Iquitos, Piura, Tacna, and Trujillo). The fundamental objective is to promote and to disseminate information about the stock market's activities, providing investors in all regions throughout the country with greater access to information and to existing investment alternatives.

At the international level, an agreement has been signed with the Peruvian chancellery for disseminating information on the stock exchange movement through embassies and consulates throughout the world. Furthermore, institutional cooperation agreements have been signed with various foreign stock exchanges such as those of Mexico, Madrid, Lisbon, and Thailand.

Prospects

It is expected that the stock market will continue to play a very important role in the country's economy. During the coming years, there are solid prospects of growth, given the existence of clear and transparent rules and the accelerated modernization of the Lima Stock Exchange. Investment returns will benefit from the greater stability of the economy, and will continue to be attractive in comparison to other securities markets. Economic recovery in various sectors of the economy will be reflected in higher stock prices and various other securities market indicators. There will be a continued increase in participation by institutional investors, such as Administrators of Pension Funds, that will support the growth in domestic saving and therefore contribute to the expansion of the stock market. The Lima Stock Exchange will continue to implement new services and new investment instruments to encourage the connection to global financial markets. The futures and options markets will be implemented to encourage investment in derivatives, offering investors the possibility of covering the risk of variations in the prices of certain assets and combining various trading strategies.

One of the segments less exploited by most of Peruvian companies is the primary market. The Lima Stock Exchange will seek greater participation in this area, trying to consolidate the market for new issues of either fixed or variable income. It should be mentioned that, given the legal framework of Short Term Instruments of Public Offering, it is expected that companies will use this financial instrument to finance working capital and issue more commercial paper.

In sum, the technical elements of market modernization have interacted with an effective national economic recovery to produce an active and growing securities exchange. It is anticipated that this will continue in the future.

Part Three

Innovations in Microfinance

MICROFINANCE: AN EMERGING MARKET WITHIN THE EMERGING MARKETS

Marguerite S. Berger

An Emerging Market?

In the early 1970s, before the term "emerging markets" became current, international development agencies and a few academics were already beginning to look with interest at the myriad of hawkers, peasant farmers, home-based workshops, and service providers that make up a large part of economic activity in Latin America, Asia and Africa.[1] Today, even as capital markets in these regions hang in the balance, a few forward-looking investors have joined the development bureaucrats and not-yet-defunct scribblers in identifying opportunities for investment in what we now call "microfinance," the provision of financial services to the owners of these tiny businesses.

Microfinance qualifies for the label "emerging market" because it represents a developing market for private investment. Microfinance institutions (MFIs) are enterprises that are just beginning to access capital on customary terms in countries with underdeveloped financial markets. The clients of MFIs

[1]The International Labor Office, which conducted a study of employment in Kenya in 1972, was one of the first development institutions to look to microenterprises as a source of employment generation in developing countries, using the term "informal sector"to describe what we now call "microenterprises."

are businesses just beginning to access capital from institutional sources in these markets.

What has happened to produce this transformation in the way we view microenterprises and their financial services? And what is the future of the fledgling microfinance industry? The past 30 years have seen a shift in the way we think about microfinance, in the economic and regulatory policy framework within which it operates, and in the development of products and institutions capable of offering microfinance services on a sustainable basis. This paper explores these developments, focusing on the case of Latin America.

What is Microfinance?

Only recently coined, the term "microfinance" is already being used in many different ways. For our purposes it is defined as financial services — credit, deposits, insurance and others — for microenterprises. Microfinance and microcredit are often treated as synonyms, although microfinance refers to an array of financial services on a micro scale, including but not limited to credit. This paper focuses on the credit side of microfinance, which is its most developed side, especially in Latin America.

As shown in Table 1, microcredit differs significantly from traditional commercial lending in that loans are of smaller sizes, mature earlier, and rely on character rather than collateral as a guarantee.

Two caveats must be borne in mind with regard to the definition of microfinance. Although the central feature of microfinance is its clientele, microenterprises, this does not imply that these clients borrow only for business purposes. Given the informal nature of most microenterprises, where household and business activities often overlap, it is common for such borrowers to seek loans for consumption as well as production. The secret to microcredit is finding ways to make credit decisions and to manage the risk of lending to customers who have neither a verifiable salary nor assets that can be easily valued or seized.

The second caveat concerns the nature of microenteprise. The lower bound of this concept is here defined as any economic activity where the owner risks his or her own resources to produce a product or generate

Table 1. Distinctive Features of Microfinance

Area	Traditional Finance	Microfinance
Lending Methodology	(1) based on collateral (2) more documentation (3) less labor intensive (4) loans are usually serviced monthly, quarterly, or yearly	(1) based on character (2) less documentation (3) more labor intensive (4) loans are usually serviced/repaid in weekly or bi-monthly installments
Loan Portfolio	(1) fewer loans (2) loans larger in size (3) collateralized (4) longer maturity (5) more stable delinquency	(1) more loans (2) loans smaller in size (3) uncollateralized (4) shorter maturity (5) more volatile delinquency
Institutional Structure and Governance (of regulated financial institutions)	(1) profit maximizing institutional and individual shareholders (2) creation by spin-off from existing regulated institution (3) centralized organization with branch offices located in cities	(1) mainly non-profit institutional shareholders (2) creation by conversion from NGO or formation of new entity (3) decentralized set of small units in areas with weak infrastructure

Sources: Adapted from Rock and Otero, 1996; and Behrenbach and Churchill, 1997.

an income. This defines as enterprises many activities that some would not consider worthy of the term. The upper bound of the definition is usually arbitrarily set by the number of employees the enterprise supports or its total assets. Employment is somewhat easier to measure; five or ten workers are the most commonly used cutoffs. But microfinance clients at any one point in time may include businesses larger than this, since some longstanding customers grow beyond this size.

The Economic Potential and Limitations of the Microenterprise Sector

The microenterprise sector represents a huge untapped market for the financial service industry in developing countries. There are more than fifty million microenterprises in Latin America and the Caribbean. Over 80 percent of the region's businesses have fewer than ten employees, and they employ more than 120 million people. Though insufficient reliable data exist, and conditions vary widely across countries, studies show that microenterprises employ a significant share of the labor force, ranging from one-third in Panama to almost 60 percent in Bolivia. Their share of national output ranges from less than 10 percent to nearly 50 percent, depending on the country (Berger and Guillamón 1996).

According to the International Labor Office, microenterprises accounted for roughly half of the region's employment by the mid 1990s (see Table 2 below), while the public sector and enterprises with over ten employees accounted for only 44 percent (the remaining 6 percent was in domestic service). Moreover, the share of employment in microenterprises has been growing steadily since the 1970s.

Despite their sheer numbers and their important contribution to output and employment in developing countries, few microenterprises are able to obtain loans or other services from banks, credit unions or finance companies. It is estimated that fewer than 5 percent of microenterprises in Latin America have access to institutional sources of credit (Barry 1995). A new sense of the possibilities of the microenterprises' niche market has coincided with an evolution toward a more businesslike approach to the structure, management, and objectives of successful MFIs, a group still largely dominated by non-profit foundations.

Microenterprises are found in all fields of economic activity, including commerce, agriculture, manufacturing and services, but they are most prominent in the retail trade and service sectors. Microenterprises are characterized by informality in organizational structure and compliance with regulations, use of family labor, rudimentary technologies, discontinuities in production, the combination of different industrial and occupational categories in one unit, and the overlapping of household and business activities.

Although size parameters are the main elements used to define the microenterprise sector, strict adherence would quickly illustrate their arbitrariness. This sector is extremely heterogeneous and varies dramatically in terms of size and composition in different countries throughout the region. At the lower end of the spectrum are subsistence level household/firms

Table 2. Microenterprise Employment in Latin America, Mid 1990s

Country	Economically Active Population (EAP)	Self-employed Micro-entrepreneurs (% of EAP)	Micro-enterprise Workers (% of EAP)	Total Micro-enterprise Work Force (% of EAP)	Number Employed in the Micro-enterprise Sector
Argentina	14,345,171	27.0	18.1	45.1	6,469,672
Bolivia	2,530,409	37.1	19.0	56.1	1,419,559
Brazil	59,420,165	23.4	24.5	47.9	28,462,259
Chile	5,219,300	23.7	20.6	44.3	2,312,150
Colombia	11,669,274	26.4	30.9	57.3	6,686,494
Costa Rica	1,187,005	17.8	23.1	40.9	485,485
Ecuador	3,359,767	31.5	15.0	46.5	1,562,292
Honduras	1,728,599	31.5	15.1	46.6	805,527
Mexico	33,651,812	30.7	20.9	51.6	17,364,335
Panama	940,301	19.5	12.9	32.4	304,658
Paraguay	1,097,724	22.3	34.9	57.2	627,898
Peru	2,945,101	35.2	16.2	51.4	1,513,782
Venezuela	7,537,817	27.3	14.5	41.8	3,150,808

Source: ILO Latin American and Caribbean Office, *Panorama Laboral 95*.

that depend exclusively upon family labor, with no distinct separation between household and firm finances. At the upper end of the scale are firms that have more in common with their counterparts in the small enterprise category — they utilize relatively sophisticated production technologies and are directly linked to larger firms in the modern sector of the economy through diverse supplier-client relationships.

Few microenterprises will grow beyond two to three employees, but they are nevertheless part of the continuous process of creation and destruction of businesses that lead to improved productivity and growth. The smallest microenterprises often labeled as "survival" or subsistence businesses, may remain at the bottom because they have low levels of capitalization, they are new start-ups, or they have suffered a crisis. These businesses may have a similar size, and they may be equally precarious, but the solutions to their problems are different, and are not solely related to their size.

Many microenterprises experiencing modest growth are actually in a process of consolidation at a low level, and are not transformating into small- or medium-size businesses.[2] A third type of microenteprise already shares some characteristics with the small and medium business sectors. These are the businesses that are set to grow at a rapid pace and consolidate at a larger size. However, just because they are in a dynamic phase does not mean that they cannot be reduced to the survival state by external or internal management crises.

Are Microentrepreneurs Poor?

Studies show that owners and workers of microenterprises are a very diverse group, and that the relationship between microfinance and poverty is a complicated one (Gulli 1998). As shown in Table 3, most owner/operators of microenterprises do not live below the poverty line. The workers of

Table 3: Poverty Incidence in the Microenterprise Sector (% of poor in each category)

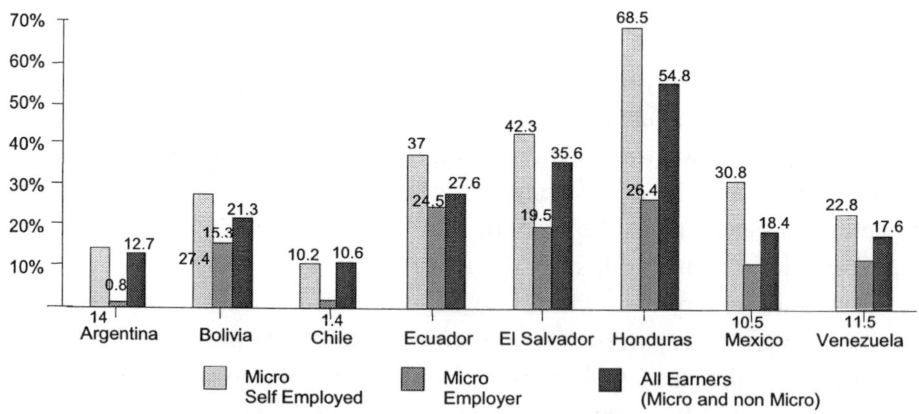

Source: Orlando and Pollack forthcoming.

[2]This pattern of growth within the small business sector is found within the industrialized countries as well. In the United States, where both birth and death rates in the small business sector are very high, the term "gazelles" is used to refer to those few small businesses that account for the bulk of the *growth* of jobs and output in the sector as a whole.

microenterprises are poorer than those in other businesses or the public sector, but in some countries the incidence of poverty of microenterprise workers is lower than that of self-employed owners (with no employee).

For the private sector investor looking for emerging market opportunities, the question remains whether the microenterprise sector is a profitable niche with untapped customers for financial services. For the Inter-American Development Bank, the World Bank and other development agencies, the issues are whether microfinance can reach the poor on a significant scale and still make a profit, and whether increasing the availability of credit to the poor and/or those microenterprises that employ them can have a significant impact on poverty (Gulli 1998).

Between Poverty and Profits: Competing Paradigms of Microfinance

The 1970s saw the emergence of a new way of looking at microenterprises, a shift from the earlier negative paradigm of "the informal sector" — an underground economy of illegal activities, tax evaders and disguised unemployment — to regarding it as a source of livelihood for the poor in developing countries (International Labor Office 1976).

While the informal sector had been seen as a transitional segment of the economy divorced from the "mainstream," as well as a problem for development policy and programs to overcome, the new paradigm focused on this sector as a potential source of employment that required and deserved public sector support to become sustainable and even expand. In this context, microcredit became an important tool to help microenterprises create jobs. It was also seen by many nongovernmental organizations as a tool for improving the lives of the poor, and sometimes as an incentive to draw poor people into in other activities.

A third paradigm, which emerged in the late 1980s and early 1990s, is a move from microenterprise as a livelihood of the poor, often accompanied by charity, to microenterprise as a business. From this perspective, size, not poverty, constitutes the defining characteristic of the microenterprise sector, although advocates of microenterprise development still argue that the sector is the key to reducing poverty in developing countries. Microentrepreneurs are manufacturers, retailers and service providers that are an integral part of the economy as are suppliers and purchasers. They do not only create jobs, but contribute as well to economic growth. In this respect, microenterprise is similar to a small enterprise and it is pivotal to the economy in most developing countries. Along with this perspective is the view of microenterprises as clients or customers of institutions providing services (Otero and Rhyne 1994).

In the 1990s, governments and development donors have increased their support for microenterprise development and especially microfinance. However, the priorities and means of support have changed in line with the new paradigm. MFIs are no longer funded through donations alone — they are receiving loans and "equity investments" from their traditional donors and tapping commercial financial markets, especially in their home countries.

We are today living in a world of competing paradigms: none of the three views of microenterprise described here has disappeared. Each one colors the public policy debate about microenterprise development in a different way. However, the only one that envisions microenterprises, and consequently microfinance, as "emerging markets" is the paradigm that casts microenterprises as businesses and customers. Whether this view is accurate, and to what extent it is compatible with either of the other two, is subject to empirical confirmation. The test is now underway in Latin America where the involvement of the commercial private sector has been the greatest.

The Changing Environment: Financial Sector Reform in Latin America

Over the past ten years, the Latin American economies have experienced profound structural changes, especially in the financial sector. Changes in financial regulation in most countries in Latin America have redefined the parameters of microfinance. In some countries, such as Bolivia and Peru, changes in banking regulations have made it possible for lenders previously operating as nonprofit foundations to convert to formal financial intermediaries, thereby greatly enhancing these lenders' access to financial markets and their prospects for long term sustainability.

Most countries of the region were characterized by financial repression during the 1980s. In the late 1980s and early 1990s, sweeping reforms were carried out throughout the region, removing interest rate ceilings, reducing or eliminating directed credit, reducing barriers to entry in the financial sector (including eliminating the preferred status of government-owned banks, or even eliminating such banks), and improving banking regulation and supervision. These reforms substantially changed the structure and opportunities in the financial sector, paving the way for increased competition in the sector and increased interest in new niche markets, including small and medium microenterprises (Cuevas 1996; Westley 1995; Basch and Morales 1995).

There is growing recognition that in order for MFIs to function profitably and soundly, specific regulations will be required in such areas as capital adequacy, risk weighting of assets, provisions for bad debt and reporting requirements (Jansson and Wenner 1997). One example of the constraints placed on institutions that target microenterprise clients is the required minimum capitalization of formal financial institutions, whether they are full scale commercial banks, or regulated finance companies that may or may not be permitted to accept term or demand deposits. Table 4 shows that institutions wanting to specialize in microfinance would find it difficult to comply with the minimum capital standards and leverage their capital sufficiently to stay profitable. In Colombia, for example, a specialized MFI would require over 200,000 customers in order to satisfy both of these conditions, and this with an average loan size of $1000, which is considerably higher than that of the typical specialized microlender. The most successful microfinance bank in the region, Banco Sol, has fewer than 100,000 microenterprise borrowers. The region's other successful institutions have between 20,000 and 50,000 active microenterprise clients. The prospects are better for finance companies in the region, however, but these companies offer only a limited range of services.

Improving regulation and supervision for microfinance will be a challenge in Latin America where prudential safeguards for banks and capital markets in general have lagged behind other types of financial reform. The banking superintendencies of the region are undergoing a process of modernization and most countries' attention is devoted to implementating the recommenda-

Table 4. Minimum Capital Requirements and their Impact on Micro-Loan Portfolios

Country	Institution	Minimum Capital (US$ Million)	Capital Adequacy Ratio (%)	Minimum No. of Clients with Average Loan of US$1000
ARGENTINA	Bank	15	11.5	91,305
	Finance Company	15		91,305
BOLIVIA	Bank	2.76	8	24,150
	Finance Company	1		8,750
BRAZIL	Bank	8.5	10	59,500
	Finance Company	3.6		50,400
CHILE	Bank	13.3	11.3	82,390
	Finance Company	6.8		42,124
COLOMBIA	Bank	27	9	210,000
	Finance Company	5		38,889
ECUADOR	Bank	7	9	54,445
	Finance Company	3.75		29,167
EL SALVADOR	Bank	5.7	8.6	46,396
	Finance Company	1.5		12,210
GUYANA	Bank	7	8	61,250
	Finance Company	2		17,500
MEXICO	Bank	15.5	8	135,625
NICARAGUA	Bank	2	8	17,500
	Finance Company	2		17,500
PARAGUAY	Bank	4.6	10	32,200
	Finance Company	2.3		16,100
PERU	Bank	5.6	9.1	43,077
	Finance Company	2.8		21,539
URUGUAY	Bank	6.3	8	55,125
	Finance Company	3.8		33,250

Source: Jansson with Wenner 1997.
Notes: It is assumed that 70 percent of the institution's assets are in its loan portfolio.

tions of the Basle Committee.[3] Many superintendencies are overwhelmed by the responsibility for supervising their traditional charges in a more competitive and perhaps more volatile financial sector, and have very limited desire or ability to attend to nonbank financial institutions.

Two examples of the way a favorable regulatory environment can create opportunities for private sector involvement in microfinance are the cases of Peru and Bolivia: in 1995, both countries modified the laws governing their financial sectors to recognize and facilitate the creation of specialized non-bank financial intermediaries designed to provide services to micro and small businesses. Private Financial Funds (FFPs) in Bolivia and Small and Microenterprise Development Entities (EDPYMEs) in Peru are regulated financial institutions that offer limited banking services and have capital and reserve requirements tailored to microfinance rather than commercial banking.

In Bolivia, the first FFPs to commence operations were the Caja de Los Andes in La Paz and FASSIL in Santa Cruz. Both capture deposits and make small loans to microentreprenurs, and were capitalized by private shareholders, although Caja de Los Andes also relies primarily on nonprofit investors and international development agencies. FASSIL (a name which is similar to the Spanish word for "easy" and is spelled with two dollar signs) offers consumer credit as its primary loan product, but also lends to microenterprises for business purposes. Today there are four FFPs in Bolivia and seven EDPYMEs in Peru, and several others currently in the process of formalization in both countries. In Peru, there has been considerable interest in EDPYMEs because they are easily capitalized, have access to commercial and rediscounted sources of funds, can capture deposits (at higher levels of capitalization), offer shares to private investors, as well as provide a variety of credit instruments. CREDINPET in Lima, the first

[3]The Basle Committee on Banking Supervision is a committee of banking supervisory authorities, which was established by the central bank governors of the Group of Ten Countries in 1975. It usually meets at the Bank for International Settlement in Basle, where its permanent Secretariat is located. For further information see: Core Principles for Effective Banking Supervision, *Basle Committee on Banking Supervision*, Basle, Switzerland, 1997. A short article by A.D. Crokett (1997), General Manager of the Bank for International Settlements, also highlights these issues in the Latin American context.

Table 5. New Financial Intermediaries: Comparison of FFP and EDPYME

Areas Of Regulation	FFP (Bolivia)	EDPYME (Peru)
Minimum Capital: Capital Adequacy Ratio: Deposits: Security:	US$ 1 million 10% (10:1) savings, but not demand deposits recognizes solidarity groups, movables, and jewelry	US$ 265,000 10% (10:1) savings deposits, but only after special permission from the superintendency not defined
Maximum Loan Size:	3% of net capital (US$30,000)	5% of net capital (US$12,500)
Unsecured Credits:	1% of net capital (US$10,000)	not defined
Foreign Exchange:	yes	yes
Other Operating Restrictions:	no trust and foreign trade operations, equities, underwriting, or mutual fund management	not defined

Source: Adapted from Rock and Otero 1996; Resolución SBS No. 259–295 (Peru); Decreto Supremo 24,000 (Bolivia). Cited in Jansson and Wenner 1997.

EDPYME, was founded by a non-governmental organization (NGO) and a group of private sector shareholders. The possibility of using EDPYMEs and FFPs to provide consumer credit as well has sparked considerable interest on the part of private firms in Peru that are looking to finance the purchase of their products. This reflects the similarities between microfinance and consumer credit (although microfinance borrowers do not have verifiable salaries that can be used for the credit decision).

Commercialization of Microfinance: Fact or Fantasy?

As noted earlier, fewer than 5 percent of Latin American and Caribbean microentrepreneurs have access to formal financial services. Suppliers' credits and informal money lending are important sources of microfinance and will continue to play a key role in the future, given their advantages for overcoming the information constraints to microlending. Formal financial institutions, using their traditional credit technologies, do not serve microenterprises well because of the relatively high cost of making small loans and the lack of required forms of collateral. Microenterprises face constraints on the deposit side as well. Most microenterprises are financed through the owners' and family members' savings, but minimum deposit requirements, limited liquidity and high transaction costs limit their access and use of formal savings mechanisms.

Given the magnitude of the microenterprise sector in Latin America, the penetration of this market even by the most successful institutions — those reaching over 50,000 microenterprise clients — is still limited to a small percentage of the sector. In the past, significant subsidies for microenterpise support organizations providing loans to low income business owners have been justified by the high costs of such specialized financial activity. The optimistic vision of the future is that increasing competition will force microlenders to be more efficient. As a result, the need for subsidies will decrease and the microentrepreneurs who are customers of these financial services will enjoy the benefits of lower interest rates, increased access, and better services such as bill payment and credit cards (Vega 1998).

The resources available in multilateral and donor agencies are not sufficient to satisfy the demand for microfinance and other services. Financial resources for microenterprise development must come from the private sector. But investment in microenterprise development from financial markets will only be possible if those resources can be made available on commercial terms. Private investment in the sector's development is also deterred by unstable macroeconomic and financial sector conditions in emerging markets, the legal and regulatory framework and barriers to entry for new sources of capital (including lack of knowledge of the sector, especially of successful program experiences, and lack of appropriate credit and other technologies to serve the sector).

In Latin America, unlike Asia, microfinance has generally remained in the private sector, although in the hands of nonprofits. The state-run loan programs for agriculture and small business, prevalent in the 1960s, 1970s and early 1980s, did not reach the microenterprise level and tended to be captured by the better-off businesses within their target groups. The Latin American market has distinct characteristics (especially when contrasted with the better known Asian experience) — higher average per capita incomes, with very high inequality, historically high inflation rates, very high real interest rates (both deposit and lending rates), high spreads, and very limited financial deepening (Edwards 1995). This gives a distinct cast to microfinance in the region.

Different factors are prompting private investors' interest in microfinance in Latin America. On one hand, competitive forces and regulatory reform are pushing some institutions toward the microfinance business; on the other hand, microfinance is an opportunity pulling in institutions that can take advantage of existing core competencies or new regulations in the financial sector to develop new products for this market. Pushed by the growing competitive pressures in the financial sector, some local financial institutions are looking for untapped markets for their services or potential subsidies (see Table 6). Other institutions are discovering that their experience in consumer finance or nonprofits gives them core competencies on which to build a new business of micro-scale commercial lending. In the absence of fully functioning credit bureaux, these lenders find that a large client base can yield sufficient information to screen credit applications based on risk factors.

At present, the bulk of private sector interest in microfinance is not solely profit driven. The most common reasons offered by those formal financial institutions active in microfinance are somewhat complex, ranging from public relations, to a long term view of market development and the

Table 6. Competitive Forces Expanding Commercial Microfinance

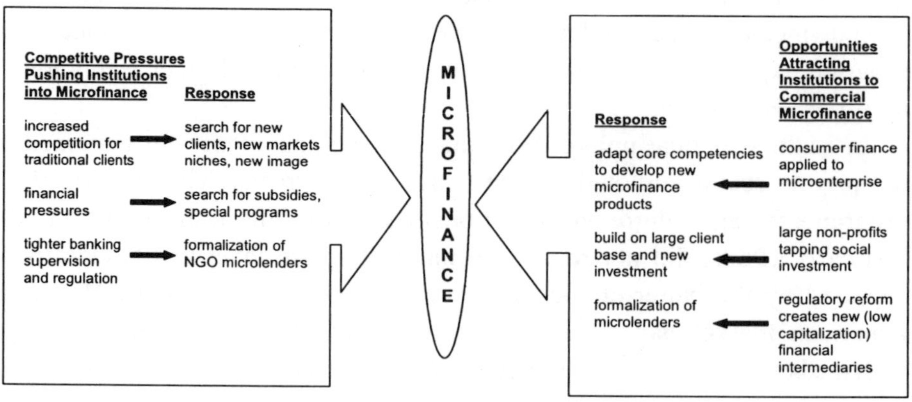

perceived need to contribute to improving economic and social conditions in their countries (Microenterprise Development Review 1998; Baydas, Graham and Valenzuela 1997). Social and philanthropic motives can also come into play, frequently mixing with public image considerations.

Some institutions are willing to invest in learning how to manage small loans and deposits using new microfinance methodologies in order to cultivate future clients closer to their mainstream profile, or to increase their interest revenues. Microentrepreneurs are willing to pay higher rates of interest because they can obtain high productivity gains from relatively small infusions of capital and they have limited access to other sources of finance. For mainstream financial institutions, however, the potential for profit is often offset by the relatively high transaction costs involved in microcredit (Wenner and Campos 1998).

Can microfinance make money? Based on the current experience in Latin America, it appears that microfinance can be profitable, with or without support from international donors. Table 7 illustrates the types of returns obtained by some of the best performing MFIs in the region.

The data presented in Table 7 show that microfinance can be profitable, although the size of the loan portfolios and total assets remain small by the standards of commercial banks, due to the small average loan size. The return on assets in some of the top performing institutions cited in the table ranges from 3 percent to 6 percent, and return on equity ranges from 14 percent in the case of Women's World Banking–Cali to 52 percent in the case of FUCAC Credit Union in Uruguay. The tendency is for return on equity to outperform industry standards, while return on assets is lower, reflecting the lower leverage of MFIs. Microcredit also tends to have lower rates of arrears, but higher administrative costs than conventional loan products. Its higher operating costs are compensated for by higher interest yields.

It appears that at its best, microcredit is a "lending technology" that allows lenders to manage the risks and costs of lending to very small borrowers who are dependent on income from self-employment or business ownership. What is less clear is whether there exists a trade-off between the ability to reach very small borrowers (including those who live below the poverty line) and profitability. It is also not clear how high up the scale of small enterprise customers these techniques will work. They appear to have built-

Table 7. Financial Performance Selected MFIs in Latin America

	Bolivia Banco Sol (Bank)	Paraguay Visión (Finance Co.)	Uruguay Fucac (Credit Union)	Peru Caja Areq. (Savings Bank)	Bolivia Los Andes (Finance Co.)	Colombia WWB–Cali (NGO)
Loan portfolio (US$ millions)	64	19	19	22	20	6
Past due > 30 days (%)	1.11	8.20	7.10	2.10	0.65	1.62
Number of clients (thousands)	76.2	12.1	10.4	36.6	29.5	10.9
Average loan size (US$)	828	1,563	1,868	593	693	539
No. of branches	34	14	2	9	11	5
Return on assets (%)	3	3	6	4	5	6
Return on equity (%)	23	19	52	36	36	14
Portfolio yield (%)	33	43	49	47	29	46
Operating expenses / average portfolio (%)	18	18	10	19	16	15
No. of clients per officer	416	205	2,072	401	518	407
Portfolio per officer (US$ thousands)	349	320	3,871	356	358	219

Source: "Standards of performance," a joint project of the Inter-American Development Bank and Private Sector Initiatives Corp. Results as of 31 December 1997.

in drawbacks when applied to larger scale clients since they are based on the experience of lending to large numbers of very small clients, creating their credit history by gradually increasing loan size, and covering relatively high operating costs with high interest rates. From the investor's point of view, both the upper and lower boundaries of this market are a concern. From the development agency's point of view, the lower bound is the main issue. As shown in Table 8, there does seem to be some trade-off between customer size (as measured by average loan size in the microloan portfolio)

Table 8. Performance and Outreach of Microfinance Institutions in Latin America

Location	Peer Group	Number	Average Loan Size	Adjusted Return on Equity	Financial Self Sufficiency	Profit Margin	Real Internal Yield	Administrative Expense/Loan Portfolio	Clients Per Loan Officer
World	Fully Sustainable	26	$428	4%	113%	10%	34%	27%	108
Lat. Am.	Large Broad Based	6	$636	4%	116%	12%	26%	26%	130
Lat. Am.	Med. Broad Based	7	$414	6%	115%	15%	45%	32%	96
Lat. Am.	Med./Low Broad Based	8	$340	–8%	83%	–23%	31%	42%	160
Lat. Am.	Small/Low Broad Based	5	$120	–17%	73%	–42%	49%	69%	96

Source: *The Microbanking Bulletin*, Issue No. 2 (Boulder, CO: The Economics Institute, July 1998).

and profitability (Rhyne 1998). However, it is not clear whether this is due to the newness of some of the institutions in the lower-end peer groups, poor credit decisions, or inherently higher costs of doing business at the low end.

New Microfinance Models in Latin America

Even readers of *The Wall Street Journal* have heard of Banco Sol, the microfinance bank in Bolivia with over 70,000 clients and an enviable financial performance, but there are many other MFIs in Latin America worthy of notice. Table 9 presents a typology of the variety of MFIs that operate in Latin America today. They range from commercial banks and finance companies with some microenterprise clients, to NGOs that give credit, but are also involved in many different non-financial activities.

Not all of the MFIs in Table 9 involve commercial interests. Commercial private sector participation in microfinance comes about through the creation of formal lending institutions from the portfolios of nonprofits (often called "upgrading") or by the entrance of commercial banks and finance companies into the microfinance market (called "downscaling"). We will review some of these experiences in greater detail below.

Up-grading. Nonprofit organizations have been lending to microenterprises in most countries in Latin America since the 1970s. Although they have operated for a long time in a gray area at the edge of legal regulations, some of these institutions have grown and transformed themselves into regulated financial institutions, providing a vehicle for private capital investment. Others have become majority shareholders in new banks or finance companies that specialize in microfinance. Banco Sol in Bolivia led this process, followed by Caja de Ahorro y Crédito Los Andes, in Bolivia, Financiera Calpia in El Salvador, Finansol in Colombia (now Finamérica), and others in Peru, Venezuela, Dominican Republic and Haiti.

However, not all NGO transformations have been successful. The region's successful microfinance institutions are only now being tested by a major economic slump. In the case of Finansol, a finance company formed by an NGO engaged in microfinance in Colombia, rapid portfolio growth masked serious problems. Corposol, the nonprofit parent of Finansol, retained the

Table 9. Typology of MFIs

	COMMERCIAL FFIs*	SPECIALIZED FFIs*	SPECIALIZED NGOs	MULTIPURPOSE NGOs
Strategy and goals	• Expansion into new markets • Institutional image	• Profitability • Social impact	• Social Impact • Cost coverage • Graduation	• Social impact • Initial cost coverage
Clients	Microenterprises in minority	Micro and small enterprises	Microenterprises	Microenterprises
Legal form	• Banks • Finance companies • Credit unions	• Banks • Finance companies • Credit unions	NGOs	NGOs
Methodology	• Individual lending • Instruments vary according to segment	• Individual and/or solidarity group lending • Leasing	Individual and/or solidarity group lending	Individual and/or solidarity group lending
Sustainability	The FFI as a whole is sustainable	Striving towards profitability and efficiency	Striving towards operational efficiency	Difficult to isolate microenterprise activities
Capital sources	• Capital • Certificates • Inter-bank loans • Clients'savings • Donor funds	• Capital • Certificates • Inter-bank loans • Clients'savings • Donor funds	• Bank loans • Subsidized • Social funds • Donor funds	• Few bank loans • Subsidized • Social funds • Donor funds
Examples	Banco del Comercio (Costa Rica) Bco. Empresarial (Guat.) FASSIL (Bolivia) Bco. del Pacífico (Ecua.) Financ. Familiar (Para.)	FIE (Bolivia) Mibanco (Peru) Los Andes (Bolivia) Banco Sol (Bolivia) Fin. Calpia (El Salv.) Multicredit (Panama)	Propesa (Chile) Emprender (Arg.) Fundasol (Urug.) Prodem (Bolivia) Funadeh (Honduras)	CARE FINCA Catholic Relief Services Various NGOs, Village Banks and grassroots org.

Source: Fernando Lucano and Miguel Taborga, "Tipologia de instituciones financieras para la microempresa en América y el Caribe," occasional paper. Washington, D.C.: Inter-American Development Bank, 1998.

*"FFI" refers to (regulated) formal financial institutions.

credit extension staff while Finansol, the commercial financial institution, served only as a booking and financing agent. Since most of Corposol's operating revenues were generated by training fees charged concurrently with loan disbursements, this created an incentive to disburse loans quickly and disregard loan collection. The institution launched an overly ambitious variety of new products using unproven methodologies, in some cases allowing two or three different types of loans per client. In addition, Finansol appears to have misrepresented its rate of asset growth to the Superintendency of Banks by using questionable accounting practices (Steege 1998).

Downscaling is the term given to commercial bank operations that reach the microfinance market. Some commercial banks, such as Banco del Pacífico in Ecuador, Caja Social in Colombia and Banco del Desarrollo in Chile entered this market out of a sense of social responsibility. Others, such as Banco Weise in Peru, offered loans to NGOs that on-lent to individual microenterprises in the past and are now experimenting with their own microfinance products and subsidiaries. Some banks and finance companies, such as Banco del Desarrollo in Chile and Financiera Visión in Paraguay, have built on existing competencies and financial products to expand their activities into microfinance. Commercial banks' cost structures and corporate culture present significant challenges, however, and specialized products, credit technology, information systems and properly trained credit officers are key to overcoming these barriers (for example, see Wenner and Campos 1998; Baydas, Graham and Valenzuela 1997).

Intermediate models. In order to overcome management problems when entering the microfinance market, some banks have teamed up with nonprofit organizations or absorbed their microfinance portfolios to jump start their entry into this market. This is the case of Bangente in Venezuela (Banco de la Gente Empresarial), that grew out of a partnership between a large existing commercial bank, Banco del Caribe, and three non-profit foundations involved in microfinance — Fundación Mendoza, Grupo Social CESAP, and Fundación para la Vivienda Popular. Bangente is a subsidiary of Banco del Caribe that will accept deposits and make loans to microenterprises. It will conduct these operations in association with its NGO partners who have considerable experience in microenterprise development. Customers will move from the NGO portfolio to the new bank, and the NGOs will then specialize in nonfinancial services for these and other customers. In its pilot project phase, loan disbursement and collection will be carried out through a single agency of the Banco del Caribe in Caracas, while loan preparation and follow-up services will be out-sourced to the NGOs.

Other examples along these lines are found in the case of Banco Solidario in Ecuador, a bank subsidiary that used technical assistance from microfinance

NGOs to get started, and now offers advisory services to microfinance NGOs seeking to upgrade their banking technology and skills, as well as microfinance services to its own clients. The case of Banco del Comercio in Costa Rica presents yet another model: it is a commercial bank that purchased outright an NGO portfolio of microloans and built on this to create a new area of operations that has proved more profitable than its traditional corporate finance activities.

Private foundations, some of which combine a mix of social and religious motivations with a philosophy of generating sufficient revenues for full cost coverage with growth, have invested as shareholders in MFIs. Fundación Social is a private foundation based in Bogotá, Colombia and controlled by the Jesuits. It has built consolidated assets of over US$1.3 billion since it began in 1911. Fundación Social entered the field of microfinance in 1991 by opening branches of its bank, Caja Social de Ahorros, in extremely poor neighborhoods. It has close to a million deposit accounts averaging $200, three quarters of its loans are in amounts less than $3000, and it is ranked among Latin America's most profitable banks.

State-owned banks. So far the state-owned banks that still exist in Latin America have been slow to enter microfinance. One notable exception is the Banco del Estado in Chile, which after watching the experience of a private Chilean bank, Banco del Desarrollo, is creating its own microfinance products and growing rapidly. Banco del Estado has a solid base of small savers drawn from the same low- and middle-income segments that include most microentrepreneurs. It may be able to build on this base, as Caja Social in Colombia is doing, to create a profitable microcredit portfolio. The municipal savings banks in Peru (Cajas Municipales), owned by the local municipal governments, are another interesting type of microfinance institution. They tend to target better-off clients and the local government as depositors, while targeting lower income microentrepreneurs for short-term loans at relatively high rates. Many of them have excellent financial performance, as illustrated by the Caja Municipal de Arequipa in Table 7.

Finance Companies. Nonbank financial intermediaries, such as finance companies and other lenders with varying degrees of regulation and supervision, may ultimately become the most important actors in commercial microfinance. Finance companies offer products similar to microcredits in terms and payment, but they generally depend on a consumer durable purchase as collateral that can be repossessed. They also use the salary of the borrower to calculate his or her ability to repay. In Bolivia, Chile, Paraguay and Peru, however, there are examples of consumer finance companies that are developing new techniques to assess and manage the risks of lending to borrowers who do not have a regular salary, and it is likely that more of such companies will emerge in the future.

Private non-bank financial intermediaries, such as consumer finance companies, small savings banks, credit unions or specialized entities like Peru's EDPYMEs or Bolivia's FFPs can offer advantages not available to a commercial bank in terms of capital, reserve and provision requirements, leaner cost structures, and greater flexibility and responsiveness. Some can also mobilize savings. Existing finance companies that have provided consumer credit have the advantage of having obtained some experience in managing numerous small transactions. Many also have extensive payment history records for their clients that can be adapted to assess the risk of lending to microenterprises using credit scoring techniques developed for other markets.

Credit Unions. Credit unions are numerous in Latin America, despite the problems they have endured over the past two decades. Their recent history is one of struggling to recover from hyperinflation and the distorting effects of past donor funding, which undermined their deposit base and eroded the repayment culture of their members. However, their focus has traditionally been on lending to salaried workers (very often, credit union membership is organized around employment in a particular firm or in the public sector) or land-owning agricultural producers. Despite targeting the popular market of middle and lower-middle class workers, they have been slow to expand services to the self-employed and microenterprise owners. Recent experiences in Guatemala and Uruguay, however, show that credit unions may become important actors in the microfinance industry in the future (Westley and Shaffer 1997; Almeyda 1996; Barham, Boucher and Carter 1996).

Innovative Models for Linking Microfinance to Financial Markets

New Products. Credit cards and smart cards are poised to become a new wave in microfinance. Credit cards offer lenders the advantages of lower transaction costs, ease of information management, and increased customer access. MasterCard and other credit card finance companies have their eye on the potential of the microcredit market. They have seen their traditional upper and upper middle class market become saturated in recent years, and are looking at lower income segments as potential clients (Ruis-Velasco 1996). In the Dominican Republic, la Asociación para el Desarrollo de la Microempresas (ADEMI), Banco Popular and MasterCard have teamed up to offer a MasterCard ADEMI Popular for members of ADEMI. Cardholders may receive cash advances, check balances, and make payments through the 60 ATMs and 45 offices of Banco Popular. The card also offers travel and theft insurance, bill payment services, and up to 12-month terms for consumer credit. Smart cards also offer the potential of facilitating transactions on both the deposit and borrowing side, but their use is currently still limited in this industry.

Deposits. So far, MFIs have lagged behind in developing products that meet microenterprise demands for instruments to facilitate payments, safeguard money and accumulate savings (Haning, Elserand and Wysniwski 1997). Commercial banks, savings banks and credit unions are far better placed than NGOs to develop these services, since NGOs are not regulated and in most countries are even prohibited from accepting deposits from the public. The same obstacles that plagued microcredit in its infancy are facing microdeposit products today — their small size implies very high administrative costs. The development of new microdeposit products will be important, however, as a vehicle for keeping good customers by offering services they want, enhancing information on borrowers to assess lending risk, creating sizeable assets to mitigate lending risk, and funding lending operations. Unfortunately, many inexperienced MFIs, unfamiliar with managing the liabilities side of a financial institution, see the last reason as the most important. Formal institutions familiar with deposit services are likely to be more cautious, even though they are in a better position to develop microdeposit products.

Developing Sources of Funding for MFIs

Until recently MFIs, which were mainly non-profit NGOs, have been almost entirely dependent on donor funding for their expansion. This has led them to concentrate on improving the asset side of their businesses — developing their lending products and credit technology, controlling arrears, and reducing administrative costs associated with lending to microenterprise. Now, these institutions, some of them newly transformed into for-profit financial institutions, are looking for ways to capitalize themselves and improve their leverage by borrowing from formal financial institutions, among other means. This is part of a new phase of development of the microfinance industry — a phase where development of the liabilities side of the balance sheet is as important as the asset side. In this new phase, for-profit institutions will come to dominate the market because they already understand the liabilities side of the business and are in a better position to raise capital. New investment facilities and instruments will be developed, and in this context, the need for better information on the performance of MFIs will be accentuated.

Investment funds: The Calvert Fund, a U.S.-based socially responsible investment fund, recently began to make loans to microfinance institutions in the United States and Latin America. Institutional investors can also pool their assets and share the risks of investing in emerging-market MFIs through two specialized funds — Profund, and a new fund created by the Banque International de Luxembourg.

- *Profund*. A specialized financial institution based in Panama with shareholders of several nationalities, Profund makes investments throughout Latin America in micro and small enterprise financial institutions. Its shareholders are mainly development institutions, such as the Multilateral Investment Fund (MIF) of the Inter-American Development Bank, but the Calvert Fund and private individuals are also among the shareholders. With US$15 million initial paid-in capital from ten shareholding institutions, Profund is now capitalized with over US$23 million in preferred and common shares. Profund supports the growth of regulated, efficient financial intermediaries by investing in or lending to new financial institutions developed by experienced non-profit small and microenterprise lenders; new financial institutions created by existing commercial banks, finance companies, and similar institutions proposing to serve small and microenterprise clients; and existing financial institutions that already serve small and microenterprise clients and are seeking to expand their operations with equity or debt financing.

- *The Banque International de Luxembourg (BIL).* The bank recently announced the creation of a fund for MFIs — both long term loans and equity investment. The fund, which targets only institutional investors, will be managed by a large European financial company, AXA.
- *Intermediary guarantees.* Intermediary guarantee funds, or guarantee mechanisms that are structured to include a third party institution as an intermediary between the financial institution providing the capital and the microborrower, have been used for microfinance since the mid 1980s (Young, Goldmark and Londoño 1998). Some networks, such as Acción International and Women's World Banking, provide guarantees to their affiliated programs. Other networks, such as Foundation for International Community Assistance (FINCA) and Opportunity International, are in the process of developing this type of microfinance guarantee fund as well. National programs also issue this type of institutional guarantee to non-formal microlenders in Colombia and Ecuador. So far, no fund of this type has been undertaken on a for-profit basis, although some appear to be able to cover their costs. The Latin America Challenge Investment Fund (LACIF), a new second-story guarantee company and investment fund for microfinance that is being financed by the Inter-American Development Bank through its MIF, will develop a guarantee mechanism that assumes 100 percent of the risk of lending to MFIs by providing guarantees in favor of local banks to permit them to lend to MFIs at lower rates of interest. LACIF may then be able to charge a premium sufficient to cover its costs and give returns to its investors (Microenterprise Development Review 1998).
- *Securitization.* Private investment in securities issued by microfinance institutions is hindered by shallow incipient markets and the small size of potential offerings. Buying and selling of securitized microfinance loan portfolios in the capital markets has yet to happen. The main impediment has not been credit risk, but rather currency and transfer risk. Recently, 24 percent of the shares of Banco Sol, a microfinance bank in Bolivia, was sold by the Inter-American Investment Corporation (IIC), the finance corporation of the IDB group, to a consortium of NGOs that had been

involved in the bank's creation. Although a private bank bid for the shares, the consortium took the opportunity to retain control of what continues to be a unique and profitable institution.

- *Increasing Transparency*. Private investors need to be able to assess the strength of MFIs easily. Uniform auditing standards, such as those being developed by Deloitte and Touche under contract to the Consultative Group for Assistance to the Poorest (CGAP) (CGAP 1998), are one piece of the puzzle. Ratings could be another important tool. Diagnostic instruments developed by commercial banks and adapted for application to MFIs have been in use in Latin America since 1993 (Saltzman, Rock and Salinger 1998). Although their continued application and refinement are creating a tool for diagnosing financial performance in terms of capital adequacy, asset quality management, liquidity and efficiency, significant work remains to be done in making comparisons across institutions and countries, and over time. PSI, a U.S.-based organization, plans to establish an agency that will rate MFIs based on a comparatively simple diagnostic technique, making this information available to investors.

Microfinance from the Market Perspective

There is no doubt that microfinance constitutes an interesting niche for a small group of emerging market investors. The commercial development of microfinance is still in its infancy. How far this market will grow remains an open question. Although the locus of microfinance is just beginning to shift from the non-profit world to private investors, what is now being called an industry does appear to have growth potential.

An enabling macroeconomic and regulatory environment has drawn lenders' interest to new financial market niches, including micro and small enterprise. Additional improvements in government policy, including controls on interest rates and use of directed credit by government lenders are needed to develop the microfinance industry further in Latin America. Reduction of barriers to entry in the financial sector, and improvements in prudential regulation and supervision of financial institutions will also help create conditions for commercial microfinance to grow.

At the institutional level, a series of innovations and changes in management practices will be required for profitable expansion of the industry. First and foremost, especially for banks and finance companies entering this market, appropriate microcredit products and technology are needed to attract customers and keep transaction costs down. Second, a significant scale of operation and growth are required to allow cost coverage, meet excess demand, and obtain profits. As is the case with consumer finance products such as credit cards, specialized management expertise and institutional structures may be required for microfinance. Banking institutions typically set up subsidiaries to handle their credit card operations because the products, cost structures, risk, liquidity management and even organizational culture are different from their other business lines. Although the basic principles of due diligence, management and control are the same as in any other economic activity, provisioning, liquidity management, and advanced information systems are areas of special concern for management of microfinance. Detailed, reliable information on the client pool is a very important part of microcredit technology.

NGOs seeking to expand and formalize their microfinance operations face another set of challenges. They will need to make progress in setting interest rates with respect to real costs, in maintaining operating costs within acceptable parameters, and in achieving a good currency match between assets and liabilities in order to hedge foreign exchange exposure. They need to create management and governance structures that take into account the interests of all stakeholders, and develop adequate controls using sophisticated management information systems, in order to be successful MFIs in the long run. Some will successfully make this transition, and others will contract as they face a shrinking availability of the external donations on which they depend. However, the current popularity of microfinance may forestall this process for several years.

A significant expansion of private investment will require widely-accepted standards of financial performance and risk for the microfinance industry as a whole. In addition to satisfying their macro level concerns such as sufficient liquidity in the financial system and a favorable regulatory environment for microfinance, potential private sector investors need to be able to assess the viability of specific MFIs or microfinance departments within their own institutions. Transparency of information and proper regulation and supervision are needed to support this process.

Microfinance from the Development Perspective: How Low Can the Market Go?

The expansion and diversification of financial services for microenterprises — whereby institutions reach out and down to smaller clients — is still a key task for the future of microfinance from the development perspective. On the one hand, technological and organizational improvements should continue, enabling MFIs to lower transactions costs. Improved information systems and supervision can also reduce their risks and improve their access to the capital needed to expand their operations. On the other hand, certain characteristics of microfinance could limit its reach and profitability. High levels of risk are associated with the high interest rates charged for microloans, a particularly severe problem now given the economic uncertainty in emerging markets. In addition, the greater problem of information and administrative cost bottlenecks at progressively lower loan sizes, the costs of regulatory compliance, and the likelihood that poor microentrepreneurs are riskier clients would limit commercial penetration of the lowest segments of the market for some time to come. Thus, while microfinance is allowing investors to tap a new emerging market within the emerging markets, its growth will ultimately depend on the industry's capacity to innovate and increase efficiency in order to serve the lowest end of the market.

References

Almeyda, G. (1996). *Money Matters: Reaching Women Microentrepreneurs with Financial Services*. Inter-American Development Bank, Washington.

Barham, B. L., S. Boucher, and M. R. Carter (1996). Credit Constraints, Credit Unions, and Small-Scale Producers in Guatemala. *World Development* **24** (5), 793–806.

Barry, N. (1995). *The Missing Links: Financial Systems That Work for the Majority*. Women's World Banking, New York.

Basch, M., and C. Morales, eds. (1995). *Expanding Access to Financial Services in Latin America*. Inter-American Development Bank, Johns Hopkins University Press, Washington.

Baydas, M. M., D. Graham, and L. Valenzuela (1997). *Commercial Banks in Microfinance: New Actors in the Microfinance World*. Microenterprise Best Practices, Development Alternatives, Inc., Bethesda, MD.

Behrenbach, S., and C. Churchill (1997). *Regulation and Supervision of Microfinance Institutions: Experiences from Latin America, Africa and Asia.* The Microfinance Network, Occasional Paper No. 1.

Berger, M., and B. Guillamón (1996). Microenterprise Development in Latin America – A View from the Inter-American Development Bank. *Small Enterprise Development* **7** (3), 4–16.

The Consultative Group for Assistance to the Poorest (CGAP) (1998). *External Audits of Microfinance Institutions: A Handbook.* The World Bank, Washington.

Crockett, A. D. (1997). Separate but Converging: International Financial Standards and National Financial Systems. In L. Rojas-Suárez, ed., *Safe and Sound Financial Systems: Who Works for Latin America*, Inter-American Development Bank, Washington.

Cuevas, C. (1996). Enabling Environment and Microfinance Institutions: Lessons from Latin America. *Journal of International Development* **8** (2).

Edwards, S. (1995). *Crisis and Reform in Latin America: From Despair to Hope.* Oxford University Press, New York.

González Vega, C. (1998). Microfinance: Broader Achievements and New Challenges. Economics and Sociology Occasional Paper No. 2518, Rural Finance Program, Ohio State University, Columbus, OH.

Gulli, H. (1998). *Microfinance and Poverty: Questioning the Conventional Wisdom.* Inter-American Development Bank, Washington.

Hannig, A., L. Elser, and S. Wisniwski (1997). *Comparative Analysis of Savings Mobilization Strategies (Overview of Four Case Studies).* Gesellschaft fur Technische Zusammenarbeit (GTZ), Eschborn, Germany.

Holden, P. (1996). The Enabling Environment for Latin American Business. *Small Enterprise Development*, September **7** 28–36.

International Labor Office (ILO) (1972). *Employment, Income and Equality: A Strategy for Increasing Productive Employment in Kenya.* Geneva.

Jansson, T., with M. Wenner (1997). Financial Regulation and its Significance for Microfinance in Latin America and the Caribbean. Occasional Paper, Inter-American Development Bank, Washington.

Lucano, F., and M. Taborga (1998). Tipología de Instituciones Financieras para la Microempresa en América y el Caribe. Occasional Paper, Inter-American Development Bank, Washington.

Mazumdar, D. (1976). The Urban Informal Sector. *World Development* **4** (8) 655–678.

The Microbanking Bulletin (July 1998), No. 2, The Economics Institute. Boulder, CO.

Microenterprise Development Review (1998), **1** (1 and 2). Inter-American Development Bank, Washington.

Orlando, B., and M. Pollack (Forthcoming). *A Study of Poverty in the Microenterprise Sector: Evidence from Latin America.* Inter-American Development Bank, Washington.

Otero, M., and E. Rhyne (1994). *The New World of Microenteprise Finance: Building Healthy Financial Institutions for the Poor.* Kumarian Press, W. Hartford, CT.

Rhyne, E. (1998). The Yin and Yang of Microfinance. *The Microbanking Bulletin*, No. 2, The Economics Institute, Boulder, CO.

Rock, R., and M. Otero (1996). *From Margin to Mainstream: The Regulation and Supervision of Microfinance.* Acción Monograph Series No. 11, Acción International, Cambridge, MA.

Ruís-Velasco, L. M. (1996). La Revolución Consumista. *América Economía* No. 103, 30.

Saltzman, S., R. Rock, and D. Salinger (1998). *Performance Standards in Microfinance: Acción's Experience with the CAMEL Investment.* Acción International, Cambridge, MA.

Steege, J. (1998). *The Rise and Fall of Corposol: Lessons Learned from the Challenges of Managing Growth.* Microenterprise Best Practices, Development Alternatives, Inc.

Wenner, M., and S. Campos (1998). Lessons in Microfinance Downscaling: The Case of Banco de la Empresa. S.A. Occasional Paper No. MIC-105, Inter-American Development Bank, Washington.

Westley, G. (1995). Financial Reforms in Latin America: Where Have We Been, Where Are We Going? Occasional Paper, Office of the Chief Economist, Inter-American Development Bank, Washington.

Westley, G. and S. Shaffer (1997). Credit Union Policies and Performance in Latin America. Working Paper No. 355, Office of the Chief Economist, Inter-American Development Bank, Washington.

Young, R., L. Goldmark, and R. Londono (1998). *Microfinance Guarantees: A Basic Primer and Review of Experiences in Latin America and the Caribbean.* Inter-American Development Bank, Washington.

LINKAGES BETWEEN RURAL FINANCIAL MARKETS, POVERTY ALLEVIATION AND CONSERVATION OF SOILS AND FORESTS: THE CASE OF MADAGASCAR

Manfred Zeller, Cécile Lapenu, Bart Minten, Eliane Ralison, Désiré Randrianaivo, and Jean-Claude Randrianarisoa[1]

Introduction

Most of the poor in developing countries depend directly or indirectly on agriculture for their livelihood. While the share of the world's population that is poor has declined in recent decades, the number of people earning less than a dollar a day has increased. In rural areas, populations growing at 2 to 3.5 percent annually continue to exert pressure on natural resources. Much-needed increases in farm production can in principal come about in two ways: expansion of cultivated area or increases in yields. We term the former agricultural extensification since it does not require increases in agricultural productivity by using modern inputs, such as high-yielding

[1]The financial support of this research by the United States Agency for International Development (USAID) is gratefully acknowledged (Cooperative agreement 63-0118-A-00-6039-00).

seeds and mineral fertilizers. The second is called intensification (Boserup 1965; Ruthenberg 1980; Pingali, Bigot, and Binswanger 1987).

Shifting cultivation is a prime example of extensification. When rapidly growing rural populations follow the low-input extensification strategy, the result is declining soil fertility because of the falling number of fallow years. The decline in fertility, in turn, accelerates the speed with which forests, bush and grassland are taken into (re-)cultivation — reducing progressively the fertility of soils. Indeed, one can observe Malthusian vicious cycles in rural areas of developing countries, and similar vicious cycles were experienced in the past, for example, in eighteenth century Europe. Here, it proved possible to avoid the Malthusian consequences of declining fertility through the development of technology and new institutional arrangements. The successful transformation of agrarian societies in the wake of the industrial revolution during the nineteenth century shows that mass impoverishment and degradation of natural resources can be avoided by following the intensification strategy, that is, by the adoption of high-yield crop and livestock technology that produces, year after year, more crops and animal products per unit of land.

The adoption of improved agricultural technology by farmers requires capital. In principle, capital can be raised through equity or through debt. Both are facilitated with improved access by farmers to financial institutions that offer savings and credit services (Zeller and Sharma 1998). The focus of this paper is the effects of financial market access on rural development. Can improving rural financial markets help to alleviate poverty by enabling peasants to choose more environmentally sustainable pathways to development?

After surveying certain aspects of rural development in Madagascar, we discuss selected trends in resource use, environmental degradation, agricultural productivity, rural wages and access to financial and commodity markets and public services in the sample communities. Next, we develop a conceptual framework that lays the basis for our econometric analysis and that investigates the linkages between financial market access, environmental degradation, poverty alleviation, and growth. The paper concludes with a discussion of the results of the model and their implications for policy and further research.

The Critical Triangle of Rural Development: The Case of Madagascar

Vosti and Reardon (1997) conceptualize a critical triangle that links three development objectives: economic growth, poverty alleviation, and environmental sustainability. These authors emphasize the importance of simultaneous consideration of all three development objectives, plus possible links between and trade-offs among them. They also stress how the agroecological, technological, and socioeconomic environments influence these linkages and trade-offs. The present analysis builds on Vosti and Reardon's insights, emphasizing in particular the role of access to financial institutions.

In recent years, Madagascar has become internationally known for its rich and unique biodiversity that is threatened by rapid deforestation. The export of hardwoods and plantation crops, shifting cultivation, overgrazing, charcoal production, bush fires, and the pressure of the poor to clear more land for food production all have contributed to massive destruction of primary forests[2] during this century (Gezon 1997; Jarosz 1993).

Since the mid 1980s, Madagascar has been a focus of international conservation efforts. Donor institutions such as the World Bank and U. S. Agency for International Development devised large loan and assistance programs for Madagascar that had explicit environmental objectives. Already in 1984, the Government of Madagascar drafted the National Strategy for Conservation and Development, implicitly recognizing the critical triangle mentioned above by including environmental conservation, economic development, and human needs into their frame of reference.

Changes in Rural Development: A Descriptive Analysis

It is worth noting that despite the massive investment in environmental projects and institutions in Madagascar during the past ten years, few data sources were generated during this time that linked agroecological data with

[2]Primary forests are the natural tree vegetation. Secondary forests comprise all types of tree growth that occur after primary forests have been destroyed by humans or by natural disasters.

socioeconomic data. The existence of such combined data bases is a precondition for in-depth analysis of the underlying determinants of rural development, economic growth, poverty alleviation, and environmental sustainability. The national household survey, Enquête Permanente auprès des Ménages (EPM), conducted in 1993 by the National Statistical Office (INSTAT), has few questions that touch upon the critical triangle. With the exception of the data set collected by the authors, there are no statistically representative data, even on a regional scale, that contain both agroecological and socioeconomic data.

Data Source and Sampling Frame

In 1997, the International Food Policy Research Institute and the Ministry of Scientific Research (MRS) in Madagascar designed and implemented a survey that covered 188 communities in five agroecological regions of the country.[3] While the general purpose of the survey was to document past trends in rural development and to explain how they have responded to liberalization of agricultural commodity and rural financial markets, several sections were added to cover changes in the natural resource base.[4] The respondents to the survey were the mayor of the village and other community leaders. The survey modules dealt with many aspects of rural development. Common to most questions was that the respondents were asked to provide information for the situation prevailing during 1997 when the survey took place, and for the situation prevailing ten years previously.

In order to improve the efficiency of the sampling, two stratifying variables were used: the size of the village (above or below median of all villages in the agroecological region), and the terciles of the distance from the village to the next national road. These stratifiers are exogenous variables in the

[3]These villages represent five agroecological regions of Madagascar: Fianarantsoa Highlands, Fianarantsoa coastal and escarpment region, Majunga Lowland and Majunga Highland areas, and the *Vakinankaratra*, a diverse region in the central Highlands of Madagascar. The regions surveyed cover most of the major agricultural systems in Madagascar, except for the semi-arid agriculture in the south of the island.

[4]The authors thank John Pender and Sara Scherr for providing helpful comments on the design of the modules of the community-level questionnaire concerned with natural resources.

short to medium run for rural development, but influence communities' access to commodity and financial markets, information, preventative and curative health care, education, and other public services. All of these variables are generally believed to be major determinants of the direction, pattern and speed of rural development. Within each strata, the same sampling ratio for selecting survey villages was maintained, that is, the sample size of each strata was a fixed proportion of the total number of the villages in the strata. The descriptive and econometric analysis uses sampling weights reflecting the sampling procedure so as to derive representative figures and regression coefficients for the agroecological regions as a whole.

Next, we present changes over time in three selected indicators that relate to the three objectives defining the critical triangle of rural development. The second section describes changes in access to financial markets and other services that are hypothesized to have influenced the observed trends in rural development.

Major Trends Characterizing the Critical Triangle of Rural Development[5]

Rice is the major crop and also the staple food in urban and rural Madagascar. For the nation as a whole, about half of calories consumed are from rice (see SECALINE 1996; Ravelosoa 1997). Most of the rice is grown on irrigated lowland fields and less than 5 percent of national rice production is grown on rain-fed upland plots.

In Table 1, the yield (in kilograms per hectare) of irrigated rice is shown for the agroecological regions in the sample. For all regions, average rice yields declined from 1765 kg per hectare to about 1540 kg per hectare between 1987 and 1997, yet important differences across regions exist. In the *Vakinankaratra* (a mountain range encompassing the cities of Antsirabe and Betafo about 200 kilometers south of the capital Antananarivo), the yields remained the same. Major declines in rice yields can be noticed for the Majunga regions and to a lesser extent also for the *Faritany* (district)

[5]A more comprehensive presentation and discussion of the changes in indicators of rural development is contained in Zeller *et al.* 1998.

of Fianarantsoa. Insofar as rice yields can be viewed as a performance indicator for the agricultural sector as a whole, we conclude that there was either stagnation or decline in agricultural productivity.

In the community survey, we sought to ask about changes in poverty over the past ten years. Poverty encompasses many dimensions, such as food insecurity, malnutrition, illiteracy, ill health, and lack of entitlements. Most of these indicators, however, are difficult to measure through surveys if they are not obtained at the household or individual level. Moreover, we were interested in the change over the past ten years, and, therefore, had to find variables that could be easily recalled by our respondents. One such variable, we believe, is the rural wage rate. In most regions of Madagascar, rural wages are often paid in rice, and measured as the number of *kapoaka*[6] paid per day. Poor households with farms too small to feed the family engage regularly in wage labor. For example, the 1992 IFPRI/CNRE/DSA[7] survey found that 25 percent of rural households earned income as wage laborers. The average share of total household income earned from wage labor was 11 percent. For landless households, which are the poorest, wage income can be the largest single source of household income (Zeller 1993). Wage laborers usually find employment in agriculture.

Table 1 differentiates wage rates by agroecological regions. We note that wage rates have declined over the past ten years for all regions as a whole, but important differences among the regions exist. Again, the wage rate improved in the *Vakinankaratra* region, whereas the other regions experienced modest (Fianarantsoa) or severe declines in wage rates (especially the Majunga Plateau). Insofar as wage rates determine the ability of the poorest of the rural poor to feed their families in Madagascar, we can conclude that food insecurity and rural poverty has increased.

The change in soil fertility is the third indicator shown in Table 1, reflecting the environmental objective of the critical triangle. Community leaders were asked how the fertility of the upland (*tanety*) in their community has changed.

---

[6]This common measure is the tin can used by Nestle Company for its condensed milk that holds 285 grams of white rice.

[7]Three institutions participated in this survey: The International Food Policy Research Institute (IFPRI), the Centre National de Recherche sur l'Environnement (CNRE), and the Direction de la Securité Alimentaire (DSA) of the Ministry of Agriculture in Madagascar.

Table 1. Indicators of Economic Growth, Poverty and Resource Degradation: Rice Yields, Wages for Rural Laborers, and Fertility of Upland Soil, by Region and Year

	Majunga: Plaines		Majunga: Plateaux		Fianar: HT		Fianar: Côte/Falaise		Vakinankaratra		All regions	
	1987	1997	1987	1997	1987	1997	1987	1997	1987	1997	1987	1997
Yield, irrigated rice	2664.3	2245.5	1927.1	1469.7	1704.6	1611.4	1475.3	1213.2	1853.7	1851.9	1765.3	1539.5
Number of kapaoka of rice paid per working day	9.5	8.5	14.7	8.0	4.2	3.7	6.1	5.0	5.3	6.7	7.6	5.7
Index for change in fertility of upland soil		1.3		1.2		0.3		0.9		0.9		0.8

Source: IFPRI/FOFIFA Community Survey 1997.

Note: The index for soil fertility has the value 2 if no change over the past 10 years. The other values recorded are: 3 = improved, 1 = reduced, 0 = severely degraded.

The categorical variable 'soil fertility' has the following values: 3, if soil fertility improved over the past ten years; 2 if it did not change; 1 if it were degraded somewhat, and 0 if it became severely degraded. Averages below 2, therefore, reflect deterioration in the soil fertility. It is apparent from Table 1 that soil fertility significantly decreased on average for all regions, with major degradation observed in the Fianarantsoa Highlands (HT), the *Vakinankaratra* and the coastal and escarpment area of the *Faritany* of Fianarantsoa. More modest losses have occurred in the *Faritany* of Majunga. This is compatible with our finding that yields from rain-fed rice, either grown in already cleared upland (*vary tanety*) or in upland after burning (*vary tavy*) have declined considerably during the past ten years (see Minten *et al.* 1998).

The rice yield, wage rate, and soil fertility variables serve as indicators of the trends in agricultural or rural economic growth, in poverty, and in environmental degradation, respectively. Overall, the data reveal quite disturbing trends. Only one of the five regions improved in two of the three criteria over the ten-year period.

Trends in Access to Financial Markets and Other Determinants of Rural Development

Access to microfinance institutions. As in most low-income countries in Sub-Saharan Africa with poor infrastructure and customary land tenure, the formal banking sector has barely penetrated rural Madagascar. Until 1986, the state-owned Banque pour le Développement Rural (BTM) was the main institution providing loans to farmers. An urban-biased traditional lending technique, the use of titled land as collateral, and the rent-seeking behavior of the wealthy and powerful (who monopolized the subsidized loans provided by the BTM) prevented most of the smallholders from borrowing. The BTM, like the other banks in the country, continues to play a negligible role in the life of the peasant household. Apart from the requirement of tedious paperwork and collateral, which poor households cannot understand or provide, the one-way travel time of the average smallholder to the nearest bank branch is 4.75 hours. In other words, it takes an entire day for the average peasant to apply for a loan. As can be seen from Table 2, this travel time is more

Table 2. Participation in Microfinance Programs and Travel Time to Finanical Institutions, by Region and Year

	Majunga: Plaines		Majunga: Plateaux		Fianar: HT		Fianar: Côte/Falaise		Vakinankaratra		All Regions	
	1987	1997	1987	1997	1987	1997	1987	1997	1987	1997	1987	1997
Rainy season travel time in hours to nearest bank	2.56	2.55	8.88	9.30	1.93	1.92	3.96	5.30	3.35	3.16	4.33	4.75
Rainy season travel time in hours to nearest post office or postal savings bank	2.43	2.48	7.95	8.52	1.38	1.55	2.88	3.93	2.91	2.79	3.59	4.04
Percent of households participating in credit	0.00	22.75	0.00	3.61	0.00	18.32	0.00	0.06	0.00	25.65	0.00	11.37

Source: IFPRI/FOFIFA Community Survey 1997.

than it was ten years ago. Average travel times to the nearest post office and postal savings bank have also increased. The increase in travel time is presumably caused by the deterioration of roads from villages to the rural centers where the postal offices and rural bank branches are located.

During the late 1980s, several development projects, mostly located in high-potential agricultural areas such as at Lake *Alaotra* and Lake *Itasy* as well as in *Marovoay*, began to promote the formation of credit groups with joint liability. However, these early group-based agricultural credit projects had little ambition to contribute to development of sustainable financial systems as they neglected rural savings as well as institution-building. In the early 1990s, a number of village bank programs and credit and savings cooperative societies were eventually introduced and subsequently expanded, especially in the *Vakinankaratra*, the *Fianarantsoa* Highlands, at Lake *Alaotra* and in *Marovaoy* (Fraslin 1997). These more recent institutions emphasize the provision of savings services and the accumulation of equity capital for member-based ownership of institutions at the community level.

One can distinguish three types of member-based financial institutions currently operating in rural Madagascar. These are village banks, mutual savings and credit cooperatives, and specialized group-based agricultural credit programs. In village banks, a large group of members (between 30 and 100) pay membership fees. The bank is physically located in the village and usually offers checking and savings deposit services. The village bank, most often through the support of a non-governmental organization (NGO), obtains external lines of credit from the BTM. Village banks are more complex than credit groups, but less formalized and regulated than savings and credit cooperatives, which are governed by the cooperative law. Village banks, therefore, offer more flexibility to their members in determining the rules of conduct, for example, the level of interest rates for loans and savings deposits. Savings and credit cooperative societies have been recently promoted by the World Council of Credit Unions (WOCCU) and the Canadian NGO Société Desjardins. However, their outreach is so far quite limited, and the survey areas of our sample did not include villages reached by cooperative systems.

Finally, credit groups consist of 5 to 20 members who all are held liable for repayment of loans to any member of the group. As it is the case with groups of the Grameen Bank in Bangladesh, which pioneered and extended the group-based lending approach on a large scale, future access to credit to all members is denied if only one member defaults. In contrast to the Grameen Bank's groups, the approach usually followed in Madagascar does not target poor women nor does it offer complementary services, such as skills training, nutrition education, and political and social education. Instead, farmers with average or above average incomes are likely to participate in the credit groups in Madagascar.

There are more than 15 different group-based agricultural credit programs. Most of them are by now supported by the private agribusiness sector that processes certain products, such as cotton, tobacco, milk, wheat or brewery barley. The agribusinesses' incentive to form and nurture credit groups is to secure and expand a reliable supply of crops that meets their quality standards.[8]

The community survey obtained information on the existence and size of all types of member-based financial institutions in the village. With this information, a variable was defined that measures the density of village-level participation in member-based financial institutions. This information was only obtained for 1997, but it is safe to assume that none of the villages had access to similar organizations ten years before since they were all formed after 1987. Table 2 shows that 11 percent of households participate in member-based financial institutions. The participation is much higher in the regions where NGOs first intervened.

Access to agricultural input and output markets. Survey data not shown here for lack of space show that access to markets for seed rice and farm equipment improved, while access to mineral fertilizer, pesticides, herbicides, vegetable seeds and veterinary inputs worsened over the survey period. Particularly noteworthy is the large decline in access to fertilizer markets. However, the access to agricultural output markets improved somewhat, in particular for rice.

Community access to public services. One of the survey modules enumerated the travel time from the village to over fifteen public services that are

---

[8]For further information on the structure, conduct, outreach and repayment performance of credit groups and village banks in Madagascar, see Fraslin (1997) and Zeller (1998).

provided by the central or local governments. The travel time in the rainy season — using the commonly used modes of transport in the village — ranges between two and four hours. Travel time to access a public phone booth is highest among all public services. It takes an average of two hours to travel to either the nearest primary and secondary school, or the nearest health post or hospital. Compared to 1987, the average travel times for all regions taken as a whole in 1997 were either the same or slightly higher.

Availability of land and population growth. Our finding that rice yields have stagnated or declined is evidence that an intensification strategy (that is, using more inputs such as fertilizer and high-yield seeds to increase productivity) had not been chosen by rural households and communities. Table 3 shows that rural communities have substantially increased their cultivated area during the ten years covered by the survey, confirming the choice of an extensification strategy. While rice land area grew an average of 5.3 percent for all regions, the area of cultivated upland (*tanety*) increased by about 24 percent. Since the population in the survey regions grew by a weighted average of 3.1 percent per year over this time, or by more than 31 percent over the previous ten years, the growth in arable area is below that of the growth of the population.

The expansion of the agricultural frontier came at the expense of forest, bush, and grassland. The largest losses were for primary forests. Primary forests shrank by 33 percent between 1987 and 1997. The loss in secondary forests was about 28 percent whereas the loss in grass and bushland (*kijana*) was about 20 percent. However, on average for all regions, 59 percent of villages report that there is still additional land available for expanding upland cultivation. Only half of villages have the possibility of expanding irrigated land (*tanimbary*), and only 35 percent of villages can expand both types of land. These latter villages are located in less densely populated areas. Despite the possibilities for expansion of upland, the average holding of upland per household declined from 1.74 hectares in 1987 to 1.28 hectares in 1997. Clearly, growth in population has outpaced growth of agricultural land in many communities, and pressures for agricultural intensification have tended to increase over time.

We conclude that about half of the villages in the survey regions can still choose between extensification (cultivating new land) and intensification

Table 3. Indices of Change in Area of Grassland, Forest, and Arable Upland and Irrigated Lowland during Past Ten Years

	Majunga Plaines	Majunga Plateaux	Fianar HT	Fianar Côte/Falaise	Vakinankaratra	All regions
Index for change in kijana area 1987=100	79.22	86.70	67.50	86.48	84.33	79.91
Index for change in primary forest area 1987=100	83.46	88.45	43.28	72.96	69.84	67.35
Index for change in secondary forest area 1987=100	80.42	79.83	63.19	76.25	67.54	71.96
Index for change in tanety area 1987=100	131.58	129.63	134.19	107.26	119.79	123.96
Index for change in tanimbary area 1987=100	112.60	104.58	105.66	104.04	105.66	105.32

Source: IFPRI/FOFIFA Community Survey 1997.
Note: The figures are indices for which the value 100 was given for the area held in 1987 by the community. For example, an index of 120 implies a 20% average increase in the area of the sample villages belonging to a particular region.

(using the arable land more productive and sustainable) in the near future. These more land-abundant communities can maintain their living standards with their low-input agriculture for some time, while continuing to expand the area they cultivate and degrading soils. While this extensive expansion of agricultural production may meet subsistence needs in the short run, the continued degradation of forests, watersheds, and soils has implications for future agricultural productivity, health and nutrition (von Braun 1997). The remaining half of the villages no longer have the possibility of further land expansion. In order to maintain or improve their living standards, households in these land-constrained villages must choose between two other strategies: (1) agricultural intensification, increased trade, and diversification into off-farm enterprises, or (2) migration.

A Causal Diagram of the Critical Triangle

Three major strategies by which households and communities seek to secure their livelihood are distinguished in this analysis. The first is the extensification strategy, that is, to continue with low-input, low-output agricultural technology by expanding cultivated land area and reducing fallow years, thus negatively affecting soil fertility. The second strategy is to intensify agricultural production and increase yields by exploiting access to financial and commodity markets, thus adopting more capital-intensive, higher-yielding technology and reaping the benefits of interregional specialization. Migration is the third major strategy that we observe from the data. As our data cover only rural villages, we measure rural out- and in-migration. The migration strategy is similar to the extensification strategy — if migrants are attracted by the possibility of farming new land — since the pressure on natural resources is simply shifted from one region to another.

Hence, our conceptual framework stipulates three endogenous outcome variables, rice yield, wage rates, and changes in soil fertility, that are influenced by three strategies leading to different paths of rural development. The villagers' choice of strategy is, of course, endogenous as it is influenced by the access to financial markets, by the endogenous wage rate, rice yields, and soil fertility, by the socioeconomic and agroecological characteristics of the region, and by the access to commodity markets and public services.

Figure 1 presents a causal diagram of the three different strategies and the resulting three outcomes that reflect the critical triangle of rural development. Arrows between the variables represent relationships. A positive sign implies that an increase in the value of the variable from which the arrow originates is expected to induce an increase in the value of the other variable. For example, we hypothesize that higher lowland rice yields will decrease the incentives for further expansion of upland since the returns to lowland rice production become relatively higher. This relationship is reflected by an arrow with a negative sign. Let us consider first the arrows that feed into the upland area from the other endogenous outcomes or strategies. These arrows come from access to financial markets, the wage rate, soil fertility of upland, and the net immigration rate.

First, improved access to financial markets — reflected either through lower interest rates, lower transaction costs for the clients, or higher amounts available to borrow — will make the capital used in rice production and in upland fields less costly. With the reduced cost of capital, the profitability of these enterprises rises, leading to increases in yields in both lowland

Figure 1. Causal diagram of the critical triangle of rural development

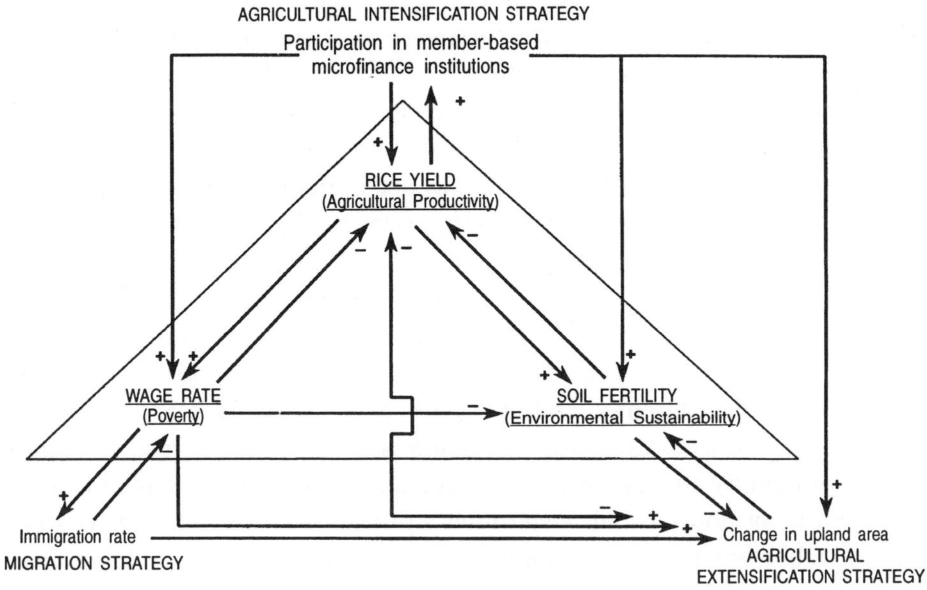

and upland areas. Second, with increasing wage rates, farm households will tend to choose more labor-extensive crop production technologies: as cultivation of irrigated rice is more labor-intensive than upland production, higher wage rates will induce lower labor input and therefore lower yields of rice, but increased expansion of upland area. Third, the expansion of upland area is expected to be positively influenced by a higher net immigration into the village since migrants are expected to cultivate new lands not already occupied by villagers. Fourth, and last, expansion of upland cultivation will have negative effects on soil fertility due to shorter fallow periods for already cultivated land or result in increased cultivation of marginal or infertile land. The negative arrow from soil fertility to upland area change reflects the vicious, unsustainable cycle of extensification and soil degradation — lower soil fertility will induce farmers to abandon fields after only a few harvests and seek new farmland to cultivate.

As noted above, soil fertility is expected to decrease if the level of wages in the village increases. As most investments in conserving soil fertility are labor intensive (for example spreading manure, planting trees or terracing land), rising labor costs will reduce the relative profitability of soil-conserving investments. Moreover, we hypothesize that increased participation in member-based financial institutions will improve soil fertility since it reduces the cost of capital and increases its availability for investment in conservation.

In the causal model of Figure 1, the net immigration rate is perceived to be a function of the endogenous wage rate. We hypothesize that villages with high wage rates will attract migrants. As more migrants come into those high-wage villages, they will increase the supply of labor and therefore push wage rates down, an effect that is expressed through a negative arrow.

It is hypothesized that wage rates will be influenced by two other endogenous variables in addition to immigration: access to financial markets and lowland rice yields. As access to financial markets improves, the cost of capital to the community and its households decreases, thus increasing the marginal return to labor and pushing wage rates up. Similarly, if yields of irrigated rice (a labor-intensive crop) increase, the marginal return to labor used in rice production increases, resulting in an increase in wages.

Lowland rice yields are influenced by four variables. Two of them, improved access to financial markets and wage rates, have already been discussed. We further expect that increases in food and cash crop production on upland will reduce incentives for households to intensify rice production, in particular if that rice production is more capital and labor intensive than upland production and if ample opportunities to expand upland continue to exist. The same type of argument can be made for the expected effect of soil fertility of upland on lowland rice yields. If upland soils are fertile and productive, and one can get good harvests on upland, little economic incentive exists for increasing yields of irrigated rice.

We choose to model the access to member-based financial institutions as an endogenous outcome variable for the following reasons. First, as mentioned above, financial institutions that reach rural households in Madagascar have only been formed during the past ten years. This is the period we are focusing on in the analysis. The placement of financial institutions is driven by a variety of factors that determine directly or indirectly the loan repayment performance or the transaction costs for the financial institution and the client.[9] Second, as Pitt, Rosenzweig, and Gibbons (1995) demonstrate, failing to correct for the possible non-random placement of government programs can result in substantial biases in the estimates of the programs' effects. In the case of Madagascar, one can observe that placement of financial institutions was concentrated mostly in areas with high agricultural potential and above average infrastructure (Zeller 1993). More particularly, we hypothesize that lowland rice yields are a good indicator of agricultural productivity, and that financial institutions tend to place programs in villages with above-average lowland rice yields in order to increase the average loan repayment performance. There are, as Pitt *et al.* (1995) argue, other variables that determine the placement of programs. Yet, these variables are not in the data set. In this case, simple ordinary least squares of cross-section data may overestimate or underestimate the effect of access to credit on yields. For example, Pitt *et al.* (1995) find in their analysis that the proportion of households in villages with a school has a negative and significant impact on male school attendance at the district level when using the incorrect simple ordinary least squares procedure for the cross-section data. In order to control for endogenous placement of programs, Pitt *et al.* (1995) use a fixed-effects model that sweeps out the unobservable characteristics. In this model, the effect of the placement of schools on male school attendance is positive and significant.

The causal diagram in Figure 1 could be extended by including additional endogenous variables. In the very long-run, everything is endogenous. We choose only the six endogenous variables shown in Figure 1. The main reason is that the ten-year period considered in this analysis is sufficiently short so that access to public services and infrastructure, such as roads, are likely not to change much because of regional growth or other endogenous processes.

[9]See, for example, Sharma and Zeller (1999) for an analysis of placement of branches of three major NGOs in Bangladesh: the Grameen Bank, BRAC, and the Association for Social Advancement. Their analysis shows that, while these NGOs seek to maximize outreach to the poor, they end up placing branches in districts with above-average infrastructure and economic potential in order to improve loan repayment and reduce transaction costs to sustainable levels.

Econometric Model and its Results

This section presents the econometric model and results from its estimation. The model uses long-term recall data that provides information on state and flow variables for 188 communities. In total, about 110 variables have been observed at two points in time through the recall technique. The measurement error on some of these variables can be quite large. Due to the lack of other secondary data, we are not able to correct for measurement error. However, as the data collection has been supervised by the authors, we feel quite confident about the accuracy of the data.

The Model

With information on endogenous strategies and outcomes at two points in time, the potential biases resulting from unobservable characteristics — for example, those that influence the placement of member-based rural financial institutions — can be avoided by using a fixed-effects model (Pitt *et al.* 1995). Figure 1 shows a total of six endogenous variables that depend on each other. To obtain consistent and unbiased estimates, we apply a two-stage least squares model with fixed effects (Greene 1993).[10]

The structural equations of the model are:

1. Participation in member-based financial institutions $(Y_1) = f(Y_2, X_i, \text{BANK})$
2. Rice yield $(Y_2) = f(Y_1, Y_4, Y_6, X_i, \text{TSTRIZ, PEREAU})$
3. Net immigration rate $(Y_3) = f(Y_1, Y_4, X_i, \text{TRANHUMD, MONEYTRA})$
4. Wage rate $(Y_4) = f(Y_1, Y_2, X_i, \text{SHARINCO})$
5. Change in upland $(Y_5) = f(Y_1, Y_2, Y_3, Y_4, Y_6, X_i, \text{TSTPAT, A34BACC2, MARKMAN})$
6. Change in soil fertility $(Y_6) = f(Y_1, Y_2, Y_5, X_i, \text{CONFLICK})$

where X_i is a vector of exogenous variables not necessarily mutually exclusive for the six endogenous variables. The other variables listed in the equation

[10]The model is estimated with LIMDEP, using a two-way fixed-effects model that, in addition to village-specific fixed effects, measures time-specific effects of the two years, 1987 and 1997 (see Greene 1995. LIMDEP Version 7.0, Chapter 17.4, 309–314).

serve as instrumenting variables to identify the estimation.[11] The names, definitions, means, median and standard deviation of these and all other variables used in the regression model are shown in Table 4.

Interpretation of Results

Tables 5–10 list the results of the regressions for each of the six equations 1–6, respectively. With very few exceptions, all signs of regression coefficients are as hypothesized. In general, the models for participation in member-based financial institutions (Table 5) and the rate of net immigration (Table 7) have a low adjusted R^2 of 0.15 and 0.16, respectively. The other models have higher explanatory power with an R^2 ranging from 0.34 (Table 9) for the change in upland to 0.68 for rice yield (Table 6). The results are robust to changes in the specification of the model.

Determinants of Community Access to Member-based Financial Institutions

We begin the interpretation with the regression explaining the density of participation in member-based financial institutions (OUTREACH) (Table 5). The participation can be perceived as the joint outcome of determinants of supply and demand for financial services. The model estimates these determinants in a reduced form as we are not interested here in studying the formation of financial institutions. The community's participation in member-based financial institutions improves its access to formal credit and savings options. The regression results indicate that increased formal market participation significantly increases with higher yields (YLDRICI)

---

[11]To test whether these instruments are good ones, an F-test was performed to test the joint significance of the instrumental variables in the first-stage regression. The F-statistic is the ratio of the explained variation in the dependent variable and the unexplained variation, adjusted for the number of independent variables. The probability of error resulting from the F-test for the estimated coefficients of the instrumental variables is 0.74 for equation (1) (OUTREACH), 0.07 for equation (2) (rice yield), 0.00 for equation (3) (net immigration RNETIMIG), 0.08 for equation (4) (wage rate), 0.02 for equation (5) (change in upland), and 0.49 for equation (6) (soil fertility).

Table 4. Descriptive Statistics of Variables Used in Regressions (n=376 from 188 villages)

Name of variable	Definition	Mean	Median	Standard deviation
OUTREACH	Percent of households participating in credit program	5.68	0.00	29.28
RNATPOP	Annual natural population growth rate in percent	3.56	3.45	3.33
RNETIMIG	Net annual immigration rate in village in percent	0.01	0.00	0.87
WAGERATE	Number of kapoaka of rice per labor day	6.67	5.00	4.36
CHTAN	Index for increase in tanety area, 1987=100	111.98	100.00	25.55
YLDRICI	Yield irrigated rice	1,652.40	1,500.00	760.22
SOILFERT	Soil fertility change, 3=improved, 0=very degraded	1.40	2.00	0.80
ACCINPUT	Mean of indices of access to seven agriculture input markets, 100=1987	0.99	1.00	0.26
A34ACC1	Change in access to fertilizer dealers during past 5 years, 1=no change, 0=worse, 2=better	0.92	1.00	0.42
A34BACC2	Change in access to buyers of upland crops, 1=no change, 0=worse	1.04	1.00	0.46
MARKRIZ CCI	Interaction term: price of rice × index of access to rice markets (ABACCI)	89.43	59.52	78.44
MARKMAN CC2	Interaction term: price of manioc × index of access to nonrice agriculture output markets (A34BACC2)	96.90	50.91	109.64
BANK	Rainy season travel time in hours to nearest bank	4.54	3.00	6.19
BANKRISK	Interacted term: BANK times number of covariate risks in last 10 years	33.00	0.00	75.13
MONEYTRA	Rainy season travel time in hours to nearest post office or de caisse de épargne	3.81	2.00	5.25
DELEC	Electricity in village, 1=yes, 0=no	0.05	0.00	0.21
EDUC	Rainy season travel time to education institutions	2.09	1.33	2.67
HOSPITAL	Rainy season travel time to hospital or health post	2.11	1.50	2.86
PEREAU	Percent of rice land irrigated	50.01	60.00	37.81
SHARINCO	Share of primary income source in village income	60.43	60.00	16.20
PRIZ	Consumer price of 1 kapaoka of white rice	63.30	60.00	38.85
PRICAUTR	Interaction term: price of rice (PRIZ) × rice self-sufficiency index (autoriz)	73.11	50.71	86.79
FOKDENS	Number of people per sq. km in village	231.19	92.86	469.21

Table 4. Continued

Name of variable	Definition	Mean	Median	Standard deviation
POPDENS	Number of people per square km in firaisana	67.43	34.83	103.26
LANDLT1	Number of households in village owning less than 1 hectare of upland (tanety)	29.59	20.00	29.93
LANDSCAP	Interaction term: social capital (SOCCAP) with LANDLT1	2,211.52	0.00	14,235.01
SOCCAP	Social capital: number of present informal groups × years of existence	68.24	0.00	360.96
PRICAUTR	Interaction term: price of rice (PRIZ) with LANDLT1	1,945.07	1,000.00	2,677.87
AUTORIZ	Index of rice self-sufficiency of village, 100=1987	1.07	1.00	0.41
TSTPAT	Possibility of extension of tanety, 1=y, 0=n, 1987=1	0.79	1.00	0.41
TSTRIZ	Possibility of extension of rice land, 1=y, 0=n, 1987=1	0.75	1.00	0.43
TSTRITA	Interaction term: TSTPAT × TSTRIZ	0.67	1.00	0.47
CONFLICK	Number of conflicts about grassland/kijana	0.15	0.00	0.97
TRANHUMD	Distance in km to cattle grazing area	28.35	10.00	34.57
PRICEREL	Consumer price of rice divided by price of manioc	0.80	1.10	1.69
WATPAT	Interaction term: WAGERATE × TSTPAT	5.00	5.62	5.07
OUTRINPU	Interaction term: ACCINPUT × OUTREACH	5.85	0	27.11
OUTRFER	Interaction term: A34ACC1 × OUTREACH	5.56	0	28.81
FOODPOOR	Interaction term: LANDLT1 × PRIZ	2,189.2	1,200.0	2,760.3

Source: IFPRI/FOFIFA 1997 Community Survey.
Note: All descriptives in this and the following tables are weighted averages, using the sampling weights computed for the stratified random sampling frame.

in the village and with higher social capital (SOCCAP). The former effect is likely to be a supply-driven one as program managers seek to place institutions in villages with high economic returns so as to improve loan repayment rates as one of the most visible performance criteria of microfinance program. As most credit programs target agricultural enterprises, rice yields could be a good predictor of such returns. The effect of social capital is

Table 5. Determinants of Participation in Member-based Financial Institutions

Variables	Coefficient	Standard Error	t-Value
YLDRICIR	0.12817E-01	0.71157E-02	1.801**
BANK	–0.21288	0.72728	–0.293
DELEC	15.190	22.492	0.675
SOCCAP	0.18258E-01	0.11007E-01	1.659**
FOKDENS	–0.10264E-01	0.13716E-01	–0.748
LANDLT1	0.20022	0.17806	1.124
LANDSCAP	–0.16480E-03	0.28227E-03	–0.584
Constant	–19.687	13.338	–1.476*

Notes: Dependent variable is OUTREACH with mean of 5.68 and standard deviation of 29.28.
Number of observations: 376. Degrees of freedom = 179.
R^2 0.59 and adjusted R^2 = 0.15.
* and ** indicate significance at the 15% and 10% level.

interpreted as a demand-side effect — social capital encourages and promotes villagers' participation in semi-formal credit groups or cooperative societies. Social capital is measured by the number of informal self-help groups, multiplied by the number of years of their existence during the previous ten years. Informal group action is expected to benefit participation in other groups since experiences gained in the formation and management of informal groups make it easier for community members to perform similar functions in member-based microfinance institutions.

The identifying variable in the regression is the travel time from the village to the nearest bank branch (BANK). Its coefficient has the expected negative sign but is highly insignificant. All credit programs in Madagascar rely to some extent on branches of the commercial or the agricultural banks for depositing savings, and, in many instances, for channeling lending funds from the donor to the village groups. As the travel time from the village network to the bank influences the transactions costs of the program, and credit programs are presumably concerned about cost recovery, villages close to a bank branch appear to have a higher chance of obtaining access to credit. Villages with electricity or with more landless households have a positive, but also insignificant effect on the access to credit.

We conclude from this regression that villages with high agricultural productivity seem to be targeted by the financial institutions. As most member-based financial institutions in Madagascar lend for agricultural and food-processing activities, this result is immediately intuitive.

Determinants of Lowland Rice Yields

Table 6 shows the results of the regression concerning rice yields. Again, all signs are as expected. Yields significantly increase with improved access to credit (OUTREACH). The coefficient is very robust to alternative specifications of the model, and is significant at the 1 percent level. The direct marginal effect of an increase of 1 percent more households in the village being member of a microfinance institution raises average lowland rice yields at the community level by 20 kilogram per hectare. This produces an elasticity of lowland rice yields with respect to credit access of 0.07. This positive and significant effect would not occur if capital were not a binding factor in the farm sector of Madagascar. As Zeller (1994) shows, informal and formal lenders alike frequently ration loans, and about half of the rural sample households have been subjected to credit rationing.

The access to fertilizer markets (A34ACC1) has the expected positive effect on lowland rice yields, but is insignificant. When multiplying access to fertilizer (A34ACC1) with access to financial markets (OUTREACH), the interaction term (OUTRFERT) has a negative coefficient significant at the 10 percent level. This implies that the effect of access to credit on yields diminishes at the margin as access to fertilizer markets increase. Similar reasoning holds for the effect of fertilizer when the access to capital markets improves. This result suggests that access to fertilizer dealers acts as a substitute for access to financial institutions, and vice versa. Indeed, fertilizer dealers have been found to advance loans for fertilizer, and obtain repayment when buying the harvest.[12] Moreover, some of the microfinance programs provide credit in kind, mostly in the form of seed and fertilizer.

This finding is in line with the negative, though highly insignificant coefficient of the change in upland area (CHTAN) and soil fertility of upland (SOILFERT). With higher soil fertility of upland, mostly found in the hillsides

---

[12]See, Zeller (1993) and Barrett (1997) for a discussion of interlinked credit-cum-marketing transactions in rural Madagascar.

Table 6. Determinants of Yields of Irrigated Rice

Variables	Coefficient	Standard Error	t-Value
CHTAN	–0.47583	3.5631	–0.134
SOILFERT	–36.605	114.32	–0.320
WAGERATE	–30.095	32.101	–0.938
OUTREACH	20.107	7.6738	2.620***
OUTRFERT	–12.407	6.6113	–1.877**
PRIZ	–3.6858	2.7553	–1.338
MARKRIZ	0.39802	0.94583	0.421
MARKMAN	0.45386E-01	0.46810	0.097
TSTRIZI	–95.094	91.067	–1.044
A34ACC1	136.62	105.60	1.294
PEREAU	2.8289	2.6442	1.070
PRICEREL	83.247	21.707	3.835***
PRICAUTR	–1.1088	1.7382	–0.638
AUTORIZ	269.62	256.21	–1.052
Constant	2177.7	588.08	3.703***

Notes: Dependent variable is YLDRICIR with mean of 1652.40 and standard deviation of 760.22.
Number of observations: 376. Degrees of freedom = 172.
R^2 0.86 and adjusted R^2 = 0.69.
*,**, and *** indicate significance at the 15%, 10%, and 5% level.

and slopes, and a greater possibility of expanding upland, the lower the incentive to intensify rice production, for example, through investments in improving existing irrigation and drainage systems. Similar results are obtained for the possibility of expanding irrigated lowlands (TSTRIZI). If a community still has additional area that can be terraced for irrigation, the yields of rice are on average 95 kilograms per hectare lower than in land-constrained villages. Again, if further land expansion is possible — be it upland or lowland, less incentive for agricultural intensification exists. These results empirically confirm the Boserup's induced innovation model: when land becomes scarce and its opportunity cost rises, rural households and communities seek to adopt technology and alter their institutional arrangements for the management of land in order to increase its productivity and return. As expected, higher wages (WAGERATE) reduce the yield of labor-intensive rice, although the coefficient is insignificant. The elasticity of rice yield with respect to the wage rate is 0.12.

In summary, the most important determinants of the rice yield is the access to financial markets and the availability of idle land that can be used for expanding cultivated land.

Determinants of Migration

The dependent variable net immigration (RNETIMIG) is the average annual rate of net immigration into a village over the previous ten years. Table 7 shows the regression results. As expected, migrants respond to wage differentials, although this relationship is highly insignificant. The elasticity of immigration with respect to wage rates is measured at 1.74, that is, a 1 percent increase in wage rates in a village increases the net immigration rate into this village by 1.74 percent. In contrast, the net immigration rate (with a mean of 0.13 percent per year for all villages) increases by an absolute 0.66 percent if a village has the possibility of expanding both upland and irrigated lowland (TSTRITA). In other words, villages with ample land have a five times higher net immigration rate compared to villages with constraints for future land expansion. The size of this coefficient shows

Table 7. Determinants of Migration

Variables	Coefficient	Standard Error	t-Value
WAGERATE	0.17356E-01	0.70694E-01	0.246
WATPAT	–0.87747E-01	0.52580E-01	–1.669**
TSTRITA	0.66022	0.39019	1.692**
HOSPITAL	0.12580	0.85311E-01	1.475*
EDUC	0.38938E-01	0.83788E-01	0.465
MONEYTRA	–0.12592	0.46989E-01	–2.680***
POPDENS	0.13163E-03	0.20789E-02	0.063
TRANHUMD	–0.58849E-03	0.29993E-02	–0.196
SOCCAP	0.36156E-03	0.45638E-03	0.792
LANDSCAP	–0.12310E-04	0.11700E-04	–1.052
FOKDENS	0.84745E-03	0.60349E-03	1.404
Constant	–0.25177	0.59452	–0.423

Notes: Dependent variable is RNETIMIG with mean of –0.07 and standard deviation of 1.21.
Number of observations: 376. Degrees of freedom = 175.
R^2 0.61 and adjusted R^2 = 0.16.
*,**, and *** indicate significance at the 15%, 10%, and 5% level.

that rural-to-rural migration is largely driven by the possibility of further expanding the agricultural frontier. The negative coefficient on the variable distance to grazing areas for cattle (TRANHUMD) supports this finding.

Migrants significantly prefer villages that have lower travel time to institutions for transferring money or sending letters (MONEYTRA). As migrant families maintain their ties with their extended family in the home region, sending and receiving money and letters are important. Each additional hour of travel time to the post office or savings bank (caisse d'épargne) reduces the net immigration rate by 0.12 percent. This translates into an elasticity of 7.

Controlling for all other factors, migrants seem to prefer villages with higher population density, either at the village (FOKDENS) or at the level of district (*Firaisana*) (POPDENS). While the former is significant at the 20 percent level, the latter is not. Social capital (SOCCAP) has a positive, but insignificant effect on the rate of immigration from the village. With an increasing percentage of households owning less than one hectare of upland, the positive effect of social capital on immigration diminishes (LANDSCAP). In other words, as more virtually landless households live in the village, pressure on idle land presumably increases and a countervailing power against further immigration may begin to gain strength, reducing the positive effect of social capital on immigration at the margin. Just as trade unions seek to protect the wages of their members, the landless class in rural villages may be able to form coalitions and exert a political voice that perhaps undermine and work against the interest of the land-rich households for importing cheap labor from other regions.

Determinants of Rural Wages

An improved access by the community to financial markets (OUTREACH) increases the wage rate although the estimated coefficient is insignificant. Villages with higher population density (FOKDENS) and higher diversification of income sources (SHARINCO) have significantly higher wage rates. These results appear to be caused by the wage-enhancing effects of increased diversification of the rural economy that comes along with higher population density and, linked with this, lower transaction costs in trade.

As can be seen from the regression coefficient (RNETIMIG) in Table 8, rural migration depresses wages in villages that receive migrants and increases wages in villages that sent migrants. This result confirms the previous argument that the landless class in migrant-receiving villages may negatively be affected by migrants and therefore build up political and social coalitions that dampen further immigration. As expected, since most wage laborers perform labor services for agricultural enterprises, improved agricultural productivity — measured by the yields of the major crop (YLDRICI) — increases the wage rate (through the increase of the value of the marginal product from labor used in agriculture). The elasticity of the wage rate with respect to yields is 0.33.

Table 8. Determinants of Rural Wage Rate

Variables	Coefficient	Standard Error	t-Value
RNETIMIG	–0.45322	0.38361	–1.181
YLDRICIR	0.13507E-02	0.12537E-02	1.077
OUTREACH	0.87814E-02	0.26850E-01	0.327
FOKDENS	0.27656E-02	0.15360E-02	1.801**
PRIZ	–0.21659E-02	0.17181E-01	–0.126
AUTORIZ	2.4720	1.6974	1.456*
PRICAUTR	–0.21634E-01	0.10671E-01	–2.027***
SHARINCO	–0.59400E-01	0.30764E-01	–1.931**
Constant	6.3875	3.5893	1.780**

Notes: Dependent variable is WAGERATE with mean of 6.67 and standard deviation of 4.36.
Number of observations: 376. Degrees of freedom = 178.
R^2 0.7961 and adjusted R^2 = 0.56.
*,**, and *** indicate significance at the 15%, 10%, and 5% level.

As expected, the consumer price of rice has a negative effect on the wage rate. Since wages are paid in rice, an increase in the price of rice will result in a lower quantity of rice per labor day, if all other factors are held constant. Finally, with an increased self-sufficiency index of rice (a traditional indicator of prosperity of a village), the wage rate increases (see coefficient for variable AUTORIZ). This positive effect becomes smaller at the margin with an increasing price of rice (PRICAUTR).

Determinants of Expansion of Upland

Table 9 shows the regression results for the change in upland. All signs of the coefficients are as hypothesized. Holding everything else constant, the agricultural extensification strategy gains in importance for villages with better access to financial institutions (OUTREACH), with higher wage rates (WAGERATE), and with higher net immigration (RNETIMIG). Less forest and bushland is taken under cultivation if lowland rice yields are higher (YLDRICI) or if soil fertility of upland is higher (SOILFERT). While the direct effect of access to financial institutions (OUTREACH) on upland expansion is positive (an absolute 1 percent more of credit program participants increases upland area by 0.247 percent), the indirect effects of improved credit access through other endogenous variables are negative with the result that credit access actually reduces upland expansion. The indirect effects can be calculated from the regression coefficients for credit access (OUTREACH) on other endogenous variables, multiplied by the regression coefficient of the endogenous variable for upland in Table 9. As this has important policy implications, we discuss these results. From Table 6 we see that credit access improves rice yields (the coefficient of 20.1 kilogram per hectare for a one percent increase in participation in credit programs). In turn, one additional kilogram of rice reduces upland expansion by 0.026 percent. Assuming constant marginal returns, the indirect effect is a reduction of 0.52 percent of upland area with an absolute 1 percent increase in households participating in member-based credit programs. The indirect effects of credit access on upland expansion, through higher wage rates and higher soil fertility, are 0.017 and –0.106, respectively. The combined effects, both direct and indirect, of a 1 percent increase in the number of households participating in a credit program in the village is then a reduction of 0.36 percent in upland area. In other words, improved access to credit markets promotes agricultural intensification and preserves soils and forests.

The effect of population growth (RNATPOP) is very small. A 1 percent increase in the mean population growth rate increases upland by only 0.0092 percent. This shows that other factors play a much more important role in explaining expansion of the upland area at the expense of forests and bushland. Research in other countries also shows that the effect of population growth on the expansion of cultivated area and resource degradation is

Table 9. Determinants of Expansion of Arable Upland

Variables	Coefficient	Standard Error	t-Value
YLDRICIR	−0.26405E-01	0.14709E-01	−1.795**
SOILFERT	−14.013	6.3488	−2.207***
WAGERATE	2.0264	1.4973	1.353
RNETIMIG	1.4897	3.2619	0.457
OUTREACH	0.24726	0.24391	1.014
TSTPAT	16.705	5.4775	3.050***
DELEC	−28.826	23.325	−1.236
AUTORIZ	−21.228	14.796	−1.435
PRICAUTR	0.17182	0.87940E-01	1.954**
PRIZ	−0.25321	0.14753	−1.716**
MARKRIZ	0.37519E-01	0.48049E-01	0.781
MARKMAN	−0.12102	0.44332E-01	−2.730***
A34BACC2	19.863	9.5550	2.079***
RNATPOP	0.55790	0.70146	0.795
PNATPAT	−0.41441	1.1443	−0.362
PRICEREL	2.0634	1.3793	1.496*
Constant	159.26	36.857	4.321***

Notes: Dependent variable is CHTAN with mean of 111.98 and standard deviation of 25.55.
Number of observations: 376. Degrees of freedom = 170.
R^2 0.70 and adjusted R^2 = 0.34.
*,**, and *** indicate significance at the 15%, 10%, and 5% level.

mediated by and often overshadowed by pressures arising from changing market, policy, or institutional conditions. (See, for example, Cropper and Griffiths 1994; Foster *et al.* 1997; Jodha 1985.)

Finally, more land is put under the spade (*angady*), if the village still possesses the possibility to extend its agricultural frontier in the future, that is, after 1997 (TSTPAT). The increase in upland is 16.7 percent higher in such villages in comparison with those that cannot expand anymore. With higher prices of rice (PRIZ), the crop competing with upland crops such as cassava, the agricultural extensification strategy loses significantly. However, this direct effect of the rice price needs to be seen in conjunction with the result for the relationship between rice and cassava price (PRICEREL). Here, if the rice price increases in relation to the price of cassava, more of upland is cultivated. In other words, if calories from rice become relatively more expensive compared to calories from cassava, the food deprived will seek to produce more of cheap cassava and mine the hills.

With improved access to markets for nonrice crops (A34BACC2) that are usually cultivated on upland, the village seeks to expand its upland area: with an increase by one in the qualitative indicator for access to nonrice markets, the upland area increases by an absolute 19 percent. The positive effect of access to nonrice crop markets significantly diminishes at the margin with a higher consumer price of cassava (MARKMAN). The results further suggest that the expansion of arable land can be slowed down by rural electrification (DELEC). Electricity provides an alternative energy source for the few that currently can afford it. More importantly, access to electricity enables a range of food processing, trading and off-farm enterprises that increase the demand for labor and offer alternative employment for the poor.

Determinants of Soil Fertility of Upland

The descriptive analysis showed that soil fertility has declined over the past ten years. What caused this degradation? As shown in Table 10, holding all other determinants constant, an increase in upland (CHTAN) significantly reduces soil fertility (SOILFERT). Two effects explain this result. First, as more land is put into cultivation, more and more infertile soils are taken. Second, as the demand for land increases, the time for fallow is reduced, giving upland less and less time to regenerate.

As expected, improved lowland rice yields, that is, agricultural intensification, has a positive effect on soil fertility of upland as higher productivity of lowlands reduces the incentives to mine upland soils. An increase in the index for soil fertility of upland by 0.2 percent is associated with a 1 percent higher yield of lowland rice.

The results show that soil fertility can also be enhanced by improving the community's access to financial markets (OUTREACH).[13] Given that rural households in Madagascar face credit constraints, improved access

[13]As Pender and Kerr (1996) point out, improved access to credit (or higher initial liquid assets of the household or village) is not expected to have an effect on conservation investment and soil fertility if capital markets are perfect, that is, if every household can borrow and save as much as it wants at the prevailing market rate. However, empirical evidence leads to the rejection of the assumption of a perfect credit market in rural Madagascar.

Table 10. Determinants of Soil Fertility on Upland

Variables	Coefficient	Standard Error	t-Value
CHTAN	–0.82909E-02	0.39462E-02	–2.101
YLDRICIR	0.17701E-03	0.24547E-03	0.721
OUTREACH	0.76829E-02	0.13813E-01	0.556
OUTRINPU	–0.19943E-01	0.12347E-01	–1.615
EDUC	–0.41241E-01	0.37853E-01	–1.090
ACCINPUT	0.59672E-02	0.21238	0.028
CONFLICK	–0.56723E-01	0.54192E-01	–1.047
AUTORIZ	0.35286	0.18792	1.878
RNATPOP	0.23778E-02	0.18927E-01	0.126
PSQRNAT	0.75183E-03	0.15944E-02	0.472
LANDLT1	–0.59350E-02	0.42577E-02	–1.394
FOODPOOR	0.16124E-04	0.28418E-04	0.567
LANDSCAP	–0.68352E-05	0.62478E-05	–1.094
SOCCAP	0.53611E-03	0.29026E-03	1.847
Constant	1.9094	0.73036	2.614

Notes: Dependent variable is SOILFERT with mean of 1.40 and standard deviation of 0.80.
Number of observations: 376. Degrees of freedom = 172.
R^2 0.77 and adjusted R^2 = 0.50.
*,**, and *** indicate significance at the 15%, 10%, and 5% level.

to credit reduces the opportunity costs of capital, leading to lower discount factors or time preference rates when valuing future income streams against current ones. A major hypothesized determinant of the decline in soil fertility is the high time preference rate that poor households use for discounting the value of future use of soils.

A third potential option to preserve soil fertility is to improve access to input markets (ACCINPUT). Yet, the coefficient on this variable is highly insignificant. As was the case for yields, the interaction term between input and credit access is negative, indicating that the two types of access can act as substitutes for each other (see significant result for OUTRINPU).

Population growth (RNATPOP), and its squared term (PSQRNAT), leads to improved soil fertility, perhaps indicating that as land gets scarcer through population growth, institutional arrangements and response mechanisms can be found to improve soil fertility. However, these results are highly insignificant. More conflicts over common property resources (CONFLICK) in the village during the previous ten years are used as an indicator of insecurity of land tenure. As tenure insecurity increases, investment in the maintenance of soils is reduced as the investor cannot be sure to be able to reap the benefits of his or her investment. The sign of the regression coefficient confirms this hypothesis although the result is not statistically significant. Lower access to school education, reflected by the travel time from the village to primary and secondary schools combined (EDUC), appears to have a negative influence on soil fertility.

Finally, social capital of the village significantly contributes to preserve and maintain soils (SOCCAP). The results seem to confirm the notion that common property management requires collective action, and that collective action in turn necessitates social capital. The percentage of households holding less than one hectare of upland (LANDLT1) has a positive, but highly insignificant effect on soil fertility. This positive effect of relative landlessness is reduced with an increasing consumer price of rice (see interacted variable FOODPOOR). Moreover, the positive effect of social capital on soil fertility diminishes with an increasing percentage of households owning less than one hectare of upland (interacted variable LANDSCAP). It is interesting to note that the rice self-sufficiency index in the village (AUTORIZ) has a significant and positive effect on soil fertility, confirming our hypothesis that a high dependency on risky and highly seasonal markets for buying rice increases consumption and production risks that negatively impact the overall investment capacity of households. In other words, if one has to rely on uncertain provisions of rice by the market, one wants to reduce this dependency by growing more food even if this is at the expense of soil fertility and future food production.

The results suggest that improved access to financial and agricultural input markets helps to preserve soil fertility, and — through the negative effect of soil fertility on change in upland — to slow down the expansion of agriculture into fragile hillsides.

Implications for Policy

In Madagascar, as elsewhere, the agendas of environmental preservation, economic growth, and poverty alleviation are linked: pursuing one without regard to the other two is a path to failure in the long-run (Vosti and Reardon

1997). Addressing this critical triangle means putting rural households and communities first. Policies that only stress the environmental objectives and do not take into consideration the concern of the poor for improved income, food security, health and nutrition, are likely to fail in achieving any one of the three objectives on a sustainable basis.

The critical triangle — and its specific problems and ramifications in Madagascar — point to one overarching issue that needs to be better understood — what makes households and individuals choose the environmentally more sustainable intensification strategy over the extensification strategy, and how can macroeconomic and sectoral policies and institutional and technological innovations in the financial, agricultural, health, and education sector contribute to make the intensification strategy more attractive in the short and long run.

The analysis in this paper points to a number of implications for policy and further research. Access to member-based financial institutions, such as credit groups and village bank, seems to play an important role in enabling an agricultural intensification strategy in Madagascar. We find that access to financial institutions has significant positive effects on lowland rice yields and on soil fertility of upland. However, participation in member-based financial institutions also led to the expansion of upland, as capital becomes cheaper and more available to farmers. The combined effect of access to financial institutions on upland is the sum of the direct effect on upland change and the indirect effects of credit access through higher yields, higher soil fertility and higher wages. The sum of all effects shows that increasing the percentage of households participating in a microfinance institution by one percent reduces upland area by 0.36 percent. We conclude therefore that promoting microfinance institutions for rural households can have beneficial effects on agricultural productivity, poverty and natural resources. Other strategies complement the development of microfinance institutions, and are likely to reinforce each other.

Our research indicates that improving rural infrastructure will reduce transactions costs in accessing commodity markets, thereby enhancing interregional trade and producing gains from specialization and trade. The results of our econometric analysis suggest a positive effect of improved access to markets for rice and agricultural inputs on rice yields, on soil fertility of upland and on the reduction of newly cultivated hillsides. Yet, improved access to output markets for nonrice crops that are grown on upland seems to lead to an expansion of cultivated upland in the short-run. As such market access increases, farm-gate prices increase while farmers' transaction costs for selling and buying crops decrease, ultimately pushing up the value of land. Investments in soil conservation will consequently become more economical. Neglecting the build-up of rural infrastructure and markets would only condemn rural villages and households to continue with the low-input, low-output, land-mining agricultural strategy.

Because of lack of data, the analysis has not focused on a number of factors that deserve further research. These include (i) the interdependence between food security, health and nutritional status and related pathways of rural development; (ii) the linkages among livestock, cropping and off-farm income generation within the household and village economy; and (iii) the role of land tenure and of informal and formal institutions guiding the villagers' strategies, including the informal institutional arrangements to respond to idiosyncratic and covariant food insecurity and health risks at the community level.

References

Barrett, C. (1997). Food Marketing Liberalization and Trader Entry: Evidence from Madagascar. *World Development* **25** (5), 763–777.

Boserup, E. (1965). *The Conditions of Agricultural Growth: The Economics of Agrarian Change under Population Pressure*. Aldine Publishing Co., Chicago.

von Braun, J. (1997). The Links Between Agricultural Growth, Environmental Degradation, and Nutrition and Health: Implications for Policy and Research. In S. A. Vosti and T. Reardon, eds., *Sustainability, Growth, and Poverty Alleviation: A Policy and Agroecological Perspective,* Johns Hopkins University Press, Baltimore, 1–15.

Cropper, M., and C. Griffiths. (1994). The Interaction of Population Growth and Environmental Quality. *American Economic Review* **84** (2), 250–254.

Fraslin, J. H. (1997). Quel Crédit pour les Agriculteurs? *Economie de Madagascar* **2**, 153–174.

Foster, A., M. Rosenzweig, and J. Behrman (1997). *Population Growth, Income Growth and Deforestation: Management of Village Common Land in India.* Typescript, Brown University, University of Pennsylvania, Providence and Philadelphia.

Gezon, L. (1997). Institutional Structure and the Effectiveness of Integrated Conservation and Development Projects: Case Study from Madagascar. *Human Organization* **56** (4), 462–470.

Greene, W. H. (1993). *Econometric Analysis.* Prentice Hall, Englewood Cliffs, New Jersey.

Greene, W. H. (1995). LIMDEP Version 7.0. Chapter 17.4, 309–314.

Hossain, M. (1988). Credit for Alleviation of Rural Poverty: The Grameen Bank. IFPRI Research Report No. 65, Washington.

Jarosz, L. (1993). Defining and Explaining Tropical Deforestation: Shifting Cultivation and Population Growth in Colonial Madagascar (1896–1940). *Economic Geography* **69** (4), 366–379.

Jodha, N. (1985). Population Growth and the Decline of Common Property Resource in India. *Population and Development Review* **11** (2), 247–264.

Minten, B., C. Randrianarisoa, M. Zeller (1998). Niveau, Evolution et Facteurs Déterminants des Rendements du Riz à Madagascar. *Cahiers de la Recherche IFPRI/FOFIFA sur les Politiques Alimentaires,* IFPRI/FOFIFA working paper series No. 8, Centre National de la Recherche Appliquée au Développement Rural (FOFIFA), Antananarivo, January.

Pitt, M., M. Rosenzweig, and D. Gibbons (1995). The Determinants and Consequences of the Placement of Government Programs in Indonesia. In D. Van der Walle and K. Nead, eds., *Public Spending and the Poor,* The World Bank, Washington.

Pender, J., and J. Kerr (1996). *Determinants of Farmers' Indigenous Soil and Water Conservation Investments in India's Semi-arid Tropics.* Environment and Production Technology Division (EPTD), IFPRI, Discussion paper No. 17, August.

Pingali, P., Y. Bigot, and H. P. Binswanger (1987). *Agricultural Mechanization and the Evolution of Farming Systems in Sub-Saharan Africa.* Johns Hopkins University Press, Baltimore.

Ravalosoa, R. J. (1998). *Les Disparites Économiques à l'Heure de la Decentralisation: Une Image Regionale de la Consommation des Ménages en 1993/94.* Projet Madio, INSTAT, Document 9637E.

Ruthenberg, H. (1980). *Farming Systems in the Tropics.* Third edition, Clarendon Press, Oxford.

SECALINE (1996). *Evaluation de la Situation Alimentaire et Nutritionelle a Madagascar.* Ministry of Agriculture, Government of Madagascar, Antananarivo, June.

Sharma, M., and M. Zeller (1999). Locational Criteria of Non-Government Organizations Providing Credit to the Poor: The Experience of Bangladesh. In D. Bigman, and H. Fofack, eds., *Geographical Targeting for Poverty Alleviation: Methodology and Applications*, Regional and Sectoral Studies Services, World Bank, Washington.

Vosti, S. A., and T. Reardon, eds. (1997). *Sustainability, Growth, and Poverty Alleviation: A Policy and Agroecological Perspective.* Johns Hopkins University Press, Baltimore.

Zeller, M. (1993). *Credit for the Rural Poor: Country Case Madagascar.* Final report to German Agency for Technical Cooperation (GTZ), IFPRI, Washington, October.

Zeller, M. (1994). Determinants of Credit Rationing: A Study of Informal Lenders and Formal Credit Groups in Madagascar. *World Development* **22** (12), 1895–1909, and in *Economie de Madagascar* **2**.

Zeller, M. (1998). Determinants of Repayment Performance in Credit Groups: The Role of Program Design, Intragroup Risk Pooling, and Social Cohesion. *Economic Development and Cultural Change* **46** (3), 599–620

Zeller, M., and M. Sharma (1998). *Rural Finance and Poverty Alleviation.* Food Policy Report, International Food Policy Research Institute (IFPRI), Washington.

Zeller, M., C. Lapenu, B. Minten, D. Randrianaivo, E. Ralison, and C. Randrianarisoa (1998). Vers une Meilleure Compréhension du Triangle Critique entre Croissance Économique, Réduction de la Pauvreté et Durabilité de l'Environnement. *Cahiers de a Recherche IFPRI/FOFIFA sur les politiques alimentaires,* IFPRI/FOFIFA Working Paper Series No. 19, Centre National de la Recherche Appliquée au Développement Rural (FOFIFA), Antananarivo, September.

BRIDGING THE GAP BETWEEN REGULATED FINANCIAL INSTITUTIONS AND LOW-INCOME BORROWERS

Eric Weaver

Executive Summary

Microlending (loans under $50,000) is on the upswing among regulated financial institutions in the United States. The reasons for the increase include increasing competition within their traditional core businesses, the impact of the increasing pace of bank mergers, advances in technology and changes in strategy that have made it possible to carry out microlending profitably for the first time, early indications that the microlending business may be even more profitable than anticipated, and evolution in the enforcement of the Community Reinvestment Act (CRA).

The principal barriers to making small loans profitably in the past were high transaction costs relative to loan size and excessive risk. Banks and other savings institutions have been able to overcome those barriers through the use of high-tech credit scoring systems to streamline the loan evaluation process, standardized products, and risk-based pricing models.

The impact of increased microlending by regulated financial institutions on low-income borrowers, is not clear. Low-income borrowers tend to need smaller commercial loans, which in the past were essentially unavailable from regulated financial institutions. The fact that such loans are now available is clearly a positive development. On the other hand, credit scoring systems may still filter out many low-income borrowers, due to lack of personal net worth, lack of track record (that is, length of time in business), and lack of credit history or poor credit history.

Lenders for Community Deveopment (LCD) is a for-profit multi-bank community development corporation, owned by 23 financial institutions with operations in Santa Clara County, California. LCD was incorporated in December of 1993 in order to help meet unmet credit needs in Santa Clara County and East Palo Alto, and began lending operations in March of 1995. LCD works closely with the nonprofit Community Foundation of Silicon Valley and the nonprofit Catholic Charities of Santa Clara County to deliver its products, and has up until now relied exclusively on private-sector dollars to fulfill its mission.

LCD's community needs assessment activities have identified the following critical needs in the communities it serves:

- the need for small business loans under $50,000; and
- the need for earlier stage loans not secured by real estate collateral for businesses owned by women, minorities and low-income people;

LCD provides small business loans of between $5000 and $50,000, from a $991,500 pool of funds invested by member banks. The pool is projected to grow to just under $1.6 million by the end of the year 2000. Outreach, loan packaging and technical assistance for the LCD program is provided by the nonprofit Catholic Charities of Santa Clara County, and by independent consultants. LCD's small business lending is targeted to low-income, women and minority-owned businesses, and to businesses located in low-income census tracts. As of October 1998, LCD had made 67 small business loans totaling $1,382,345.

LCD's strategy for bridging the gap between regulated financial institutions and low-income small business borrowers consists of the following:

- overcoming the problems inherent in lack of scale through reliance on existing bank systems for marketing, loan documentation and loan servicing;
- subsidizing transaction costs through partnerships with non-profit organizations and consultants funded by charitable contributions, obtaining below-market capital from member banks, cross-subsidy between LCD's affordable housing and small business lending programs, and use of volunteer labor from local bankers; and

- managing risk through risk-sharing among member banks, extensive technical assistance to borrowers, and loan guarantees from outside parties.

In the future, LCD management hopes to experiment with the use of small business credit scoring systems, in combination with subsidy and technical assistance, to increase loan volume and efficiency in reaching low-income small business borrowers.

The Trend Toward Increased Small Business Microlending

Small business lending emerged in the 1990s as an area of intense focus for U.S. banks. Large commercial banks, which historically have left the smaller end of the small business lending market to local community banks, are targeting smaller businesses and loan sizes. Meanwhile, savings and loan associations, which have traditionally focused on housing and consumer lending, are beginning to step into the market for smaller business loans. This trend is being driven both by market forces and by changes in the enforcement of the CRA, which requires regulated financial institutions to make credit available to people of all income levels within their market areas.

Meanwhile, the economic development community in the United States, inspired by the success of microenterprise lending programs in the developing world, has been diverting an increasing amount of energy and resources into small business. U.S. practitioners have been learning over the past decade how to borrow concepts from microenterprise programs in developing countries, adapt them to meet conditions in the United States, and put them into practice. This confluence of events presents a significant opportunity to increase the flow of capital from regulated financial institutions into businesses owned by low-income people and/or located in low-income communities.

Why All the Interest in Small Business Lending in the Banking World?

Probably the most important factor driving banks, as well as savings and loan associations into small business lending is that large sectors of their traditional markets are turning to other sources for capital. Traditionally, commercial banks did much of their lending to corporate America. Banks were the only place a large company could go to borrow very large amounts of money. Nowadays, however, with increasingly efficient capital markets, large and even middle-market companies can work through investment banks and other intermediaries to sell stocks or bonds, and obtain capital more cheaply than it can be offered by banks. In the current banking environment, margins on loans to the Fortune 500 are so thin that only a few big banks can generate enough loan volume to stay in the business.[1]

Meanwhile, savings and loan associations, which are regulated under an entirely different system than commercial banks, have traditionally done the vast majority of their lending in the single-family home-mortgage market. In the past decade, they too have seen their traditional core customers turn to other sources, principally non-regulated mortgage brokers who sell single family home loans to Fannie Mae (Federal National Mortgage Association) and Freddie Mac (Federal Mortgage Corporation). These days, virtually any single family home mortgage that conforms to Fannie Mae or Freddie Mac standards is sold on the secondary market, and savings and loan associations cannot offer rates on portfolio loans that are competitive with secondary market rates. At the same time, as regulated institutions, they have a hard time competing with unregulated mortgage brokers. Unregulated brokers can compete more efficiently for the fee income associated with brokering loans for Fannie Mae and Freddie Mac because they do not bear the cost of regulation. Thus, more and more savings and loan associations are beginning to make forays into the small business lending market where they believe yields will be higher. Currently, savings and loan associations are restricted to making consumer loans and real estate loans, and at least 65 percent of an savings and loan association's portfolio must be in real estate. As we will see, it is not hard to fit small business microloans into the consumer loan category, which is what the savings and loan associations are doing. In the near future, it is likely we will see some kind of move to combine the regulation of banks and savings and loan associations into a single system, which would likely mean an end to restrictions on the makeup of the savings and loan associations' loan portfolios.

---

[1]Interview with Michael Gallagher, Wells Fargo Bank, San Jose, California.

Consolidation is the name of the game in banking today. Analysts predict that within a decade or so, the United States will have 10 to 20 nationwide mega-banks, and a few thousand small community banks. Financial institutions that are neither very large nor very small are unlikely to survive. For the shareholders of medium-sized regional institutions, then, the best strategy is to try to make the institution as attractive a candidate as possible for acquisition. According to some, this is a major impetus driving some savings and loan associations into small business lending. The theory is that by making their portfolios resemble more closely those of commercial banks, they will be more attractive acquisition candidates.[2]

Traditional wisdom in banking has long held that it is not possible to make money at the small end of the small business lending market, especially for large retail banks (Rifkin 1995, 42–45). Most banks tended to have unwritten rules regarding loan size, and borrowers seeking less than $100,000 (or $250,000, or $500,000, depending on the bank) tended to be turned away for one reason or another. The reason for avoiding very small loans should be obvious. Under traditional methods of evaluating loan requests, the same amount of time and effort (that is, cost) has to go into evaluating a $50,000 request as when evaluating a $500,000 one, while the payoff in terms of interest and fees is much smaller.

In the early 1990s, however, just as banks were desperately looking for new markets in which to make loans, technological advances and creative thinking began to turn conventional banking wisdom about small business lending on its head. As will be discussed later in this paper, advances in technology, along with the realization that techniques pioneered in consumer lending can be applied to small business lending, have radically reduced the cost of delivering small business loans.

Banks that have moved rapidly into the small business lending market and employed the high-tech, consumer-lending-style strategy are realizing that small loans to small businesses can be very lucrative. According to a banking analyst with Donaldson, Lufkin and Jenrette, Wells Fargo Bank, one of the pioneers in the new strategy, generates a return on assets of 2.9 percent from its small business loan portfolio, more than twice

[2]Interview with David Johnson, Glendale Federal Bank, Glendale, California.

the return on an average bank's portfolio (Rifkin 1995, 42–45). Needless to say, Wells Fargo's positive experience so far has led other lenders to follow suit.

The CRA was originally passed by Congress in 1977 as an answer to the problem of redlining in home mortgage lending. Essentially, the act requires regulated financial institutions to assess and respond to the credit needs of all segments of their designated market area, regardless of borrower income or neighborhood conditions, while still working within the boundaries of safety and soundness as prescribed by bank regulators. Under the CRA, bank regulatory agencies examine banks and rate them on their compliance with the act, just as they examine and measure the quality of the bank's loan portfolio and risk management systems. For the first decade or so of the CRA's existence, it was perceived as a piece of legislation that essentially had no "teeth." Even if a bank received a rating of less than "satisfactory" (there are four rating categories: outstanding, satisfactory, needs improvement, and substantial noncompliance), no penalty was imposed on the bank. In 1990, the regulations governing enforcement of the CRA were strengthened in two key ways. First, bank regulatory agencies began to make CRA ratings public, which created the potential for public relations problems for banks with poor ratings. Secondly, the regulators began to solicit public comment on bank performance, and created a link between CRA ratings and applications for bank mergers and acquisitions. Suddenly, bankers faced the spectre of having mergers and acquisitions — which have been happening at an ever accelerating pace over the past decade — held up due to protests by community groups or poor CRA ratings from regulators. Banks and savings and loan associations began to place much more emphasis on CRA compliance.

CRA was passed mainly as a way to combat redlining in housing lending. The application of the law to business lending activities has been more recent, but the trend has definitely been toward increasing scrutiny of the activities of business lenders, with the key questions being whether the lender is making enough small business loans in low-income areas within its market area, and whether the lender is making enough smaller loans. The assumption behind the latter question is that low-income borrowers are more likely to need smaller loans than higher income borrowers.

In 1995, the Clinton administration completely revamped the CRA regulations. These regulations make the importance of small business lending within low-income communities much more explicit and, more importantly, for they first time they required lenders to collect data on their small business lending activities by census tract and loan size. Unless Congress reverses the Administration's actions (a step that looked quite possible in 1995, but now looks increasingly unlikely), the new CRA regulations will significantly increase the pressure on business lenders to find ways to make small loans in low-income areas.

Although the CRA does not touch on race or gender, many bank-sponsored small business lending programs (including that of LCD) have focused on outreach to women and minority business owners, in addition to focusing on low-income communities. The reasons behind this have more to do with fair lending laws (which are also receiving greater emphasis in recent years than they had previously) than the CRA, but the net result is that efforts to reach low-income, minority and women business owners are often lumped together.

Barriers to Making Smaller Loans

From a profitability perspective, there are two principal barriers to making small business microloans: transaction costs and risk.

One of the key problems inherent in making small loans is that there is very little money to be made on any one loan because of high transactions costs. For instance, the loan fee on an average small business loan might be 2 percent of the loan amount — $1000 for a $50,000 loan. If the $50,000 loan is a three-year term loan, the bank might earn $8000 in interest over the life of the loan (assuming an interest rate of prime plus 2 percent), which amounts to $4000 after subtracting the bank's cost of funds (assumed to be prime minus 3 percent). Even without discounting the profit that trickles in over three years, the bank's gross profit on the loan is a mere $5000. The gross profit on a $500,000 loan, on the other hand, would be closer to $50,000. Meanwhile, banks have traditionally used the same complex process to make the $50,000 loan as to make the $500,000 loan, relying on an analysis of both micro- and macroeconomic factors, as well as a substantial amount of documentation to insure that the borrower would live up to the terms of the loans and that the collateral was well secured. Issuing the loan might involve several days of work by a loan officer and several hours of work over the life of the loan by the bank's note department.

What further complicates the picture is that smaller loans tend to be made to smaller, younger, less well-capitalized businesses. Good lending decisions depend most importantly on good information. Good information means audited financial statements, a written business plan and the like. A business looking to borrow a small amount of money is most likely a small operation, with the business owner doing the books in her spare time, or perhaps waiting until tax time to do any accounting at all. The loan officer is lucky to get any kind of financial statement, much less audited ones. So, if the loan officer wants to make the loan, she needs to put in even more time with the borrower than she might with a representative of a larger company seeking a larger loan — often assisting the borrower to compile the information necessary to evaluate the loan request.

Smaller loans are both more and less risky than larger business loans. The risk on any one loan is less because the dollar amount is less. On the other hand, since the business is most likely younger, there is a shorter track record and a less predictable cash flow to repay the loan. Length of time in business and a history of stable cash flows are believed by most lenders to be the best indicators of lending risk. Timothy Bates (1993, 41) has shown that an enterprises's chance of remaining in business increases as the business grows older.

There is also the problem that smaller enterprises, by their very nature, are less likely to succeed than larger ventures. Bates also found that scale, in and of itself, is an important predictor of long term small business viability. He demonstrates that the single greatest disparity between his samples of young white and young black businesses lay in the fact that whites tended to begin their ventures with more capital, and thus on a larger scale, than did black businesses (Bates 1993, 41). Common sense suggests that the same would hold true for low-income versus high-income business ventures. Thus, profit-seeking lenders tend to shy away from smaller loans to younger businesses for good reasons.

How Banks Overcome Barriers to Making Smaller Loans

Although improvements in technology are usually given credit for the sudden explosion of small business lending on the part of banks, it is my belief that the key factors that have led banks to rethink the possibility of making very small loans were more philosophical than technological. First, and most importantly, was the realization that traditional methods of evaluating business loans were not well-suited to the smaller end of the market. According to Beth Raphael of Bank of America,

> Most small business owners are sole proprietors, have been in business less than five years, employ fewer than ten people, and visit their local bank frequently. They *are* the business. In other words, small businesses have more in common with individual consumers than with larger companies. It makes sense to attract them with retail-like approaches (Raphael 1994, 78–82).

I would add that it also makes sense to evaluate their loan requests with a retail-like approach.

A second important insight (made possible by technology) was that it makes sense to try to manage risk, rather than simply avoid it. Generally, banks have targeted loan loss rates of under 1 percent. With a high-tech, high volume lending approach, it appears possible to target much higher loan loss rates, price the loans accordingly, and still make a profit.

As previously described, the method used to evaluate larger business loans tends to be slow and expensive — in fact, evaluating a single request involves essentially three separate analyses: of the business, of the owner or guarantor, and of the industry. The product delivered to the borrower tends to be a specialized one, tailored to meet the particular needs of one business. Evaluation of consumer loan requests (think of credit cards), on the other hand, can be done in as little as a few minutes. The method used is called credit scoring, and it relies on a massive database of information on the credit histories and financial profiles of people who have used consumer credit. Essentially, a credit scoring system uses computer-generated models to match the applicant's credit and personal net worth information with information in the database, compare them to a lender's preprogrammed preferences regarding risk and likely profitability, and arrive at a rapid decision.

A lender can customize a credit scoring system to target a specific level of risk, and can program in preferences across a wide array of variables.

While credit scoring systems can achieve startling reductions in transaction costs, not every lender can make use of them. Using a credit scoring system requires a very high volume of lending to be effective. First, volume is required because the technology has high fixed costs (but very little in the way of variable costs) that must be spread across many loans. A lender has to invest not only in technological equipment, but also has to invest in data. The more loans made, the more information available to incorporate into the database. High loan volume is also critical to the effort in managing risk. If a lender is targeting an 8 percent loan loss rate, it is important to attract a lot of loans quickly to build up enough of a portfolio to weather the inevitable losses. As an example, Wells Fargo introduced its $50,000-and-under business line of credit in 1993, and booked $300 million in loans. By 1995, Wells' loan portfolio had grown to $1.2 billion, with an average loan size of $20,000.[3]

Another limiting factor with credit scoring is that it can really only be employed for very standardized loan products — like credit cards or lines of credit. In adopting a high-tech, rapid decision model, a lender sacrifices flexibility in structuring loan terms to meet an individual borrower's needs. This will inevitably mean that some loans will not get made that might have in the past. On balance, though, there can be no doubt that more bank money is flowing into smaller small business loans than ever before.

One important component of traditional loan structuring that has become much less important under the new approach is collateral. Lenders that are using a high-tech, high-volume approach to small business lending are doing most of the lending on an unsecured basis. This makes sense because the cost of actually liquidating collateral if a loan goes bad tends to be very high anyway, and, on a small transaction, the cost of liquidation is likely to outweigh the benefit to the lender. Eliminating collateral requirements also speeds up both the loan evaluation and the loan documentation processes.

With a strategy of risk management, as opposed to risk avoidance, pricing is obviously critical. Historically, banks have tended to target the same

---

[3]Interview with Michael Gallagher, Wells Fargo Bank, San Jose, California.

level of risk (very little) with every business borrower, and offered every borrower the same interest rate. With credit scoring, banks are using the technology to cluster borrowers into risk brackets, and offering graduated pricing. Wells Fargo Bank now offers small business credit priced as high as prime plus 6.75 percent, whereas in the past it was very rare to see small business loans priced higher than prime plus 2 or 3 percent.[4]

As will be discussed in the next section, making loans to low-income business owners continues to present unique obstacles to regulated financial institutions, even under the high-tech, high-volume approach. One of the ways banks and savings and loan associations have attempted to overcome these obstacles is through investments in lending intermediaries, an approach pioneered in the 1980s in the area of affordable housing. Through investments in intermediary organizations, like loan consortia and multi-bank community development corporations, banks (especially small-and medium-sized banks) can share the risk and expense of community development lending, while avoiding the need to develop in-house expertise in the field. In California, multi-bank community development corporations for small business lending are now up and running in San Diego, Riverside County, Orange County and San Jose, and a state-wide multi-bank community development corporation has also been established.

Impact on Low-Income Business Owners

The issue most important to those of us involved in economic development is the impact of the high-tech, high-volume lending approach on low-income small business borrowers and low-income communities. I have not seen any data on this question, so all I can offer are my thoughts on the matter.

The good news with the new approach is that smaller loans are being made, and the system being used is more objective (that is, less reliant on personal judgment) than the old system. For this reason, credit scoring should have a net positive impact on the problem of lending discrimination,

[4]Interview with Michael Gallagher, Wells Fargo Bank, San Jose, California.

which tends to disproportionately affect lower-income applicants.[5] Fewer applicants will be denied credit because they are members of minority groups or because they do not speak proper English. In addition, one reason low-income borrowers have had trouble obtaining credit in the past is that they tend to lack assets that can be pledged as collateral. Banks that are now making small business loans of under $50,000 are tending to make them on an unsecured basis, which is surely positive news for low-income borrowers. It is inarguable that many more small businesses are getting credit today than a few years ago, including businesses owned by low-income individuals. Whether or not this trend is leading to more job creation and wealth within low-income communities remains to be seen.

The bad news is that credit scoring systems being used by banks for small business lending still tend to filter out many low-income applicants. Although credit history and performance are the most important evaluation factors, personal net worth is also factored into the decision, which is clearly a negative where low-income borrowers are concerned. The reason for considering personal net worth is obvious: a lender feels more comfortable making a loan to someone who has personal assets that could be used to pay back the loan if the business venture fails.

Another factor related to credit scoring that might negatively impact small businesses is that banks are increasingly measuring and emphasizing the profitability of the entire relationship in deciding whether to grant a loan request. Credit scoring systems can be programmed to determine how likely an applicant is to use the bank's payroll service, or how much money the applicant is likely to leave sitting in her checking account, earning no interest. Small business owners are not usually very efficient at cash management, so a loan that might be only marginally profitable might actually lead to a very profitable relationship. Wells Fargo estimates that it gets back three dollars in deposits for every dollar it lends to small business (Rifkin 1995, 42–45).

---

[5] I say net positive impact because I am sure there are some built-in biases with credit scoring systems. Nevertheless, I think the overall impact of going to a computerized system of credit analysis should be positive for groups that have historically faced discrimination in lending.

The reality is that low-income people, including those running small businesses, are more likely to have either poor credit histories or no credit history at all than those with higher incomes. The reason for this should be clear: it takes money to borrow money, and if a borrower has personal assets, she will be considered less likely to default if the business venture fails. For borrowers with poor or no credit history, the fact that banks are now making small loans is irrelevant because they will not score well enough under a credit scoring system to get a loan.

Summary

High-tech and high-volume lending, while it is leading to more small loans being made, is not really being used to target low-income communities, at least to my knowledge. The possibilities for doing so are intriguing, but the limitations are also evident. For one thing, the computerized nature of credit scoring, with its deemphasis on human decision-making, means the end of what little technical assistance commercial lenders used to offer to their customers. Virtually all U.S. microlenders agree that some kind of technical assistance and training needs to be closely linked to the provision of credit to increase the borrower's chances of success and reduce risk to the lender. Also, most credit scoring systems are still screening out businesses with less than a two-year track record since the length of time in business is one of the best indicators of loan repayment risk. On the other hand, because of the CRA, the mere fact that banks are making more and more microloans to small businesses means that they will have to find ways to extend those loans to low-income communities.

Lenders for Community Development

Despite significant advances in the ability of banks to serve the needs of those seeking small amounts of capital, and despite increasing pressure from federal regulators for small business lending to occur in low-income communities, significant obstacles exist in trying to invest in low-income business ventures. LCD is an example of one attempt to overcome some of those obstacles.

Background

The LCD Mission Statement reads as follows:

> LCD is a bank-owned corporation which develops and administers lending programs in response to community credit needs. Our mission is to complete the cycle of reinvestment by investing local bank deposits in community-oriented ventures. We implement our programs in partnership with community organizations, and involve community representatives in the management of our business activities.
>
> LCD fulfills its mission by providing financing for small businesses and for community-based developers of affordable housing. We recognize the vital roles our customers play in building and preserving a healthy community, and are committed to work with them to ensure the success of their endeavors. In addition, LCD seeks to improve the flow of information between local financial institutions and the community at-large through an active program of community outreach and education.

LCD is a for-profit, multi-bank, community development corporation based in Santa Clara County, California. In June 1992, representatives of several Santa Clara County financial institutions joined together — under the sponsorship of the Community Foundation of Santa Clara County (now called Community Foundation Silicon Valley) and Silicon Valley Bank — to examine ways they might collaborate to better meet community credit needs and comply with the requirements of the CRA. Initial research for the project was conducted by a Stanford Business School summer intern, Cheryl Cole. Her work was coordinated by the Community Foundation and Silicon Valley Bank, and funded by Silicon Valley Bank and the Packard Foundation.

Throughout the summer of 1992, Cole facilitated group meetings, assessed community credit needs, researched models for multi-bank collaborations around the country, and performed extensive community outreach. As part of her assessment of community credit needs, Cole conducted a survey of Santa Clara County small business owners and interviewed small business service providers, government officials and developers of affordable housing in the county.

Based on this research, participating bankers and community representatives chose to focus on creating an entity that could provide microloans for small businesses unable to obtain bank financing, and financing for development of affordable housing. In September 1992, an Organization Committee was formed to recommend an organizational structure for the multi-bank/thrift effort. In addition, two technical committees were formed to make recommendations about specific lending products — a Technical Committee on Small Business Lending and a Technical Committee on Affordable Housing Lending. A full-time Project Coordinator, Eric Weaver, was hired by Silicon Valley Bank in October 1992.

In December 1992, the Organization Committee presented a proposal recommending that the participating financial institutions form a multi-bank/thrift community development corporation (CDC) as the best vehicle through which to make community development investments. The committee asked interested institutions to make founding capital contributions ranging from $1000 to $5000 according to a tiering system based on bank size, to provide seed capital for the CDC.

In January 1993, the original Organization Committee developed into a larger Steering Committee. By June 1993, 16 financial institutions had made initial capital contributions to the proposed CDC. Initial capital contributions were converted to equity stock after the CDC received regulatory approval. In March 1993, the Technical Committee on Small Business Lending and the Technical Committee on Affordable Housing Lending presented proposals for the CDC's lending programs to the participating institutions. The committees requested that the institutions make conditional commitments to the CDC's lending programs. Participating institutions initially committed $530,000 to a pool for small business microloans and $3.2 million to a pool for interim loans for affordable housing. The lending pools have since grown to $991,500 and $6.82 million respectively, and participating banks have indicated their willingness to double the size of the current pools.

In August 1993, Saratoga National Bank submitted an investment proposal to the Comptroller of the Currency seeking approval for new debt and equity investments in the CDC, to be renamed LCD. The Comptroller issued an opinion letter approving the investments as "qualified community development investments" in October 1993. The approval from the Comptroller was important because banks are typically not permitted to make equity investments, with investments for community development purposes being one of the exceptions. With that approval obtained, LCD was able to be incorporated as a California Corporation in December 1993.

LCD's first Board of Directors meeting was held in March 1994, and Weaver was elected President and Executive Director of the company. The remainder of 1994 was devoted to creating the framework necessary for LCD to achieve its goals. Tasks accomplished during this period include:

- obtaining an application for a California Commercial Finance Lenders License;
- negotiating funds pooling agreements that govern the operations of LCD's two lending pools;
- forming loan committees;
- recruiting banks to provide loan servicing and fund administration for LCD loan pools; and
- fund-raising for LCD's non-profit partner organizations.

LCD's lending activities began in early 1995. As projected from the beginning, LCD's small business loan program got off to a faster start than the affordable housing program. LCD's first small business loan — a $17,000 loan to a Latino-owned aquarium store — closed in March 1995. One year later, 14 loans were on the books, totaling $375,470. All loans made to date have been to small businesses in one of LCD's target populations: either woman-owned, minority-owned, located in a low-income census tract, or owned by low-income individuals. (LCD also booked $518,300 in affordable housing loans in its first year, but this paper will not focus on LCD's affordable housing lending activities.)

Despite the fact that it was not expected to ever generate profits, LCD was incorporated as a for-profit corporation, rather than as a nonprofit. This was done because under the for-profit model, the member banks can actually own and control the CDC, which will help insure their long term commitment to the project. Such ownership would not be legally possible under the nonprofit model. The downside is that the for-profit LCD is not likely to directly receive charitable contributions (because donors are not able to deduct their contributions from their taxable income). The LCD strategy for mitigating this problem has been to work in partnership with

501(c)(3) nonprofit organizations, which can receive grants, depending on these organizations to perform certain functions to support LCD's lending programs.

Meanwhile, in order to balance LCD's community commitment versus its corporate objectives, provisions were incorporated into the corporate bylaws to insure accountability to the communities to be served. LCD's bylaws state that at all times the board of directors shall consist of at least 25 percent community representatives, as shall any other bodies with lending authority. (Currently, LCD's Small Business Loan Committee has lending authority, and includes community representatives, while the Affordable Housing Loan Committee acts only in an advisory capacity to the LCD Board, and does not include community representatives.) Additionally, the LCD Articles of Incorporation include a provision stating that no dividends shall be paid to member banks in the first three years, and that any dividends paid after that time must be invested by member banks in other public purpose activities.[6]

LCD's "products" are innovative lending programs designed to allow local bank deposits to be invested into local low-income communities and constituencies that have historically lacked access to credit. LCD loan programs meet the interlocking goals of several kinds of institutions: the member banks' goal of complying with the CRA, the goal of philanthropic investors to increase access to capital for low-income and minority communities, and the goal of non-profit housing developers and small businesses to obtain types of financing not available from conventional financial institutions.

LCD's small business lending program targets businesses that are unable to obtain conventional bank financing in four categories:

- businesses owned by low-income individuals (earning less than 80 percent of area median income);
- businesses operating in low-income census tracts;
- businesses owned by members of ethnic minorities; and
- businesses owned by women.

---

[6]In fact, bank investors in LCD understand that they are unlikely to ever see dividend income from their equity investments.

Market Research

Businesses owned by low-income people, women and minorities tend to be relatively smaller, on average, than other businesses, and hence tend to have smaller capital requirements. Sixty-eight percent of respondents to a question about loan sizes on LCD's 1992 survey of small business credit needs indicated a need for loans under $50,000. Meanwhile, a 1996 survey of local banks showed that of the top 25 banks issuing Small Business Administration-guaranteed loans in Santa Clara County, only seven included loans under $20,000 within their target loan range, while another seven refused to process requests under $50,000. These survey results coincide with anecdotal information gathered from both bankers involved in LCD and small business owners suggesting that loans under $50,000 are not really on the "radar screen" of most banks.[7]

Similarly, low-income, minority and women-owned businesses have tended to have more difficulty obtaining adequate capital in the early years of their operations due to the lack of personal savings, less investment from friends, family and business associates, lack of credit history, and lack of experience.[8] Again, banks are not well-positioned to respond to this problem, given lending policies that focus on the length of time in business, amount of owner's equity, and collateral requirements. In essence, LCD found that a mismatch exists between the current products offered by local banks and the needs of a subset of small business that the banks increasingly seek to serve. LCD's microloan program for small business responds to the mismatch by

[7]Note that this situation has changed substantially since 1992, with large retail-oriented banks now aggressively seeking to make small loans. However, these banks are using credit scoring systems, and the businesses targeted by LCD tend not to score well due to poor or the lack of credit history, lack of experience, and absence of personal and business assets.

[8]While there is a wealth of research on discrimination in home mortgage lending, there is very little hard research on lack of access to credit among women and minority small business owners in the United States. The main reason for this may be that banks are not required to (in fact, not allowed to) collect data on the gender and ethnicity of small business borrowers. Research conducted in South Carolina between 1988 and 1992 by Burton and Associates, Inc. showed that African-American small businesses were either disproportionately denied credit by banks or received insufficient credit extension (Burton 1995). Bates (1993) and California Reinvestment Committee (1994) reached similar conclusions.

offering smaller loans designed to be accessible to younger, less well-capitalized businesses.

Loan Policy and Underwriting Standards

The loan policy and underwriting criteria for the LCD Small Business Microlending Program are summarized below, with commentary inserted in brackets:

Purpose of Loan

The primary reason for making the loan should be that it will assist the company in expanding, and/or creating, or retaining jobs in our market area. Eligible purposes will include:

- cash flow/working capital
- equipment purchase
- inventory
- debt consolidation
- leasehold improvements
- business acquisition

Ineligible purposes will include:

- payments to partially secured creditors who would likely sustain a loss without the new financing
- payments to owners, partners or shareholders
- buyouts
- speculation in any kind of property
- investments for purposes other than those eligible purposes listed above
- loans to restricted membership groups or organizations

Type of Loan

All loans will be made on an amortizing basis (fully amortized principal and interest). No lines of credit will be considered. [This is primarily because the cost of monitoring a line-of-credit product are too high for LCD to handle, given the small scale of its operations.]

Loan Amount

Loans will be from $5000 to $50,000. [In practice, LCD has made several loans smaller than $5000 because there has been a demand for them.]

Geographic Area

Loan applications will be considered from companies located within the designated service area of LCD.

Term

The term of the loan will be determined based on the specific purpose of the loan and the borrower's ability to make payments. [The purpose of the program is to make loans that are affordable to the small business borrower. In some cases this will mean granting a longer than conventional term to match cash flow.] Standard terms will run from one to five years, with amortization tied to cash flow.

Borrower Eligibility

To be eligible, a business must be in existence for at least a year. (In some cases this requirement may be waived.) The program will only fund businesses that are the borrower's primary business. Both the borrower and the business must have good credit ratings. Some borrowers will be required to participate in small business counseling at the discretion of the LCD. LCD will not fund small business counseling, but will assist borrowers to utilize existing counseling programs.

One or more of the above eligibility requirements may be waived at the discretion of the loan committee if one of the following conditions applies: 1) the business owner is receiving ongoing technical assistance that represents, in the judgment of the loan committee, a significant enough credit enhancement to warrant such a waiver; or 2) another organization (that is, foundation, local government, nonprofit, etc.) is absorbing a percentage of the lending risk to a sufficient degree that, in the judgment of the loan committee, such a waiver is warranted.

Discretionary Fund

Up to 10 percent of the loan pool shall be designated as a discretionary fund. At the discretion of the Loan Committee, the discretionary fund may be placed into loans that do not conform to these underwriting standards so long as the loans are consistent with the mission of LCD. [The purpose of the Discretionary Fund is to allow LCD to make start-up loans of under $5000 to borrowers who have good credit, sound business plans, and who are receiving technical assistance from an organization with which LCD has a relationship.]

Pricing

The rate on a loan will be determined by the term of the loan and an assessment of the loan's risk, with the minimum rate being prime plus 3 percent, fixed. The longer the term, the higher the rate. [In order to actually break even on its small business lending operations, LCD would need to charge a much higher rate on its loans. Because subsidy is available, LCD has elected to charge a lower rate and pass the savings on to borrowers, thus increasing their chances of success.] At loan closing, borrowers will pay a loan fee equal to 3 percent of the loan amount, or $250, whichever is greater. The loan fee may be financed out of loan proceeds. Borrowers will pay any out-of-pocket costs.

As should be evident, LCD's loan policy for small business lending is extremely flexible, allowing the loan packager to structure a variety of different kinds of financing to meet the needs of the target population. The loan policy does not even mention collateral requirements or required financial ratios, which is intentional, and in stark contrast to bank underwriting standards, with or without credit scoring.

Technical Assistance

Due to the volume of loan requests received under this program, as well as the disadvantageous economics associated with microlending on a small, local scale, LCD cannot afford to provide technical assistance to borrowers directly. Instead, LCD relies on a series of partnerships with existing programs to provide technical assistance to borrowers. LCD's primary partnership is with the nonprofit Catholic Charities of Santa Clara County, which provides loan packaging and limited technical assistance to LCD borrowers. When extensive technical assistance is required, LCD refers borrowers to local providers of small business technical assistance. Another piece of LCD's technical assistance strategy is to assign each small business borrower a volunteer "loan monitor" who meets with the borrower on a quarterly basis to review financial performance and insure compliance with loan covenants. The majority of the volunteers come from LCD member banks.

Results of LCD's small business lending efforts are summarized in Table 1. The period covered is from March 1995 through October 1998.

Table 1. Lending Effort of Lenders for Community Development

Overall	
Number of loans closed:	67
Dollar volume of loans closed:	$1,382,345
Average loan size:	$20,632
In Low/Moderate-Income Census Tracts	
Number of loans in low/moderate income census tracts:	42
Percent of loans in low/moderate income census tracts:	63
To Minority-Owned Firms	
Number of loans to minority-owned firms:	53
Percent of loans to minority-owned firms:	79
To Woman-Owned Firms	
Number of loans to woman-owned firms:	27
Percent of loans to woman-owned firms:	40
To Business Owners Earning Less than 80 Percent of Area Median Income	
Number of loans to business owners earning less than 80 percent of area median income:	59
Percent of loans to business owners earning less than 80 percent of area median income:	88
Job Creation	
Estimated (based on borrower projection) number of jobs for low-income people created by LCD loans:	169

Cost of Delivery

Table 2 compares figures for LCD's first year of lending (1995–1996), with figures for 1997 and 1998. The figures for operating costs do not include cost of funds and loan servicing fees. (Servicing is performed by one of LCD's member banks.) These amounts have been subtracted from the overall revenue to yield the net revenue number.

Table 2. Costs, Revenues, and Profits of Lending by LCD

	1996	1997	1998[1]
Number of loans	15	20	17
Operating cost of program	$97,628	$145,910	$114,050
Cost per loan	$6,508	$7,295	$6,708
Net revenue from program	$17,500	$33,739	$45,603
Net revenue per loan	$1,167	$1,687	$2,683
Program deficit	$80,128	$112,171	$68,447
Deficit per loan	$5,341	$5,609	$4,026

[1]Ten months only.

LCD's Strategy

Although banks have shown in recent years that it is possible to make very small loans to businesses profitably, there still exists a gap between the products that have been developed and the needs of low-income small business owners. Lending to very small, undercapitalized companies, often with unsophisticated management, frequently involves even higher transaction costs, smaller loan sizes and greater risk.

Part of the reason LCD incurs higher transaction costs per loan than banks is that LCD does not have the loan volume that banks do. Keeping loan volume down is actually a conscious strategy on the part of LCD for three reasons. The first is the need to combine credit provision with technical assistance, which works best when the loan officer (that is, the generator of loan volume) is providing at least some of the technical assistance.

The second reason is that LCD expects to have a relatively high percentage of problem loans (given the level of risk being targeted), but does not intend to simply abandon borrowers who get into trouble. In the future, LCD staff will need to devote a substantial amount of time to workouts and post-loan crisis management with borrowers. This contrasts with the strategy of a large retail bank using the high-tech, high-volume strategy, which is simply to target higher risk borrowers, price accordingly and be prepared to write off a certain percentage of the portfolio, with minimum effort going into workouts.

The third reason is that community development lending works best on a local level. LCD makes riskier loans than banks do, but the program is only successful if the borrowers are successful. This means reducing risk by insuring that the borrowers have the support they need from local technical assistance organizations, volunteer loan monitors and LCD staff. A local focus is also key to accessing below-market capital and charitable contributions from banks. The CRA stresses a bank's service within its own delineated community, and banks are much more interested in supporting a program that lends in their backyard than they are in one which lends statewide.

In essence, lack of scale is both a good thing and a problem. Limiting the number of borrowers and the geographic focus helps the program achieve its goals, but it also reduces the number of loans across which LCD can spread the cost of its operations. LCD's principal strategy for alleviating the problem of lack of scale is to rely on its member banks to perform loan documentation, servicing and marketing. By "piggybacking" on the banks' systems and branch networks, LCD avoids the need to create its own note and servicing departments, and to do extensive marketing.

The main way LCD addresses the problem of transaction costs is through accessing subsidy. Loan packaging and technical assistance are provided to LCD borrowers by a nonprofit partner organization, Catholic Charities, funded by grants from corporations and foundations. Over $150,000 in grant funding has so far been donated to support the program.

Another important source of subsidy is below-market investments from member banks. LCD member banks which invest funds into the LCD small business loan pool receive a return of about 4–5 percent on their money — well below the rate at which LCD could borrow on the open market. Member banks have also made equity investments in the company totaling over $250,000, without expecting to ever earn dividends — another important source of subsidy.

In the future, LCD also expects to see some cross-subsidization between the affordable housing lending program and the small business lending program. The affordable housing loans LCD makes are much larger and much less risky than the small business loans, and will generate a profit. Depending on how profitable the affordable housing lending is, LCD may actually be able to make grants directly to its nonprofit partner.

The final source of subsidy to the program is the volunteer time of local bankers. Bankers serve on the loan committee and board of directors and serve as volunteer loan monitors, meeting with borrowers on a quarterly basis to assess their progress.

Commercial banks and savings and loan associations are learning to manage risk through computer modeling of borrower behavior and risk-based pricing. LCD currently does not make use of computer-based approaches to risk evaluation, other than examining credit reports on the owners of small businesses applying for loans. Although the problems with credit scoring as applied to low-income borrowers have already been discussed, LCD may in the future explore the possibility of "piggybacking" on the custom credit scorecards developed by member banks.

The LCD model does not rely on risk-based pricing, for two reasons. The first is that the participating banks and foundations are primarily interested in seeing LCD clients succeed. Offering a subsidized interest rate helps the small business borrower's bottom line. The second reason relates to the perception of LCD in the community. Most small business borrowers have a limited understanding of the economics of microlending. To the small entrepreneur, $25,000 seems like a lot of money, and it is hard enough to believe that a lender is not making a profit on a loan of that size at an interest rate of prime plus 3 percent (the rate charged by LCD), much less a rate of prime plus 6 or 10 percent, which is what LCD would need to charge to break even. LCD's goal is not to make money, but to assist small business owners, and a part of being able to assist them is gaining their trust.

Part of the reason LCD can afford to take more risk is that the risk inherent in the portfolio is actually being shared among the 23 member banks that have invested in the portfolio. If loan losses exceed the targeted level of 10 percent, each investor's portion of the loss is comparatively small. (To date, losses have totaled 2.27 percent of loan originations.) LCD also seeks to reduce risk in its portfolio by obtaining loan guarantees from outside parties. Currently, LCD has several loans in its portfolio that have been guaranteed by the City of San Jose, the City of Menlo Park and a local foundation.

Summary

The barriers to small business microlending presented by transaction costs and risk are even more significant for community development lenders than for regulated financial institutions. LCD has employed a variety of traditional strategies to overcome these obstacles, but has made only limited use of new technologies that have been developed for microlending in the private sector. The small scale of LCD's lending program, along with the limitations of credit scoring systems, may present challenges in adapting these technologies for use by a lender like LCD. Nevertheless, LCD management hopes to experiment with the use of small business credit scoring systems, while still accessing subsidy and providing technical assistance, to increase loan volume and efficiency in reaching low-income small business borrowers.

References

Bates, T. (1993). *Banking on Black Enterprise.* Joint Center for Political and Economic Studies, Washington.

Burton, D. J. (1995). An Innovative Approach to African-American Business Development. *B&E Review*, July–September, 24.

California Reinvestment Committee (1994). No Credit for Those Who Need It: Uncle Sam Ignores Small and Minority Business. U.S. Small Business Administration Lending in California and the United States. San Francisco.

Raphael, B. (1994). Restructure for Profitability. *Bank Management*, November–December, 78–82.

Rifkin, G. (1995). Loan Rangers. *Forbes*, December 4, 42–45.

Part Four

Capital Markets in Transition Economies

SYSTEMIC RISK: AN OVERVIEW WITH APPLICATIONS TO TRANSITIONAL ECONOMIES

Philip F. Bartholomew and Gary Whalen

Introduction

Over the past decade, the term "systemic risk" has come into widespread use to describe what to many is — or should be — the primary concern of banking supervision and regulation. As sensitive as the financial systems of developed economies seem to be to systemic risk, the systems of transitional economies in Eastern Europe, the former Soviet Union and elsewhere are, at least potentially, even more vulnerable, given the nascent state of their financial regulation.

It is remarkable, in view of the extensive literature on banking and related financial topics and the detailed public policy discussions that have followed the notable financial calamities of the past two centuries, to find that, even today, there is no precise, widely accepted definition of systemic risk and little agreement on what comprises a "systemic event." Systemic risk is in very general terms, the risk of a collapse or major malfunctioning of the banking or financial system that results in significant costs to the real economy, as opposed to the failure of one or a few individual banks. The economic nature and causes of such collapses are, however, still relatively poorly understood. Such an understanding is vital to constructing an effective regulatory regime.

Although the term, systemic risk, is relatively new, the important distinction that it draws between individual bank failure and the malfunctioning of the financial system clearly dates back at least to Adam Smith (1776), who defended banking regulation despite its being, in his words, "a manifest violation of that natural liberty which it is the proper business of law, not to infringe, but to support." As Smith noted, ". . . those exertions of the natural liberty of a few individuals, which might endanger the security of the whole society, are, and ought to be, restrained by the laws of all governments; of the most free, as well as of the most despotical." A more up-to-date and explicit statement of the distinction was provided by Dale Tussing (1968, 101), who noted the potential linkage between bank failures and their effects on "the payments mechanism, on depositors and borrowers, or through them on third parties."

The financial events and public policy issues that scholars and regulators discuss today under the rubric of systemic risk have long been discussed using the terms "manias," "panics," "crashes," and "crises." Each of the terms mentioned above has a fairly definite and widely accepted meaning. A mania is a period of euphoria characterized by speculation that leads to a "bubble" — a divergence between the market price of one or more assets and the price that would be dictated by economic fundamentals. At some point, some event or new information suggests to better-informed investors that the bubble cannot be sustained and they sell out, precipitating a panic, or a broad flight from the objects of speculation to cash. This, in turn, produces a sharp decline, or crash, in their prices. If sufficiently severe, the results of this sequence of events are deemed a crisis, although a number of scholars would confine that term to cases in which a generalized run on banks produces a sharp contraction in bank reserves and the money supply (Friedman and Schwartz 1963; Schwartz 1986). Indeed, largely for that reason, Anna Schwartz has opposed using the term systemic risk at all, arguing that it "could be dispensed with, with no loss to the analysis of putative disruptions of the payment and settlement system, the essence of a financial crises" (Schwartz 1994, 3).

Although we would not make any strong assertions regarding the first use of the term systemic risk, we have not found any that predates the early 1980s, notwithstanding Minsky's use of the term "systemic fragility" as early as 1977 (Minsky 1977). A 1983 paper discussing deposit insurance reform addressed the question whether the 1982 failure of Penn Square Bank was a "localized or a systemic problem in banking" (Carroll and Rolnick 1983, 253). The first explicit use of the term systemic risk to describe the traditional concern with instability in the financial system that we have been able to find was in a 1984 paper by then Federal Reserve Governor Andrew Brimmer (Brimmer 1984), although the term has been used for many years in discussions of the payments system in the somewhat narrower sense of "the expectation that failure of one bank to settle will cause another bank or banks to fail as well" (see, for example, Mengle 1985, 19). Several papers on financial instability that appeared in subsequent years either did not use the term at all or used slight variants of it. A 1986 study of safety and soundness regulation commissioned by the American Banking Association contained references to a "systemic problem" and a "systemic collapse" (Benston *et al.* 1986). The next use of the term in its broader sense that we have found was in a 1986 presentation by George J. Vojta of Bankers Trust Company (Vojta 1986, 250). As recently as 1988, a broad-gauged essay on the regulation and supervision of risk in banking avoided the term, using instead the variant, "system risk," to refer to the same concept (Benston and Kaufman 1988, 3). Since then, the term systemic risk has come into commmon usage.[1]

Although an important concern for financial systems in developed economies, the issue of systemic risk is even more important for public policy in transitional economies. Financial regulations for such economies need to address clearly the desired allocation of risk among participants in domestic financial markets, determine liability procedures for international transactions, and specify the appropriate role of the regulatory authority in monitoring and enforcing financial regulations. Based on the calamitous lessons from Western economies and the spectacle of the ongoing financial crisis in the economies of Eastern Asia, it is vital for transitional economies to put the "right" policies in place from the start, in order to ensure that

[1]Interestingly, however, searches of economics and finance textbooks as late as the end of last year yielded only one that contained an explicit definition of systemic risk. Even that exception proved to be a typographical error, as the definition given was for "systematic risk," a financial concept quite distinct from that of systemic risk.

the domestic financial system is able to withstand the strains of an increasing volume of transactions from the restructuring of the financial system and the macroeconomy.

This paper is designed to provide a critical overview of the literature on systemic risk for the purposes of applying lessons learned about such risk to the design of financial regulations in transitional economies. It defines systemic risk, discusses its nature and the various forms that it can take, offers some broad evidence of its magnitude and pervasiveness and the degree to which it varies over time from developed economies (principally the United States), as well as evaluates the alternative explanations for its existence. It concludes with a brief summary of current views concerning its significance for public policy toward banking. The paper is intended, then, to be a guide for policymakers in transitional economies in the creation or reform of their financial regulations regarding systemic risk.

The paper is organized as follows. The next section describes the various definitions of systemic risk appearing in the literature on financial regulation, with specific reference to externalities, "contagion" effects and monetary contractions. The third section offers our expanded definition of systemic events and of systemic risk, illustrated by examples from the United States and Scandinavia. The fourth section discusses the existence and magnitude of "real" effects from systemic risk and collapse in financial markets. The fifth section discusses changes in systemic risk over time. Factors influencing the seriousness of systemic risk on real and financial activity are analyzed in following section. The seventh section examines the alternative policies regulators might adopt to minimize the losses from systemic risk in financial markets. Differences in financial crises are categorized in the penultimate section and concluding remarks appear in the final section of the paper.

Systemic Events

A rigorous definition of systemic risk must include an exact specification of what is meant by "systemic" as well as what is meant by "risk." The first of these requires that one distinguish events that are systemic from those that are not, on the basis of the quantitative importance, the geographic extent, or some other criterion. The second simply requires making explicit the sense in which the word "risk" is being used, since that word is used in several distinct, albeit related senses both in everyday speech and in finance and statistics. The problem of choosing a particular measure of risk has been discussed in detail in an earlier paper (Bartholomew and Whalen 1995). The primary focus in this paper will be on defining and identifying systemic events.

Externalities and "Systemic Events"

As noted above, the term "systemic" in systemic risk refers to an event having effects on the functioning of the banking, financial, or economic system, rather than just one or a few institutions. Among the few aspects of a definition on which we have been able to discern wide agreement are that a systemic event involves some element of externality — that is, it entails costs to parties other than the stockholders, depositors, and other creditors whose financial decisions may have contributed to the event — and that it must have a sizable effect on the real economy, resulting in a loss in aggregate output. A prominent banking scholar recently defined systemic risk as "a type of externality whereby one [financial] firm's failure can induce failures elsewhere, to the extent that the financial system's overall efficacy is impaired for at least a short period" (Flannery 1994, 1). However, it remains to be determined just how large a proportion of the system must be affected and how severe the effects must be to qualify as "systemic." Moreover, it is important to emphasize that, for many students of systemic risk, the magnitude or pervasiveness of an event is not the key factor in determining whether it should be considered systemic.

Contagion as a Criterion for Defining Systemic Risk

Relying in part on a medical definition of systemic that emphasizes the "successive" infection of additional parts of the body, George Kaufman (1992) would restrict the term systemic risk to situations involving the transmission of effects from one institution to another — that is, to cases of contagion. Thus, Kaufman would exclude from his definition of a systemic event the effects on the financial system of an economy-wide supply shock that, by dramatically raising interest rates, adversely affects all banks simultaneously.

In our view, the problem with Kaufman's definitions is the exclusion of a wide range of financial market pathology that would seem to be of legitimate concerns to public policy. The identification of a systemic event with contagion is too narrow even if one accepts the constraint that the notion of a systemic event should correspond closely with the medical analogy from which it was derived. As Donald Hester noted in private correspondence quoted by Todd and Thomson (1990) in a paper on the too-big-to-fail doctrine, ". . . contagion and systemic risks are medical terms with meanings which are quite different. Contagion refers to the spread of disease and systemic risk refers to a simultaneous collapse of different elements or organs" (Todd and Thomson 1990, 13, fn. 1).

Monetary Contractions as the Source of Systemic Events

Other scholars, such as Schwartz (1986), would define a systemic event narrowly as a sudden contraction of the money stock or bank credit, although this appears to be less a matter of doctrine than an empirical judgment that major financial disturbances are always, or virtually always, associated with such contractions. Again, it would seem unwise to exclude from the definition of systemic risk a major financial crisis with important effects on the real economy just because it did not meet the criterion of having originated in a monetary disturbance phenomenon, particularly in view of the many factors that affect the behavior of financial markets.

A Broader Definition of Systemic Events

Given our purpose of including in the definition of a systemic event all, or at least the vast majority, of cases that would warrant public intervention, we would be inclined to include any event that brought about a severe malfunctioning of the entire system, irregardless of how it originated and whether or not it involved contagion — that is, whether it originated with one or a few institutions and infected other institutions successively. In particular, the definition should include events that simultaneously affected all institutions, or all institutions of a given type, in the financial system.

That the inclusion of such events is a substantial, rather than a trivial, consideration is suggested by at least two recent episodes. The first was the accelerating inflation and subsequent abrupt reversal in monetary policy in the United States in the early 1980s that produced extremely steep rises in interest rates and declines in the prices of real property. These, in turn, were the proximate causes of the thrift debacle and, less directly, of the sharp increase in the bank failure rate beginning in 1982. Because the thrift industry continued to function and the payments system was not threatened, many observers would not characterize the thrift debacle as "systemic." However, the pervasiveness of problems within the thrift industry, the large number of failures, and the magnitude of the ultimate costs to taxpayers suggest that, absent deposit insurance and a more accommodative monetary policy after 1982, the thrift debacle might very well have led to a major malfunctioning of the financial system, with or without contagion.

Another example of what might reasonably be designated as a systemic event affecting all the banks in a country simultaneously was the Scandinavian banking crisis of 1991. Following the deregulation of lending in 1984, Norwegian banks greatly expanded their loan portfolios. In 1986, the economy was hit by declining oil prices and a tightening of fiscal and monetary policy. The result was widespread loan losses that resulted, in 1991, in the failure and nationalization of the second and third largest banks in the country and a government bailout and partial nationalization of the largest bank. These three banks, together with a number of smaller commercial and savings banks that failed, accounted for about 60 percent of the assets of the entire banking system. A related banking crisis in Sweden at the same time affected about 40 percent of the banking system.

The fact that depositor contagion was not a factor in these cases — although, according to a study of the Norwegian crisis, there was contagion in the equity market — was probably the result of the government's decision, in the absence of a preexisting government deposit insurance system, to provide a 100 percent guarantee to all creditors. Given the breadth of the crisis, the costs to the industry-funded savings bank and commercial bank guarantee funds, and the implicit costs to the government from the provision of guarantees and direct lending by Norges Bank, it is difficult to argue that the crisis was too small or localized to qualify as systemic. Thus, while we agree that most episodes involving widespread contagion should be considered systemic events, we do not believe either that the source of the disturbance or the presence or absence of contagion should be the decisive criterion in determining what is and is not a systemic event.

Significance of Systemic Risk

Closely related to the failure to agree on the definition of systemic risk is the continuing disagreement on the quantitative significance of systemic risk, not only currently but historically. Those who believe that, because the financial system is inherently unstable, government and central bank intervention on a regular basis is both necessary and desirable tend to believe that financial systems frequently face systemic risk. Those who believe that intervention should be used sparingly feel that systemic financial crises are rare. As one might expect, those charged with maintaining the stability of the financial system are much more likely to deem a given disturbance a systemic event than are academics viewing the event with detachment after the fact.

Differing Views on the Significance of Systemic Risk

As a recent paper discussing the common features of banking problems in various countries around the world recently observed, "Central bank governors tend to behave as though 'they know one when they see one,' or as if systemic is defined by when those at the central bank think that an event could develop into a system-wide problem" (Caprio and Klingebiel 1996).

At the opposite pole is the view expressed by Benston and Kaufman (1994) and by Kaufman (1986, 1996) that the financial system is much less fragile than is commonly supposed, in the sense that the incidence of failure in banking has been generally lower than that in business, and that the consequences of bank failures are frequently less serious and far-reaching than the failures of comparably sized businesses of other types.

Kaufman (1988) even has good things to say about bank runs, noting that in all but a few cases, they have served as a useful source of discipline that has led to the closing of insolvent banks while leaving well managed banks untouched.

Perhaps the most extreme statement of the view that systemic risk in the total absence of banking regulation and supervision would be a minor problem was presented by Benston (1996) who asserted that banking regulation existed primarily to restrict competition among banks and other financial institutions and that it served no useful purpose other than to provide research topics for professors specializing in financial institutions. He did acknowledge a legitimate role for central banks, but only to ensure, through open market operations to maintain the reserves of the banking system, that depositor withdrawals did not result in a contraction of the money stock. Other economists who have downplayed the importance of systemic risk include Merton Miller (1993), Robert Mackay (1995), and the late Fischer Black (1995).

Indeed, the critics of the current system of banking supervision and regulation go beyond saying that systemic risk would be of little concern in the absence of regulation; they assert that systemic risk has been significantly worsened by the very policies designed to mitigate it. According to Kaufman (1996, 26), "Although systemic risk may exist without government regulation, on net, the probability of instability occurring in banking and the intensity of any resulting damage are likely to be greatly increased by some government policies adopted in the name of preventing systemic risk." He argues that this has, in fact been true for the United States. "But the evidence, at least for the U.S., is quite clear. The cost of systemic risk before the introduction of the safety net under banking in 1914 was far smaller than the cost of bank failures since then" (Kaufman 1996, 26–27).

Some Reservations About the "New View" of Systemic Risk

If true, these are damning indictments of the current system of supervision and regulation. We would submit, however, the case is far from being as airtight as these statements would suggest. The first and obvious point is that it was the perception, not only of bankers but of scholars and ordinary citizens alike, that the costs of financial instability in the United States in the nineteenth century warranted government intervention. That the policies and their implementation have been flawed should come as no surprise to any student of human institutions. In any case, the "safety net" that Kaufman dates from 1914 originally consisted of little beyond the "lender of last resort" function, a modified version of which even Benston still concedes is necessary. Similarly, the evidence that is "quite clear" to Kaufman is nowhere presented in his paper. But even if the costs of bank failures — however measured — have been higher since 1914, much more than a simple before-and-after comparison is required to demonstrate a cause-and-effect relationship.

There are other reasons for believing that the jury is still out on the magnitude of systemic risk in the absence of intervention. One is simply that, since at least the 1930s, we do not have any domestic examples of traditional financial crises. For example, the Federal Reserve's actions to supply liquidity to the market in the wake of the 1970 default by Penn Central on its commercial paper have been widely criticized as unwise and unnecessary, since there was no serious disruption of the market that even approached a systemic event. As Calomiris (1994) observed, however, there is reason to believe that the disturbance would have been considerably more severe in the absence of intervention. Similarly, as Caprio and Klingebiel (1996) note, even if one accepts the finding of Gorton (1988) that banking panics have typically followed, rather than preceded economic downturns, that does not preclude a causal relationship running from "a more silent form of financial distress" to economic activity. According to them, "financial distress of the banking system, when a significant fraction of the system is insolvent but remains open, is perhaps the most pernicious type . . . ." This observation may go far to explain the observation of Samuelson (1991) that, despite the effort expended in studying them, financial crises as conventionally defined appear to be a short-lived phenomena that leave little or no trace on the real economy.

Changes in Systemic Risk Over Time

Another reason for the difficulty in assessing the magnitude of systemic risk is that there is no reason to believe it remains unchanged through time. Indeed, there is reason to believe that it varies systematically both with the current outlook for the economy and for financial markets and with the vulnerability of financial institutions, as reflected in their liquidity, capitalization, exposure to interest rate risk, and degree of asset diversification. A precise assessment of the significance or magnitude of systemic risk at any given time is difficult because it inevitably hinges on a number of complex judgments on which knowledgeable individuals may differ. Judgments about the prevailing level of systemic risk depend on assessments of the probabilities of likelihoods of the following developments, all of which change considerably over time:

- the failure or near-failure of a large player or simultaneous failures of large numbers of players (bank or nonbank) in the financial system;
- the occurrence of large losses or severe liquidity problems of a considerable number of other market participants as a result of the initial failure or failures;
- the spread of severe liquidity pressures through the system as a result of contagious runs;
- significant increases in the cost or decreases in the availability of credit to a meaningful number of borrowers or severe impairment of the functioning of payments systems or financial markets;
- amplification of any initial disturbance by exogenous factors; and
- the absence of timely, effective responses by supervisors.

The listing of these specific events is not intended to suggest that any one of them is either necessary or sufficient to constitute a systemic event. They are simply elements that have been present in one or more past financial crises and that would clearly seem to affect the duration and/or severity of the event. To be sure, it is difficult to imagine a systemic event that did not include the first item on the list, the failure or near-failure of one or more large financial institutions. The particular nature of the cause of such failures would seem to be irrelevant to the identification of a systemic event, if not to its remedies. The second and third items, which may be viewed as manifestations of contagion due, respectively, to direct financial linkages between the institutions initially failing and other institutions and to runs by depositors unable to distinguish troubled institutions from healthy ones, need not be present in a systemic event but would clearly tend to exacerbate its effects. The fourth item, the effects on credit supply or the functioning of the payments mechanism, would seem to be the only one on the list that is essential to an event's designation as "systemic." It is hard to see how a financial disturbance could affect the real economy if it had no effect on either of these.

Factors Affecting the Seriousness of Systemic Risk

With the exception of those systemic events that originate in monetary or fiscal policy mistakes, there is little that policymakers can do to alter the type and incidence of any precipitating shock. At one extreme, a single large institution might be adversely affected by some external shock due to an idiosyncratic risk, that is, risk peculiar to the operations of the individual institution, as opposed to those risks common to all firms in the industry or economy. Alternatively, numerous institutions of varying sizes might simultaneously become impaired due to some shock generated externally or endogenously within the financial system. Given the size and nature of the shock, the likelihoods of the developments listed above, and therefore, the severity of systemic risk, will depend upon a small number of critical factors related to the asset and liability portfolios of individual financial institutions and the structure and technology of the industry. These factors, which have been highlighted in our earlier paper (Bartholomew and Whalen 1995), featured prominently in a recent survey of international banking in *The Economist* (Giles 1996).

Connectivity

One key factor that determines the severity of systemic risk is the extent of connectivity — the number and strength of linkages among firms and markets — in the financial sector. Greater connectivity implies larger secondary effects from some initial financial market disturbance and never greater systemic risk. The classic example is losses suffered by correspondent banks in the event of the unanticipated failure of a larger respondent. Another is settlements failure in payments systems. Linkages between institutions (banks and nonbanks), markets (for example, cash and derivatives markets, or securities and foreign exchange markets) and countries (raising legal and regulatory risks) are considerable and growing. This growth is market-driven and so cannot and should not be limited. Nevertheless, the more numerous and increasingly complicated firm and market linkages, together with increased speed of information transmission and processing, imply greater potential exposure and shorter reaction time (for both market participants and regulators) to developments in particular markets (Promisel *et al.* 1992). Market participants report increasing concern with counterparty credit risk because the volume and size of transactions are increasing, and also as counterparty credit quality is becoming increasingly difficult to assess due to the increase in linkages and the growing use of derivative and other off-balance-sheet instruments. As connectivity increases, risk exposures of counterparties become more complicated and less transparent.

Portfolio concentration

A second critical factor influencing systemic risk is the extent to which the portfolios of financial (and to some extent nonfinancial) institutions are concentrated. Greater concentration implies a higher risk of failure should an unfavorable shock occur Asset concentrations are hard to assess for several reasons. Some concentrations may reflect desirable market outcomes. For example, concerns have been raised about the extent to which a relatively small number of highly rated institutions that play a leading role in multiple markets have increased their concentrations in the derivatives business. This may be the result of inherent advantages possessed by these large institutions, but it does expose them heavily to any kind of disturbance in the derivatives markets. More traditional loan-type concentrations are inherently difficult for bankers, supervisors, and market outsiders to measure and can change relatively quickly. Partly as a result, there may be insufficient disincentives (for example, a hard-wired capital charge or supervisory penalty) to inappropriate asset concentration. A complicating factor is the tendency of financial institutions to exhibit "herd mentality." Financial institutions and other financial market participants, rationally pursuing what appear to be attractive investment opportunities, simultaneously and jointly channel credit to particular sectors and/or regions. This can result in an over-concentration in the aggregate, even though individual institutions do not exhibit imprudent portfolio imbalances. If the over-concentration fuels a speculative bubble that subsequently collapses, all creditors to this sector suffer.

Homogeneity

A third factor that affects systemic risk is actual or perceived financial institution homogeneity — the extent to which the asset and liability portfolios of institutions are similar. Greater homogeneity, in conjunction with portfolio concentrations stemming from herd mentality and/or high leverage, implies greater industry susceptibility to shocks. The thrift crisis of the 1980s was a classic manifestation of this problem, although portfolio homogeneity was only one of several important factors contributing to the crisis. Homogeneity also increases the likelihood of contagion because it makes it increasingly difficult for depositors to differentiate accurately among banks according to risk.

Information

The fourth and possibly the most important factor affecting the seriousness of systemic risk at any given time is the quantity, quality, and distribution of information available to market participants and regulators (Mishkin 1995). Indeed, the probabilities of the other crucial determinants of the seriousness of systemic risk depend heavily on information quality and asymmetries. When significant information asymmetries exist and/or the quality of information is low, there is a greater danger of inadvertent risk exposures or concentrations, contagion, credit crunches, and inadequate policy responses, and systemic risk is correspondingly greater. Unexpected bank failures are likely to be more frequent and numerous and will tend to inflict larger losses on a larger number of bank and nonbank creditors, perhaps precipitating additional failures. Creditors, unable to assess accurately the condition of apparently similar institutions, might elect to "run" on both truly troubled and truly healthy depositories (Jacklin and Bhattacharya 1988). This is rational behavior for insufficiently informed creditors whose deposits are not insured or collateralized and creates a liquidity crisis. Unless affected institutions can borrow to cover the claims of "running" creditors, otherwise solvent firms may suffer losses from selling illiquid assets at "fire-sale" prices. Although recent research suggests that contagion has been less pervasive than has often been assumed (Kaufman 1993), there is considerable evidence that it was present during several banking panics of the free banking era in the United States in the second half of the nineteenth century (Gilbert 1988; Hasan and Dwyer 1988), as well as in the 1930s.

The key role played by information conditions in determining the seriousness of systemic risk has led one leading scholar of financial crises to argue that they should be an inherent part of the definition of systemic risk. In discussing the definition of systemic risk given in our earlier paper, Frederic Mishkin (1995) suggested that it be amended as follows: "Systemic risk is the likelihood of a sudden, usually unexpected, event that disrupts information in financial markets, making them unable to effectively channel funds to those parties with the most productive investment opportunities." While we strongly agree with Mishkin's emphasis on the vital importance of information in determining both the likelihood of occurrence and the adverse impact of a systemic event, it does not seem appropriate to incorporate any one source of systemic risk into the definition of the term itself. Inasmuch as Schwartz's definition of a financial crisis involves a contraction of the money supply due to depositors' efforts to convert deposits into currency, a system-wide run based on a rational, informed assessment of the condition of the banking system would not even qualify as a systemic event under Mishkin's definition.

The availability and quality of information also influence the speed or effectiveness of any supervisory response to systemic events. The increased speed of information flow, operating through a greatly expanded number of linkages, compresses the amount of time supervisors have to analyze and respond to any given shock (Promisel *et al.* 1992). Presumably, supervisors have a compensating advantage in the form of information on the risk profiles of affected institutions (obtained through the examination process) that is as good or better than that possessed by the market. It is, however, possible — albeit unlikely — that supervisors might be confronted with a situation where some significant portion of the banking industry becomes troubled quickly.

These arguments suggest that the collapse of a bank perceived by the market to be well capitalized, well managed, and not unduly risky could reduce the public's confidence in other banks and lead to cascading bank runs. On the other hand, closure of a bank widely known to be in financial trouble should have relatively little impact on the public's general confidence in banks. Such a closure should not lead to systemic problems because creditors of the troubled bank, recognizing its condition, appropriately adjust their risk exposure prior to the failure. Thus, the state of information is a major, if not the key element in understanding how to deal with systemic problems and how to reduce the degree of systemic risk in the financial system.

Policies for Addressing Systemic Risk

Policies designed to reduce systemic risk have relied on both traditional supervision and regulation and so-called "structural" remedies, including the establishment of a "lender of last resort" to provide emergency liquidity assistance to the banking system. Because of long experience demonstrating that the provision of liquidity by central banks can limit the adverse effects of systemic events, the mere existence of a credible lender of last resort structurally reduces systemic risk. Government guarantees of some or all bank liabilities, such as deposit insurance are another means by which governments have structurally reduced systemic risk.

Recent experience suggests that there is an additional regulatory tool that can structurally reduce systemic risk and help to mitigate the moral hazard problem, namely a fixed and well-known closure rule, that is, a rule that defines under what circumstances a financial institution will be closed by regulatory authorities. Such a rule reduces uncertainty among players in financial markets and reduces the likelihood that the recognition of failure of even the largest financial institutions will increase systemic risk. Knowledge that bank supervisors, when confronted with a bank failure, will act to impose discipline on those responsible for the failure creates an enormous incentive for owners, managers, and directors to manage risk prudently. Although a number of closure rules have been suggested, there is considerable support for one similar to the prompt corrective action provisions of the Federal Deposit Insurance Corporation Improvement Act (FDICIA) of 1991. The effectiveness of such a rule presupposes both that supervisors can determine when the value of bank capital falls below a critical level and that they will take prompt action when it does so.

Among the several strategies designed to reduce systemic risk, the two that receive the most attention — the use of the central bank or some other public agency as a lender of last resort and the provision by the government of deposit insurance — come into play only after an initial disturbance has occurred and are intended to reduce the likelihood that its effects are transmitted widely and become fatal to significant numbers of financial institutions, markets, or the system as a whole. A number of other strategies, including traditional supervision and regulation as well as proposals for increased disclosure, are preventive in nature and are designed to reduce the vulnerability of the financial system to whatever shocks that may occur in the future. More recently, a number of scholars have placed heavy emphasis on the importance of assuring that supervisors move promptly to correct problems at depository institutions before they become serious and, in extreme cases, to close failing institutions before their capital becomes negative.

Lender of Last Resort

Both of the two most widely recognized means for controlling systemic risk in the current system, the lender of last resort and deposit insurance, are designed to reduce the likelihood of damaging runs, that is, contagion risk. Perhaps the most powerful tool available to central banks for limiting the losses associated with systemic events is their ability to provide liquidity when there is a generalized flight from real and financial assets to cash. The existence of a credible lender of last resort, as the Federal Reserve has proved to be in recent years, structurally reduces systemic risk. The appropriate central bank response to systemic crises is to supply adequate liquidity through open market operations, discount window lending, or some combination of the two to satisfy the needs of all parties holding acceptable collateral, valued at precrisis prices (Garcia 1988). These tools prevent runs from precipitating a sharp contraction of bank loans and deposits and associated increases in interest rates as well as the failure of solvent institutions (Schwartz 1988).

Some experts argue that because the Federal Reserve has neither the incentive nor the ability to limit discount window lending to illiquid but solvent banks, its lending policies may be either too restrictive, resulting in the failure of otherwise solvent institutions and exacerbating real economic declines, or too lenient, keeping insolvent institutions afloat and creating future moral hazard problems. These critics argue that the Federal Reserve could, and should, rely primarily on open market operations to deal with systemic events (Schwartz 1992; Todd 1988; Calomiris 1994; Goodfriend and King 1988). In the case of open market operations, the Federal Reserve relies on the market to allocate the liquidity supplied. Theory and evidence indicate that the market is effective in channeling funds to illiquid but solvent entities. Essential feedback is available in the form of movements in market rates. The effectiveness of this approach has been demonstrated in a number of recent cases (for example, the 1987 stock market break and the Drexel bankruptcy).

Deposit Insurance

Government guarantees of some or all bank liabilities, such as those provided by deposit insurance, are another device used by governments to reduce systemic risk. Deposit insurance structurally reduces the threat of systemic risk by limiting the amount of liabilities exposed to loss at depositories, thereby reducing the incentives for depositors to run. Indeed, none of the post-Great Depression financial disturbances in the United States has been exacerbated by widespread bank runs.

However, both the liberal use of lender of last resort and overly generous deposit insurance come with a cost. Liberal provision of liquidity to the banking system during periods of stringency leads banks to become dependent on central bank credit even in normal times. Deposit insurance, particularly if it is not priced to reflect differences in risk exposure, creates a moral hazard, reducing the incentive to manage risk prudently. Thus, both of the tools most commonly used by governments to control systemic risk produce undesirable side effects: in exchange for economic stability, individual banks or other financial institutions benefit from the safety net by receiving better credit terms from the market, precedents are set that may inappropriately constrain future policy, and the sharing of losses with taxpayers induces some institutions to assume additional risk. This moral hazard problem is inseparable from the existence of the safety net and strengthens the need for supervision and regulation.

Unfortunately, the desire to avoid the immediate costs of potentially systemic events — a widely observed tendency of democratic governments in many other areas of activity as well — has become so ingrained that government tends to overreact to even minor financial disturbances, placing excessive reliance on policies that preclude the closing of large banks or other significant financial institutions (Hetzel 1991; Baer 1994). As Kindleberger (1989, 182) has observed, "Actuality inevitably dominates contingency. Today wins over tomorrow."

Supervision and Regulation

The traditional approach to limiting and managing systemic risk is continuous supervision and regulation to limit the exposure of banks to credit, interest rate, and other risks, thereby reducing the likelihood of failure of individual financial institutions. Given information asymmetries, the examination process may provide supervisors with a comparative advantage in monitoring and preventing excessive credit concentrations. In principle, this could be the best defense against risks stemming from shocks related to herd mentality and speculative bubbles. Another important supervisory role is to establish capital and solvency requirements and verify adherence to them through the examination process. Supervisors can also facilitate market access to information on risk and solvency and so enlist the aid of market discipline.

However, even those most favorably disposed toward governmental or central bank intervention or the prevention or moderation of financial crises concede that supervision and regulation cannot eliminate all serious disturbances in the financial system. For example, Charles Kindleberger asked, "Can financial crisis be forestalled by strict regulation and supervision?. . . Most of the rules for sound banking are already incorporated in the regulations or are implicit in banking tradition. Many of the rules are ignored by banks and regulators alike" (Kindleberger 1989, 175). This passage is followed by a description of the many ways in which regulators have been excessively timid in their enforcement of capital and accounting standards. Kindleberger attributes much of the failure of effective supervision in reaching its theoretical potential to the division of responsibility in the U.S. financial regulatory structure.

Guttentag and Herring have suggested an alternative explanation for the occasional failure of supervision and regulation to limit the vulnerability of banks even to shocks of a size and nature that have been experienced historically (Guttentag and Herring 1986). This is the notion of "disaster myopia," which they argue is the likely outcome of two "heuristics" (learning processes) that psychologists have found to characterize human behavior in the face of low-probability events resulting in large losses. The "availability heuristic" suggests that individuals estimate the probabilities or frequencies of particular types of events based on the ease with which they can recall past occurrences. The "threshold heuristic" suggests that, in order to conserve the scarce resource of managerial attention, decision makers treat probabilities below some critically low level as if they were zero. Together, these heuristics can produce disaster myopia, which, Guttentag and Herring argue, leads both bank managers and supervisors to relax their concern with low-probability shocks as the time since their last occurrence increases and eventually to treat their probabilities as if they were zero. Indeed, such a phenomenon does appear to have been evident in the gradual erosion of post-Depression conservatism of banks in the United States and its displacement by more aggressive risk-taking.

Another important shortcoming of supervision in its task of limiting vulnerability to shocks is that ". . . regulators are likely to recognize a particular type of exposure as sufficiently dangerous to justify requiring additional capital only *after* a shock occurs" (Guttentag and Herring 1986, 30). Benston has criticized the current approach to supervision on similar grounds, specifically the inaccuracy of bank examiners' loan evaluations and the poor performance of the early warning systems devised by agencies to predict which banks are likely to encounter future financial difficulties (Benston 1973, 1975; Benston and Marlin 1974).

Perhaps equally or more serious is the problem of translating examiners' findings of management or asset quality weaknesses at institutions into prompt and effective supervisory actions. In the case of the 1973 failure of U.S. National Bank of San Diego, for example, there is clear evidence that the examiners were aware of insider loans and other problems as early as 1962, but nearly ten years went by before serious measures were taken to deal with those problems (U.S. House of Representatives 1975, 219–246). Similarly, although problems were detected at the Continental Illinois National Bank and Trust Company of Chicago at least as early as the August 1981 examination, the bank was subsequently allowed to purchase an additional $600 million dollars of highly risky, poorly documented energy-related loan participations from Penn Square Bank (U.S. House of Representatives 1984, 335). The delays in action by the Federal Home Loan Bank Board during the thrift debacle of the 1980s appear to have been even more egregious, in some cases allowing institutions to continue operating and taking on additional risks for more than a decade after they became book value-insolvent (Barth, Bartholomew and Labich 1989).

All of these examples — which are no more than an illustrative sample of the many failures of supervision over the past two decades in the United States — suggest a deeply rooted regulatory incentive problem related to the public's judgment of regulatory performance by the current failure rate. In conjunction with the time required for potential problems to show up in bank earnings and condition statements and the possibility that some institutions may actually succeed in growing out of their problems, this myopic performance standard provides regulators with both the opportunity and the temptation to postpone difficult supervisory and resolution decisions to one's successors. This basic flaw was addressed — hopefully remedied — through the adoption in the Federal Deposit Insurance Corporation Improvement Act of 1991 of a fairly well-defined closure rule.

Prompt Corrective Action

There is an often overlooked, but very important supervisory mechanism that can limit the damage associated with bank failures, thereby mitigating systemic risk, that does not entail increased moral hazard. This is a well-known, consistently enforced set of early intervention and closure rules (Benston and Kaufman 1988). Clear articulation of these rules decreases uncertainty and reduces the likelihood that recognition of the failure of even the largest financial institutions will cause systemic problems. Moreover, assuming the closure rule does not incorporate a too-big-to-fail policy, it should mitigate the moral hazard incentives associated with the existence of the safety net. Knowledge that bank supervisors, when confronted with a bank failure, will act promptly to impose discipline on those responsible for the failure creates an enormous incentive for owners, managers, and directors to manage risk prudently (Carnell 1994). In addition, regulators now have the bridge bank and final settlement payment options to deal with large bank failures. These devices allow regulators to impose manageable losses on uninsured depositors and unsecured creditors in large bank failures without restricting access to their funds.

In principle, of course, prompt corrective action is subject to the same technical problems of implementation and bureaucratic incentives for delay and forbearance that afflict supervision and regulation generally. In an effort to remedy that fundamental problem, those provisions of the Federal Deposit Insurance Corporation Improvement Act (FDICIA) of 1991 that deal with prompt corrective action were designed to limit supervisory discretion. For example, the section of FDICIA on prompt corrective action tied the intensity of supervision to an institution's capital composition and established an explicit closure rule. Some provisions of this section facilitate supervisory actions to limit risk-taking and encourage remedial actions by bank management. Other provisions generally require regulators to close institutions when their capital ratio falls below 2 percent. Although supervisors can make exceptions to this rule, they must justify and document their reasons. Moreover, Section 141 of FDICIA requires that institutions be resolved by the method that involves the least cost to the FDIC. Although the law contains a "systemic risk" exception, the invocation of that exception requires that both the FDIC Board of Directors and the Board of Governors of the Federal Reserve System recommend it by two-thirds votes and that the Secretary of the Treasury, in consultation with the President, determines that compliance with the least-cost resolution provision would have "serious adverse effects on economic conditions or financial stability." Implemented in accordance with the intent of their drafters, these provisions should have a salutary effect in disciplining bank risk taking, thereby reducing systemic risk.

Some critics of regulation are skeptical that prompt corrective action will be implemented as Congress intended. A year after the act was passed, Kane (1993, 71) argued that "regulators are carrying out their responsibilities under the act in an unfriendly spirit," citing in particular the agencies' failure "to develop either an effective measure of a bank's exposure to interest-rate risk or an effective framework for limiting the extent to which these exposures pass through to the net reserves of the BIF." Similar skepticism was expressed by Lee Hoskins (1993, 149), who asserted that "loopholes will appear and regulators will forbear." One of the first evaluations of an agency's implementation of the prompt corrective action provisions of FDICIA found evidence of delays and some reluctance to implement the provisions when other supervisory actions were available (FDIC 1994).

Nonetheless, because the federal bank regulatory agencies are still in the process of implementing some of the provisions of FDICIA, having just finalized their proposal for incorporating interest rate risk into the risk-based capital requirements and still learning how best to implement the prompt corrective action provisions, it is too early to judge their performance.

Disclosure

Because of the problems of supervision over the past decade or so, banking scholars have increasingly called for greater reliance on market discipline to limit bank risk-taking. A prerequisite for market discipline to be effective is that bank stockholders and creditors — whether uninsured depositors, subordinated debt holders, or others — possess adequate information about each bank's risk exposure. Given that the results of past studies of the degree to which differences in the riskiness of banks have been reflected in differences in the risk premia they must pay to obtain funds have been mixed (Herzig-Marx and Weaver 1979; Hannan and Hanweck 1988; Pettway 1976; Avery *et al.* 1988; Gorton and Santomero 1988), many regulators have expressed doubts regarding the effectiveness of such an approach (Randall 1989). However, these results may simply reflect the fact that, in most failures, uninsured depositors and other creditors have been made whole.

Some have argued that increased disclosure and market discipline would have the opposite effect from that which was intended, that is, they would actually destabilize financial markets. This argument highlights the fundamental conflict that exists between proposals of greater disclosure and traditional banking supervision, which relies on secrecy to prevent depositors from running on banks that have experienced serious deterioration. The conflict between these two approaches — roughly corresponding to the difference between Securities and Exchange Commission investor protection regulation and safety and soundness regulation by the bank regulatory agencies — has been highlighted in the lawsuits instituted by bank shareholders and creditors who suffered losses in the failures of banks and thrift institutions in recent years (Simons 1990). Whether banking regulation places greater reliance on market discipline or not, the appropriate degree of disclosure is a fundamental issue that will have to be fought out in the years to come.

Macroeconomic Stabilization Policies

Systemic risk can be triggered by a wide variety of events originating either inside or outside the banking system. In general, these events are the result of some sort of precipitating economic shock (for example, unexpectedly large movements in commodity or asset prices or changes in economic activity). Many, and perhaps most, of these shocks are beyond the power of public policy to control, or even influence. In a significant number of cases, however, the shocks triggering systemic risk appear to have originated in unexpected macroeconomic policy changes that resulted in rapid, persistent changes in actual or expected interest rates, foreign exchange rates, inflation, or real economic growth or some combination of the above. This was clearly the case in the early 1980s when, following a decade and a half of generally accelerating inflation, fueled both by monetary and fiscal policy and by a series of supply shocks, monetary policy turned sharply restrictive. Whether one views the more accommodative policy of the earlier years or the tight anti-inflationary policy beginning in 1979 as the major culprit, it was clearly the shift from one to the other that proved devastating for depository institutions. In the light of this experience, and numerous earlier episodes of policy instability, a number of scholars have argued that stable macroeconomic policies may be adequate to maintain financial stability and largely eliminate systemic risk. Although there is room for debate over the specific focus of a macroeconomic policy designed to maintain financial stability, Schwartz's proposal for stabilizing the price level is one that has considerable appeal and has gained a great deal of attention in recent years (Schwartz 1988).

Ideally, stable macroeconomic policies would totally eliminate financial crises, rendering questions of systemic risk academic and negating the necessity for studying the appropriate response to crises when they occur. In practice, the impossibility of completely eliminating errors in policy — or just the occurrence of exogenous shocks beyond the power of macroeconomic policies to prevent — means that we cannot entirely devote all of our efforts to perfecting macroeconomic policy or, indeed, to preventive measures of any kind.

Differences in Financial Crises

The continuing disagreement regarding the appropriate policies for reducing or containing systemic risk reflects, in large part, the failure of scholars to reach a consensus regarding the causes and cures of financial crises, banking panics, and systemic risk in recent years, particularly since the early 1980s. Considerable effort has been directed toward finding the common elements in financial crises with a view to developing a general theory of their causation and, presumably, a common approach to dealing with them. Success in this endeavor has been elusive. Thus, in his comprehensive treatise on systemic risk, E.P. Davis (1992) offered eight different theories of financial crises. These include excessive debt accumulation (Kindleberger 1978; Minsky 1972, 1977), bank panics (Friedman and Schwartz 1963; Schwartz 1988, 1992; Benston *et al.* 1986; Benston and Kaufman 1988, 1994; Goodfriend and King 1988; Todd 1988), speculative bubbles attributable to rational expectations and the existence of uncertainty (Keynes 1931), sudden credit rationing (Guttentag and Herring 1988), asymmetric information (Calomiris and Gorton 1991; Mishkin 1991), vulnerabilities associated with dealer markets (Glosten and Milgrom 1985), and excessive competition due to deregulation and the erosion of entry barriers in financial markets (Davis 1992). This diversity of opinion led Guttentag (1994, 1240) to conclude in his review of Davis's book, "that there are different kinds of crises and there is no reason why any one theory should best explain them all."

This conclusion is consistent with the frequent observation by students of financial crises to the effect that simple, universal rules for dealing with financial crises cannot be found. For example, Kindleberger (1989, 181) quoted with approval Thomas Joplin's observation, "There are times when rules and precedents cannot be broken; others when they cannot be adhered to with safety." Similarly, Hyman Minsky (1977, 152) asserted, "The only universal rule for Federal Reserve policy is that it cannot be dictated by any universal rule." Such statements either amount to assertions that the scientific method is not applicable to studying the phenomena of financial crises and systemic risk or they imply a degree of heterogeneity among crises that requires a more disaggregated approach, that is, the classification of crises into a number of more homogeneous categories from which less universal but still useful generalizations can be drawn.

We agree with the latter interpretation, and have begun our own exercise in classifying historical crises by a number of alternative criteria that appear to be relevant in determining the best policy or set of policies for dealing with each category of crises. We believe that one of the criteria that will prove most useful in this effort concerns the nature of the immediate shock — or, as Kindleberger would say, the "precipitating cause" — associated with each crisis. In particular, it would seem reasonable that it would be important to determine whether the shock was one that affected a small subset of institutions initially and then was transmitted to others or, like the sharp rise in interest rates in the early 1980s, one that affected all institutions simultaneously. Similarly, it is almost certainly important whether the shock originated on the demand side or supply side.

Recent efforts to categorize financial disturbances — some but not all of which constitute systemic events — have made considerable progress in distinguishing their common and disparate elements. For example, a study in progress at the International Monetary Fund (Garcia 1996) summarizes the views of the IMF experts on the severity, causes, and effects of recent banking problems in the countries for which they have responsibility. For the period 1980–1995, the experts identified eighteen episodes of banking problems in fourteen countries: Argentina and the United States each experienced three distinct episodes involving somewhat different sets of institutions. The experts were asked to indicate which factors, from a list supplied by the author, appeared to have contributed to the episodes in their particular countries. Thus, several factors may have been named for any given episode. The experts cited deficiencies in internal controls as contributing factors in all eighteen episodes and problems associated with the forms of ownership — state or industrial — in a large majority of the cases. They also cited low degrees of diversification in all eighteen cases, deficiencies in credit assessment in sixteen cases, unusually rapid growth in eleven cases, inadequate capital in nine cases, and excessively high costs in nine cases. Several indicators of insufficient competition, including high levels of market concentration, barriers to entry, and the absence of foreign competition, were each named in slightly more than half of the cases. Among indicators of a lack of market discipline, the experts named poor disclosure in fifteen cases, political interference in eleven cases, and full deposit insurance coverage, underfunded insurance, and a culture that favored debtors in a smaller number of cases.

Such a cross-classification of crises by origin and other important characteristics should be helpful in choosing the appropriate way in dealing with the particular type of crisis that arose. It is analogous to the efforts in macroeconomics to identify the causes of an acceleration in inflation, recession or slowdown in economic growth as a preliminary step in choosing the appropriate monetary and fiscal policy response. Assuming for the sake of argument the desirability of using discretionary fiscal and monetary policy to stabilize the economy, there is fairly broad agreement that a tightening of monetary policy is appropriate when an actual or predicted acceleration of inflation is clearly the result of excessive demand. If the accelerated inflation results from an exogenous supply shock, there is at least a plausible case to be made for a partial accommodation of the shock to avoid a sharp drop in economic activity due to secondary demand effects.

The choice of policy tools to limit the damage to the financial system and the broader economy of an incipient financial crisis should be closely integrated with decisions on macroeconomic policy, Thus, only under extreme conditions should the decision to supply credit through the discount window to some subset of financial institutions experiencing liquidity problems be permitted to override macroeconomic decisions regarding the proper rate of growth of the money supply. In many cases, the potential effect of discount window lending on money growth could simply be offset through open market operations.

In other cases, arguably including the stock market crash of 1987, a temporary but widespread increase in the demand for money may justify a temporary increase in money growth. To prevent an undesired acceleration of inflation, the temporary increase in money growth would have to be offset by a withdrawal of reserves as the demand for money returned to "normal." There is fairly general agreement that the Federal Reserve did a reasonably good job of this following the 1987 crash. In contrast, there has been considerable criticism of the Fed's actions to sustain the commercial paper market in 1970 following the announcement of Penn Central's financial difficulties. But while many knowledgeable observers have asserted that the Fed overreacted by treating as a systemic event what was really a relatively minor disturbance, others have suggested that it may have been the Fed's actions that prevented it from becoming a true crisis (Calomiris 1994). However, as Paul Samuelson has observed, "There will return times when markets crash against a background of stagflation. Then engineering more money to prevent drops in real output will add to policy dilemmas connected with increases in prices" (Samuelson 1991).

In other circumstances, there is a strong case for using public funds to avoid broader damage to confidence in the financial system, but a similarly strong presumption that such an action should not add to the total liquidity of the system. This was the case with the savings and loan "bailout," when the Congress decided that it was necessary to turn to the taxpayer to backstop the bankrupt Federal Savings and Loan Insurance Corporation. This amounted to a transfer payment from taxpayers in general to depositors of failed savings and loan associations. There was nothing in the situation to suggest that money supply growth should be accelerated, as would happen if the Fed were to supply the necessary funds through discount window lending. Even if its monetary effect were offset by open market operations, such an approach was ultimately infeasible, given the deep insolvency of the industry and the fact that the Fed only lends on a fully collateralized basis. Unwilling to accept the potential consequences of a default by the insurance fund and with no easy alternative at hand, Congress decided to deal with the problem through what was essentially fiscal policy.

These selected examples should provide useful indications of the potential value of sorting historical financial crises according the nature of their origins and other important characteristics with an eye to deriving generalizations regarding the most appropriate means for preventing, or limiting the systemic effects of future crises. Although our effort in this direction is in its infancy, we believe that it will yield some useful generalizations regarding appropriate policy in a variety of situations.

Concluding Remarks

This paper has developed a definition of systemic risk that takes account of both the magnitude and pervasiveness of losses necessary to qualify an event as systemic and its probability of occurrence. Given this definition and the ensuing discussion, several questions come to mind: How serious has systemic risk been in the past? Is it likely to be a greater or lesser problem in the future? What, if anything needs to be done? An analysis of financial market events indicates that, while financial market disturbances have been quite common in the post-Depression era, very few have risen to a systemic level (Carron 1982; Schwartz 1986). In the United States, for example, only two events in recent memory, the Continental Bank failure and the thrift debacle, appear to have even approached systemic proportions. The other notable financial institution failures, as well as many of the situations involving troubled nonbanking entities that occurred during this period (for example, the failures of the Bank of New England, First Republic, First Pennsylvania, and Franklin National; the runs on thrifts insured by the Ohio Deposit Guaranty Fund; the 1987 stock market crash; and the failure of Drexel Burnham Lambert) lacked one or more of the characteristics of a systemic event. Most of them were not sudden or unexpected and so investors and markets had ample time to react. Because it was readily apparent that the failures were the result of institution- and/or region-specific problems, there was a low probability that the failures would have caused a collapse of confidence at other solvent institutions. In these and several cases involving nonbanks — for example, the Hunt silver incident and the Penn Central bankruptcy — the potential real economic impact was small. Experience suggests that the standard remedies for the typical sort of systemic risks — the lender of last resort and deposit insurance — work well.

What is less clear, however, is the appropriate policy for dealing with the systemic risk associated with significant or substantial bank or financial institution insolvencies stemming from exposure to a common external or endogenously generated shock. Fortunately, such an eventuality appears to be unlikely. Proactive supervision, including attention to concentrations, is perhaps the best available remedy. Forbearance and expansionary macroeconomic policies designed to inflate problems away are risky and potentially costly alternative solutions to such situations. Bank regulators or policymakers face the temptation to rely on these sorts of solutions since they provide visible short-run benefits.

Going forward, what is the likelihood of the most probable precipitating event — the unanticipated failure of a large bank with large losses for numerous creditors? For the immediate future, it appears to be low in the United States. The largest U.S. institutions appear to be in relatively good shape. In particular, both their asset quality and capital levels are very good. Regulators and banks involved in payments systems have worked to shape agreements assuring the legality of netting, reducing settlement lags and providing for loss sharing (Summers 1991). Such agreements mitigate systemic risk because they ensure that the parties involved in such systems understand their risk exposure in the event of a default by one participant, sharpen their incentives to control risks, and institutionalize methods for maintaining the operation of the system in times of stress. For example, the Clearing House Interbank Payments System (CHIPS) now has a procedure in place to facilitate settlement finality. Bridge bank authority and improved techniques for resolving failed depository institutions allow supervisors to resolve bank failures, particularly large ours, in ways that permit losses to be imposed on uninsured parties without a significant reduction in the liquidity of their funds and so should reduce resolution costs to the Federal Deposit Insurance Corporation (FDIC).

As noted above, the FDICIA of 1991 contained a number of provisions that should reduce systemic risk in the United States. Although the prompt corrective action provisions of Section 131 are undoubtedly the most important, several other provisions should also prove useful. Section 308 of FDICIA required supervisors to impose restrictions on the extent of a bank's exposure to the failures of other banks through correspondent or other types of relationships. This restriction is designed to limit the risk exposure and losses of smaller banks in the event of a large bank failure, thereby closing off one channel for the transmittal of systemic effects. Section 305 of FDICIA requires federal bank and thrift regulators to develop some mechanism to adjust risk-based capital requirements for interest rate, credit concentration, and nontraditional activities risks, none of which were explicitly included in the Basle Accord risk-based requirements. Done correctly, these adjustments should reduce both the probability of failure and the cost of those that do occur.

Assuming that a large unanticipated failure does occur in the United States, what is the likelihood of contagion? The likelihood of contagion does not appear to be high, particularly in a world with deposit insurance. It is somewhat difficult for depositors to determine whether their bank is solvent. However, considerable financial information is disclosed by banks and the market does appear to be relatively efficient in processing information about bank risk, particularly if it has the incentives to do so. Thus, contagious runs appear unlikely. In the event that they do occur, the evidence suggests that solvent banks should be able to withstand temporary liquidity pressures due to contagion as long as the Federal Reserve supplies sufficient reserves to the system, either through the discount window or open market operations.

All things considered, systemic risk appears to be at a relatively low level in the United States as of mid 1996. Even if a systemic event should occur, it appears that the requisite tools and knowledge for limiting its effects are in place and ready for use. Nonetheless, financial markets and the banking system are continuously evolving in unpredictable ways and risk exposures have a way of building up without being detected by traditional supervisory approaches. Like inflation, systemic risk is never dead, although often dormant. All that is needed to revive it is a mixture of excessive optimism, poor policy, and some unexpected precipitating event. And that is why regulators and students of banking need to devote continued attention to the analysis and control of systemic risk, however negligible it may currently appear to be.

References

Avery, R. B., T. M. Belton, and M. A. Goldberg (1988). Market Discipline in Regulating Bank Risk: New Evidence from the Capital Markets. *Journal of Money, Credit and Banking* **20**, 597–610.

Baer, H., and D. Klingebiel (1995). Systemic Risk When Depositors Bear Losses: Five Case Studies. *Banking, Financial Markets, and Systemic Risk,* Volume 7 of *Research in Financial Services: Private and Public Policy*, JAI Press, 195–302.

Barth, J. R. (1991). *The Great Savings and Loan Debacle.* The AEI Press, Washington.

Barth, J. R., P. F. Bartholomew, and C. J. Labich (1989). Moral Hazard and the Thrift Crisis: An Analysis of 1988 Resolutions. *Banking System Risk: Charting a New Course, Proceedings of a Conference on Bank Structure and Competition*, Federal Reserve Bank of Chicago, 344–384.

Bartholomew, P. F., and G. Whalen (1995). Fundamentals of Systemic Risk. *Banking, Financial Markets, and Systemic Risk*, Volume 7 of *Research in Financial Services: Private and Public Policy*. JAI Press, 3–17.

Bensten, L. (1994). Statement Before the Committee on Banking, Housing, and Urban Affairs. U.S. Senate, March 1.

Benston, G. J. (1973). Bank Examination. *The Bulletin,* Nos. 89–90, New York University, Graduate School of Business Administration, Institute of Finance, May.

Benston, G. J. (1995). Comment on 'The Definition of Systemic Risk' by P.F. Bartholomew, L.R. Mote, and G. Whalen. Paper presented at the annual meetings of the Western Economics Association, San Diego, July 8.

Benston, G. J. (1977) Discussion. In Edward L. Altman, and Arnold W. Sametz, eds., *Financial Crises: Institutions and Markets in a Fragile Environment*, John Wiley & Sons, 59–61.

Benston, G. J., and J. T. Marlin (1974). Bank Examiners' Evaluation of Credit: An Analysis of the Usefulness of Substandard Loan Data. *Journal of Money, Credit and Banking* **6**, 24–44.

Benston, G. J., R. A. Eisenbeis, P. M. Horvitz, E. J. Kane, and G. G. Kaufman (1986). *Perspectives on Safe & Sound Banking: Past, Present, and Future.* MIT Press, Cambridge.

Benston, G. J., and G. G. Kaufman (1988). *Risk and Solvency Regulation of Depository Institutions: Past Policies and Current Options.* Monograph Series in Finance and Economics, Monograph 1988–1, Salomon Brothers Center for the Study of Financial Institutions, New York University, New York.

Benston, G. J., and G. G. Kaufman (1994) Is the Banking and Payments System Fragile? Presentation at the Conference on Financial Fragility, Maastricht, The Netherlands, September.

Black, F. (1995). Hedging, Speculation, and Systemic Risk. *The Journal of Derivatives*, Summer, 6–8.

Brimmer, A. F. (1984). *The Federal Reserve as Lender of Last Resort: The Containment of Systemic Risks.* Paper presented before a joint session of the American Economic Association and the Eastern Economic Association, Dallas, Texas, December 29.

Calomiris, C. W. (1994). Is the Discount Window Necessary? A Penn Central Perspective. *Review.* Federal Reserve Bank of St. Louis, May/June, 31–56.

Calomiris, C., and W. Gary Gorton (1991). The Origins of Bank Panics. In G. Hubbard, ed., *Financial Markets and Financial Crisis*, University of Chicago Press, Chicago.

Caprio, G., Jr., and D. Klingebiel (1996). Bank Insolvency: Bad Luck, Bad Policy, or Bad Banking? Unpublished paper, The World Bank, Washington, April.

Carnell, R. S. (1993). The Culture of Ad Hoc Discretion. In George G. Kaufman and Robert E. Litan, eds., *Assessing Bank Reform: FDICIA One Year Later*, The Brookings Institution, Washington, 113–121.

Carnell, R. S. (1994). *Systemic Risk.* Paper presented at the Conference on the Financial System in the Decade Ahead: What Should Banks Do? The Jerome Levy Economics Institute of Bard College, April 16.

Carroll, E. F., and A. J. Rolnick (1983). After Penn Square: The Insurance Dilemma. *Proceedings of a Conference on Bank Structure and Competition*, Federal Reserve Bank of Chicago, 243–267.

Carron, A. S. (1982). Financial Crises: Recent Experience in U.S. and International Markets. *Brookings Papers and Economic Activity* **2**, 395–418.

Chan-Lau, Jorge and Z. Chen (1988). *Financial Crisis and Credit Crunch as Result of Inefficient Financial Intermediation with Reference to Asian Financial Crisis.* IMF Working Papers, September.

Davis, E.P. (1992). *Debt, Financial Fragility, and Systemic Risk.* Oxford University Press, New York.

Diamond, D. W., and P. H. Dybvig (1983). Bank Runs, Deposit Insurance, and Liquidity. *Journal of Political Economy* **91**, 401–419.

Federal Deposit Insurance Corporation, Office of Inspector General (1994). Audit of FDIC's Implementation of the Prompt Corrective Action Provisions of FDICIA. *Final Audit Report*, September 23.

Flannery, M. J. (1994). Regulatory Responses to the Potential for Systemic Risk in the Financial Sector. Presented at the Conference on Banking, Financial Markets and Systemic Risk, sponsored by the Office of the Comptroller of the Currency, Washington, December 2.

Folkerts-Landau, D., P. Garber, and T. Lane (1993). Payment System Reform in Formerly Centrally Planned Economies. *Journal of Political Economy* **17**, 849–868.

Friedman, M., and A. J. Schwartz (1963). *A Monetary History of the United States: 1867–1960.* Princeton University Press, Princeton.

Garcia, G. (1988). Lessons from the Crash of '87: Systemic Issues. *The Financial Services Industry in the Year 2000: Risk and Efficiency,* Proceedings of a Conference on Bank Structure and Competition, Chicago, Federal Reserve Bank of Chicago, 45–59.

Garcia, G. (1996). *Regulatory and Market Discipline: International Evidence.* Paper presented at the annual conference on Bank Structure and Competition, Federal Reserve Bank of Chicago, May 2.

Gilbert, A. B. (1988). A Re-examination of the History of Bank Failures, Contagion, and Banking Panics. *The Financial Services Industry in the Year 2000: Risk and Efficiency,* Proceedings of a Conference on Bank Structure and Competition, Federal Reserve Bank of Chicago, 128–152.

Giles, M. (1996). The Domino Effect: A Survey of International Banking. *The Economist*, April 27–May 3, 1–38.

Glosten, L. R., and P. R. Milgrom (1985). Bid, Ask and Transactions Prices in a Specialist Market with Heterogeneously Informed Traders. *Journal of Financial Economics* **14**.

Goodfriend, M., and R. G. King (1988). *Financial Deregulation, Monetary Policy and Central Banking*. Working Paper 88–1, Federal Reserve Bank of Richmond.

Gorton, G. (1989). Public Policy and the Evolution of Banking Markets. *Banking System Risk: Charting a New Course, Proceedings of a Conference on Bank Structure and Competition*, Federal Reserve Bank of Chicago, 233–252.

Gorton, G., and A. M. Santomero (1988). The Market's Evaluation of Bank Risk: A Methodological Approach. *The Financial Services Industry in the Year 2000: Risk and Efficiency, Proceedings of a Conference on Bank Structure and Competition*, Federal Reserve Bank of Chicago, 202–218.

Guttentag, J. M. (1994). Book Review. *Journal of Economic Literature* **43**, 1238–1240.

Guttentag, J. M., and R. J. Herring (1986). Disaster Myopia in International Banking. *Essays in International Finance* **164**, International Finance Section, Department of Economics, Princeton University, September.

Guttentag, J. M. (1988). Prudential Supervision to Manage Systemic Vulnerability. *The Financial Services Industry in the Year 2000: Risk and Efficiency*. Proceedings of a Conference on Bank Structure and Competition, Federal Reserve Bank of Chicago, 602–633.

Hannan, T. H., and G. A. Hanweck (1988). Bank Insolvency Risk and the Market for Large Certificates of Deposit. *Journal of Money, Credit and Banking* **20**, 203–211.

Hasan, I., and G. P. Dwyer, Jr. (1988). Contagion Effects and Banks Closed in the Free Banking Period. *The Financial Services Industry in the Year 2000: Risk and Efficiency*. Proceedings of a Conference on Bank Structure and Competition, Federal Reserve Bank of Chicago, 153–177.

Herzig-Marx, C., and A. S. Weaver (1979). Bank Soundness and the Market for Large Negotiable Certificates of Deposit. *Staff Memoranda*, No. 79–1, Federal Reserve Bank of Chicago.

Hetzel, R. L. (1991). Too Big to Fail: Origins, Consequences, and Outlook. *Economic Review*, Federal Reserve Bank of Richmond, November/December, 3–15.

Jacklin, C. J., and S. Bhattacharya (1988). Distinguishing Panics and Information-based Bank Runs: Welfare and Policy Implications. *Journal of Political Economy* **96**, 568–592.

Kane, E. J. (1993). Comments. In G.G. Kaufman and R.E. Litan, eds., *Assessing Bank Reform: FDICIA One Year Later*. The Brookings Institution, Washington, 69–78.

Kaufman, G. G. (1992). *Bank Contagion: Theory and Evidence*. Working Paper Series, Federal Reserve Bank of Chicago, June.

Kaufman, G. G. (1996). *Bank Failures, Systemic Risk, and Bank Regulation*. Working Paper Series, Issues in Financial Regulation, Federal Reserve Bank of Chicago, January.

Kaufman, G. G. (1988). Bank Runs: Causes, Benefits, and Costs. *Cato Journal,* Winter, 539–587.

Keynes, J. M. (1931). The Consequences to the Banks of the Collapse in Money Values. *Essays in Persuasion, Collected Writings of J.M. Keynes*, Vol. 11, Macmillan, London.

Kindelberger, C. P. (1977). *Manias, Panics and Crashes*. Basic Books, New York.

Knight, F. H. (1921). *Risk, Uncertainty, and Profit*. Houghton Mifflin Co., Boston.

Mackay, R. J. (1995). Derivatives and Systemic Risk: Issues, Views, and Analysis. *Banking, Financial Markets, and Systemic Risk,* Vol. 7, *Research in Financial Services: Private and Public Policy*, JAI Press, 14–27.

Mengle, D. L. (1985). Daylight Overdrafts and Payments System Risks. *Economic Review*, Federal Reserve Bank of Richmond, May/June, 14–27.

Miller, M. H. (1993). Swaps and Systemic Risk in Interbank Markets. *FDICIA: An Appraisal, Proceedings of a Conference on Bank Structure and Competition*, Federal Reserve Bank of Chicago, 57–61.

Minsky, H. P. (1977). A Theory of Systemic Fragility. In E.I. Altman and A.W. Sametz, eds., *Financial Crises: Institutions and Markets in a Fragile Environment*, John Wiley, New York, 138–152.

Minsky, H. P. (1967). Financial Stability Revisited: The Economics of Disaster. *Reappraisal of the Federal Reserve Discount Mechanism*, Vol. 3, Board of Governors of the Federal Reserve System, Washington, 95–136.

Mishkin, F. S. (1991). Asymmetric Information and Financial Crises: A Historical Perspective. In G. Hubbard, ed., *Financial Markets and Financial Crisis*, University of Chicago Press, Chicago, 69–108.

Mishkin, F. S. (1994). Systemic Risk: An Information-Based View. Presented at the Conference on Banking, Financial Markets and Systemic Risk, sponsored by the Office of the Comptroller of the Currency, Washington, December 2.

Nickerson, D. (1995). Governance and Efficiency in Emerging Financial Markets. *Journal of International Trade and Economic Development*, December, 261–279.

Promisel, L. J., *et al.* (1992). *Recent Developments in International Interbank Relations*. Bank for International Settlements, Basle.

Randall, R. E. (1993). Safeguarding the Banking System from Financial Cycles. In R.E. Randall, ed., *Safeguarding the Banking System in an Environment of Financial Cycles*, Conference Series No. 37, Federal Reserve Bank of Boston, 17–64.

Samuelson, P. A. (1991). A Personal View on Crises and Economic Cycles. In Martin Feldstein, ed., *The Risk of Economic Crisis*, A National Bureau of Economic Research Conference Report, University of Chicago Press, Chicago, 167–170.

Schwartz, A. J. (1986). Real and Pseudo-Financial Crises. In F. Capie and G.E. Wood, eds., *Financial Crises and the World Banking System*, St. Martin's Press, New York, 11–31.

Schwartz, A. J. (1988). Financial Stability and the Federal Safety Net. In W.S. Haraf and R.M. Kushmeider, eds., *Restructuring Banking and Financial Services in America*, American Enterprise Institute for Public Policy Research, Washington, 34–62.

Schwartz, A. J. (1988). The Effects of Regulation on Systemic Risk. *The Financial Services Industry in the Year 2000: Risk and Efficiency. Proceedings of a Conference on Bank Structure and Competition*, Federal Reserve Bank of Chicago, 28–34.

Schwartz, A. J. (1992). The Misuse of the Fed's Discount Window. *Review*, Federal Reserve Bank of St. Louis, September/October, 58–69.

Schwartz, A. J. (1994). *Systemic Risk and the Macroeconomy*. Presented at the Conference on Banking, Financial Markets, and Systemic Risk, Sponsored by the Office of the Comptroller of the Currency, Washington, December 2.

Simons, T. (1990). Banking on Secrecy. *The Washington Monthly*, December, 31–37.

Smith, A. (1937). *Wealth of Nations*. Modern Library, New York.

Stiglitz, J. (1993). The Role of the State in Financial Markets. *Proceedings of the Annual Conference on Development Economics*, The World Bank, Washington, 19–52.

Summers, B. J. (1991). Clearing and Payment Systems: The Role of the Central Bank. *Federal Reserve Bulletin* **77** February, 81–91.

Todd, W. F. (1988). Lessons of the Past and Prospects for the Future in Lender of Last Resort Theory. *The Financial Services Industry in the Year 2000: Risk and*

Efficiency, Proceedings of a Conference on Bank Structure and Competition, Federal Reserve Bank of Chicago, 533–577.

Todd, W. F., and J. B. Thomson (1990). *An Insider's View of the Political Economy of the Too Big to Fail Doctrine*. Working Paper 9017, Federal Reserve Bank of Cleveland.

Tussing, A. D. (1968). Bank Failure: A Meaningful Competitive Force? *Proceedings of a Conference on Bank Structure and Competition*, Federal Reserve Bank of Chicago, 99–109.

U.S. House of Representatives, Committee on Banking and Currency, Subcommittee on Bank Supervision and Insurance (1975). *Hearings, Failure of the U.S. National Bank of San Diego*. 93rd Cong., 2nd Sess., November 27, 1973; December 10–12, 1974, Government Printing Office, Washington.

Vojta, G. J. (1986). Risk from a Banker's Viewpoint. Proceedings of a Conference on Bank Structure and Competition, Federal Reserve Bank of Chicago, 250–256.

ADDRESSING THE BAD DEBT PROBLEM IN THE SLOVAK ECONOMY

Michael Marrese

Overview

The authorities of the Slovak Republic and the former Czech and Slovak Federal Republic (CSFR) have redesigned institutions, incentives and regulations, as well as channeled substantial resources to create a market-based financial system in Slovakia. This study describes and assesses one aspect of that process, namely efforts to strengthen the financial position of those banks that had inherited substantial amounts of bad debt from the monobank.[1] Two points are made:

- The Slovak approach to the bad debt problem has relied on a healthy amount of self-reliance, possible because enterprise creditworthiness improved with the economic upturn and bank management (heavily influenced by the state as majority owner) has been committed to building up collateral, reserves and provisions.
- Slovakia's pragmatic and eclectic approach has embodied selective financial transfers from the authorities, self-reliance, regulatory and supervisory reform, and prudential management, and has thus far produced reasonable results.

[1]Bad debt is defined as either low-yielding relative to market levels or non-performing.

A discussion of general concepts related to the bad debt problem is found in the next section of the chapter. The origin and structure of the Slovak banking system are discussed in the third section. The fourth section documents Slovakia's macroeconomic recovery and firm-level profitability. Measures adopted by the authorities since 1991 to address solvency problems in banks — including debt write-offs in exchange for bonds, recapitalization of banks, and removal or subsidization of low-yielding loans — are described in the following section, as are policies put in place mainly in 1991 to 1992 to ensure prudent banking behavior. The sixth section evaluates the financial soundness of the banking system using "payment arrears data" and annual reports of several major banks. The seventh section utilizes a recent study prepared by the National Bank of Slovakia (NBS) and a worldwide consulting firm to provide a preliminary assessment — based on international accounting standards — of the financial position of major banks. Related to the recommendations of this study is the authorities' bank restructuring program, part of which has been implemented, namely, new regulations on loan classification and provisioning together with more extensive audits of all banks. Another element of that program, if adopted, would allow qualifying banks to provision from before-tax income. Conclusions follow in the last section of the chapter.

General Concepts

Brainard (1991) argues that at the beginning of an economic transformation, improvement of the financial position of banks should receive top priority because sustained growth requires stable prices; stable prices require financial discipline; and an effective capital market imposes financial discipline on enterprises. Brainard then points out that if financial discipline is to be attained, (a) enterprises need to be restructured in order for profitability to be a realistic condition for their survival; (b) restructured state firms should be offered for sale; and (c) the banking system needs to be reformed and recapitalized.

In general, failure to address the stock and flow aspects of the intertwined insolvency of banks and enterprises involves substantial costs. The stock problem — how to pay for the replacement of inherited bad debt — needs to be solved. Otherwise, banks may become locked in to lending to unviable firms rather than restructuring them; firms that could survive may fail because they are burdened with unrepayable debt; an excessive spread between deposit and lending rates may develop as banks endeavor to recapitalize themselves with retained earnings; the emergence of an excessive spread between deposit and lending rates could weaken the resolve of policy makers to maintain macroeconomic stability; and the introduction of prudential regulation may be delayed in order to hide overall weaknesses in the banking system. In addition, the flow problem — how to ensure that the appropriate bank management, incentives and conditions are in place to promote prudent decision making — should be addressed; otherwise, the stock problem would simply reemerge.

In practice, financial resources from either the government, central bank, or privatization agency had been commonly transferred to the large banks that inherited the bad debt because the net worth of these banks was so highly negative that adequate provisioning would have put the already indebted banks at a competitive disadvantage.[2] Simply put, investors would rather buy shares of newly established banks than shares of banks burdened with inherited bad debt. Therefore, if bank recapitalization were to occur through provisioning supported by an excessive spread between lending and deposit rates, then the market share of large banks could be eroded only gradually and state control would have to be maintained.

Given that banks would not be relying solely on their own resources for recapitalization, the timing of financial transfers becomes relevant. Begg and Portes (1993) argue for immediate recapitalization along the following lines: the government implicitly guarantees all deposits. Therefore, the liabilities of banks are implicitly the government's, so substituting interest-bearing government bonds for bad debt would not increase the liabilities of the government and would allow state-controlled banks to compete with new private banks on an even playing field. Begg and Portes go on to note that the interest on the bonds matches exactly the increase in the government's liabilities that would occur if the banks were not recapitalized.

[2]Net worth was negative in the following special sense: before bank/enterprise restructuring and assuming that loans would have been classified correctly. Many sources describe the extent of the bad debt, including Dittus (1994), Marrese (1994) and Vojtisek (1993).

Mitchell (1995) describes the full scale substitution of interest-bearing government bonds for bad debt as debt cancellation combined with recapitalization. She notes that such a combination is a compelling policy choice only in the absence of capital market imperfections, which is far from the reality of Central and Eastern Europe. Mitchell goes on to observe that debt transfer to some sort of work-out bank and self-reliance (including, provisioning by the banks themselves) have been more commonly pursued than debt cancellation plus recapitalization.

Marrese (1994) points out four problems with immediate debt cancellation and recapitalization. First, more efficient banking may develop only after bank managers have been replaced and enterprises have been restructured. These are lengthy processes, which argues against a once-and-for-all solution that may put resources in the wrong hands. Second, there is no clear delineation between bad and good loans. Therefore, the prospect of immediate debt cancellation and recapitalization, unless accompanied by appropriate incentives, may encourage solvent borrowers to claim they cannot repay, as occurred in the former German Democratic Republic after unification. Third, an overall bailout might lead economic agents to believe that such bailouts will be repeated. Fourth, a solution in which bankers — who tend to be highly paid and may well have been partly responsible for the accumulation of bad debt — bear no special share of the cost of cleaning up the situation may well be socially unacceptable.

Origins and Structure of the Slovak Banking System

Prior to 1990, the State Bank of Czechoslovakia (SBCS) not only served as the country's central bank, but acted as the country's largest commercial bank, making loans directly to firms according to priorities embodied in the government's plan. The Slovak State Savings Bank (SLSP) and its Czech counterpart placed a majority of their deposits in the SBCS, which, in turn, on-lent those resources to firms.

January 1, 1990 marked the beginning of the two-tier banking system as the SBCS allocated its commercial loans to two newly established state-owned banks — General Credit Bank (VUB) and Commercial Bank of Prague (KBP) — and to the Investment Bank, Prague (IB). At the end of 1992,

IB was divided into the Investment and Development Bank (IRB), based in Bratislava, and its Czech counterpart. In 1991, the CSFR authorities established the Consolidation Bank (KON), initially to relieve VUB and KBP of inherited low-yielding loans. KON was split at the end of 1992 into the Consolidation Bank of Bratislava (KBB) and its Czech counterpart. KBB has been restricted from accepting deposits and extending new loans, and the authorities intend to convert it into a work-out agency for bad loans. Another bank from the pre-transition era is the Czechoslovak Trade Bank (CSOB), which before 1990 handled operations and transactions in foreign currencies between domestic trading companies and foreign subjects and represented the state in international financial markets. Currently the CSOB — based in Prague with a branch in Bratislava — extends short term export and import credit, and in 1994 financed half of Slovakia's foreign trade.

Three priorities characterized the early days of the two-tier system: deregulating specialized banks, hence SLSP and CSOB were given universal banking licenses; encouraging new entrants — the number of banks grew from a handful in 1990 to 29 banks in 1994; and meeting the financing needs of agriculture — which previously received either budgetary subsidies or directed credit from the SBCS. With regard to the third priority, the Slovak Agricultural Bank (SPB) — owned by the Ministry of Agriculture, the Slovak Insurance Company, and the food industry — was created in June 1990, and has become the second largest lender to the agro-industrial sector (after VUB). In addition, Agrobank (AB), a subsidiary of the Czech Agro Bank of Prague, has been active in lending to the agro-industry.

As of late 1994, Slovakia's 29 banks consisted of the NBS, two wholly state-owned financial institutions (KBB) and the Slovak Guarantee Bank (SZBI), which guarantees loans to small- and medium-size businesses, the wholly state-owned SLSP, the majority state-owned VUB, seven banks capitalized entirely by domestic capital, four banks with majority domestic ownership, three banks with majority foreign ownership, and ten branches of foreign banks.

Despite the growing presence of new entrants, large state-controlled banks have seen their market positions erode only gradually. On the credit side, the five largest banks, as of mid 1995, controlled over 80 percent of all lending to enterprises and households: VUB with 35 percent (Sk 99 billion), SLSP with 17 percent (Sk 47 billion), IRB with 13 percent (Sk 38 billion), KBB with 10 percent (Sk 28 billion), and CSOB with 8 percent (Sk 22 billion). However, over time, IELB, SLSP, KBB and especially VUB have seen their shares of lending decline. Beyond these five large banks, Slovakia has two medium-size banks: AB with Sk 10 billion of loans and Tatrabank with Sk 4 billion of loans. All other banks had loans totaling under Sk 2 billion.

On the deposit side, SLSP's share declined steadily, but still constituted 45 percent of all deposits at the end of 1994. VUB's share has dropped slightly, while banks other than the largest four (VUB, SLSP, IRB and KBB) have been successful in attracting new deposits, from Sk 9 billion at the end of 1991 to over Sk 67 billion three years later.

Slovakia's Macroeconomic Recovery

Provisioning could not have played such a major role in bank recapitalization without the sharp economic turnaround Slovakia has enjoyed. Table 1 shows that for the period 1991 to 1995, the Slovak and Czech Republics were the low inflation countries among the eleven transition economies included in the table, and that Slovakia began its rapid economic recovery in 1994, only one year after the Czech Republic.

One frequent offshoot of an economic upturn is an improvement in the financial position of enterprises. Table 2 shows that profitability for small enterprises (up to 24 employees) was especially high in 1993 and 1994, and that their net income was increasing at a much faster rate (42 percent) than producer prices (9 percent). Financial organizations were also quite profitable in those years, although net income grew slowly in 1994. Enterprises with 25 or more employees enjoyed relatively modest profitability.

It is also noteworthy that Slovak banks have been able to provision while inflation has declined and when real interest on deposits have turned positive — both of which tend to have a negative impact on profit.[3] These observations corroborate the idea expressed below that managers of Slovakia's large banks have, on the whole, been prudent in their behavior.

[3]As inflation declines, the profit banks generate from demand deposits usually declines, *ceteris paribus*, because the negative real rate of return on demand deposits becomes less negative. Real interest rates on term deposits turned positive in April 1994, and have remained positive since.

Table 1. Changes in Real GDP and Consumer Prices in Transition Economies, 1991–1995 *(percent change relative to previous year or cumulative percent change from 1990)*

Country	1991	1992	1993	1994	1995 Proj.	Cumul. from 1990
Albania						
Real GDP	–28.0	–7.2	9.6	9.4	7.8	–13.6
CPI	35.5	236.6	30.9	15.8	7.0	639.8
Bulgaria						
Real GDP	–11.7	–7.3	–2.4	0.3	2.5	–17.9
CPI	333.5	82.0	72.8	96.0	62.6	4244.9
Czech Republic						
Real GDP	–14.2	–6.6	–0.5	2.6	4.0	–14.9
CPI	56.5	11.1	20.8	10.0	10.0	154.1
Hungary						
Real GDP	–11.9	–3.0	–0.8	2.0	1.3	–12.4
CPI	35.0	23.0	22.5	18.8	28.2	209.8
Poland						
Real GDP	–7.0	2.6	3.8	6.0	6.5	11.8
CPI	70.3	43.0	35.3	32.2	29.0	461.9
Romania						
Real GDP	–12.9	–10.1	1.3	3.5	4.5	–14.2
CPI	161.1	210.3	256.0	136.0	31.0	8817.1
Slovak Republic						
Real GDP	–14.5	–7.0	–4.1	4.8	6.4	–15.0
CPI	61.2	10.0	23.2	13.4	10.0	172.5
Russia						
Real GDP	–13.0	–19.0	–12.0	–15.0	–4.2	–49.5
CPI	92.6	1354.0	896.0	302.0	180.8	314,749.6
Ukraine						
Real GDP	–11.9	–17.0	–13.0	–23.8	–10.5	–56.6
CPI	91.0	1445.0	4730.9	900.0	346.0	6,357,962.0
Belarus						
Real GDP	–2.0	–10.0	–10.6	–20.2	–13.8	–45.8
CPI	94.0	1065.0	1188.0	2220.0	703.0	5,422,993.0

Source: IMF.

Table 2. Measures of Profit in the Slovak Republic, 1993–1994

	Net income as a percent of expenditure[1]		Net income as a percent of revenue[1]		Percent growth of net income 1994 over 1993	Percent growth of value added 1994 over 1993
	1993	1994	1993	1994		
Enterprises employing 25 or more people, excluding subsidized organizations[2]	3.8	3.7	3.7	3.6	5.2	9.7
Enterprises employing up to 24 people, excluding subsidized organizations	20.2	21.3	13.0	13.0	116.0	42.0
Nonfinancial organizations, excluding subsidized organizations	4.5	4.6	4.2	4.3	20.3	10.1
Subsidized organizations	21.4	23.8	19.1	19.1	–	–133.5
Nonfinancial organizations combined, excluding subsidized organizations	4.3	4.6	4.1	4.3	31.0	12.2
Financial organizations	13.2	13.8	11.6	12.1	–2.7	2.1
Nonfinancial and financial organizations together, including subsidized organizations	5.6	5.7	5.2	5.3	19.2	10.7

Source: Slovak Statistical Office, *Statistical Report on Basic Developmental Tendencies in the Slovak Economy for 1994 and their Prediction for the First Half of 1995.*

[1]Net income is revenue minus expenditure (including depreciation).

[2]Subsidized organizations receive subsidies from the State Budget or municipal budgets, though they also may have their own sources of revenue.

Efforts to Improve the Financial Position of the Banking System

In the early 1990s, several factors underpinned the widespread perception that the Slovak banking system was facing solvency difficulties. The demise of the Council for Mutual Economic Assistance (CMEA), the collapse of Slovakia's traditional export markets, the dismantling of the closed, planned economy and the onset of radically different relative prices initially contributed to a severe decline in output and enterprise profitability. In addition, inherited loan portfolios were heavily tilted on the domestic side to loans that were either low-yielding or soon-to-be nonperforming. On the foreign front, the State had accumulated substantial convertible-currency liabilities that needed to be serviced, yet the bulk of the State's assets, mostly denominated in nonconvertible currencies, were nonperforming. Moreover, some major banks had weak capital positions; for example, VUB reported a capital/asset ratio of less than 2 percent at the end of 1990.

Direct Actions to Improve Banks' Loan Portfolios

Since 1991, the authorities have taken a number of measures to improve the quality of the banks' loan portfolios:

- In June 1991, the CSFR Ministry of Finance shifted Sk 110 billion of "revolving credits" from VUB and KBP to the newly established KON; VUB's share, transferred to KBB (the Slovak successor of KON), was about Kcs 30 billion.[4] This allowed VUB and KBP to reduce the book value of their assets, thus improving their capital to asset ratios.
- The Slovak authorities wrote off Sk 15 billion of loans to the armaments industry and other troubled sectors from the balance sheet of VUB and other banks in 1992 to 1993. In return, the banks received bonds issued by the National Property Fund (NPF) — repayable over a five-year period at an interest rate of 2.5 percent above the discount rate.

[4]Among the loans VUB inherited were Kcs 50 billion (over 40 percent of its portfolio) of revolving inventory credits to enterprises at negative real interest rates. After a year of debate with the CSFR Ministry of Finance, KEP and VUB were allowed to "improve" their balance sheets by transforming the fixed 6 percent interest rate on revolving inventory credits into short- and medium-term credits at 20 to 24 percent. Following protests by the affected enterprises, the CSFR authorities created the KON which in June 1991 took over about two thirds (Kcs 110 billion) of the KBP's and VUB's revolving inventory credits. Simultaneously, KON granted enterprises more favorable terms on their existing loans, namely an eight-year maturity at 4 percent over the bank discount rate (equal to 13 percent in June 1991), compared to the earlier short and medium terms at 20 to 24 percent (Vojtisek 1993, 69–71).

- Selected banks were recapitalized in 1992 through issuance of NPF bonds valued at Sk 5 billion (1.5 percent of GDP) repayable within two years with no interest receivable.
- The Slovak Ministry of Finance compensated SLSP and IRB through tax deductions or subsidies at an annual cost of about 0.5 percent of GDP for pre-1990 long-term loans to households (housing loans and loans to newlyweds) at below-market interest rates.
- NPF resources have been used to assist enterprises to service their loan obligations to banks (for example, the European Bank for Reconstruction and Development EBRD/VUB loan to the aluminum company ZSNK with the NPF responsible for some of the servicing costs).
- On January 1, 1993, the Czech and Slovak Ministries of Finance took over the respective Czech (two-thirds) and Slovak (one-third) shares of the CSFR's foreign assets and liabilities from CSOB's portfolio. CSOB's balance sheet showed accumulated assets of Kcs 95.5 billion (Kcs 91.5 billion in non-convertible currencies, Kcs 4.0 billion [US$138 million] in convertible currencies) and liabilities of Kcs 74.4 billion (Kcs 14.0 in non-convertible currencies, Kcs 60.4 billion [US$2.09 billion] in convertible currencies). For most part, the assets were nonperforming, and the liabilities needed to be serviced. As a measure, the Ministries of Finance agreed to fund CSOB's uncovered exchange rate losses from engaging in state-related activities, at a ratio of 2 to 1. These uncovered losses equaled Kcs 21 billion, the difference between the net value of CSOB's assets and liabilities in nonconvertible currencies and the net value of CSOB's assets and liabilities in convertible currencies. Earlier, the Czech and Slovak NPFs donated bonds to CSOB.
- At the end of 1992, bonds worth Kcs 13.3 billion were issued to IB by the Czech (two-thirds) and Slovak (one-third) Ministries of Finance. In return, the ministries received an equivalent amount of loans, that previously had been guaranteed by the CSFR Ministry of Finance and mostly represented receivables connected with a government-sponsored construction project in a former CMEA country.[5]

[5]An additional Kc 20 billion of foreign-trade related nonperforming loans held by CSOB were taken over by a special facility at the Czech Ministry of Finance at the end of 1993.

- In May 1993, the Government directed KBB to purchase from exporters Sk 3.14 billion of "uncollectible export receivables" associated with trade disruptions/embargoes with Iraq, parts of the former Yugoslavia, and the former Soviet Union for Sk 2.2 billion. Later, the Ministry of Finance agreed to begin, in 1994, to make payments on these export receivables directly to KBB.

The above measures (Table 3 explains them in detail), though implemented on an *ad hoc* basis, were effective in improving the financial standing of banks. However, Slovak authorities, after several years of providing federal assistance to banks, have decided, for reasons of both moral hazard and social equity, to limit government intervention and to encourage banks to use primarily their own resources to deal with their problems (see Table 4). This being said, several weaknesses in the banking system suggest that some outside assistance may become necessary. For instance, the transfer of revolving inventory credit to KON (and then to KBB) improved the portfolio and capital adequacy of VUB, but KBB was not given sufficient resources to cover losses. Instead, it received long term redistribution credits of Sk 16.7 billion from the NBS and deposits of Sk 11 billion from SLSP and the Slovak State Insurance Company. KBB's solvency has become a concern because over time a large proportion of its inherited debt has become problematic — reflecting the manner in which the loans were initially granted and the incentive-numbing effect of restricting KBB from offering new credit.[6] In response, the NBS has recently started creating loan-loss provisions for its redistribution credits. Sk 2.6 billion of such provisions were made in 1994, and a similar amount was envisaged for 1995.

In addition, the authorities have not, for the most part, helped banks write off loans to the agro-industrial sector, mainly extended by VUB, SPB, AB and SLSP. Given the heavy losses agriculture suffered during 1991 to 1994, and the Ministry of Agriculture's estimate that in 1993 about 45 percent of all farms were unprofitable and not creditworthy, these loans may be problematic.

[6]At the end of 1994, revolving inventory credit represented about 60 percent of KBB's outstanding loans, with the share of doubtful and unclassified loans among the inventory credit rising from 6.5 percent at the end of 1993 to 13.6 percent at the end of 1994 (MB *1994 Annual Report* 1995, 11).

Table 3. Description of Assistance by Type of Bad Debt Inherited by Slovak Banks

I. Assistance Related to Loans to Domestic Firms and Households
A. Recognized as low yielding 1. More than 40 percent of the outstanding credits VUB inherited were revolving inventory credits issued at an annual interest rate of 6 percent, with an indefinite maturity.[1] Given inflation in 1990 of over 30 percent and expectations of continued high inflation, VUB would not have been able to compete for deposits with other banks and still remain solvent unless the low yields on these loans were somehow improved. 2. Thirty percent of the assets of Investicna a Rozvojova Banka (IRB, Investment and Development Bank, which at end-1992 took over the Slovak portion of IB's loans) and half SLSP's portfolio were long-term loans for housing and to newlyweds at interest rates much below market levels.[2,3] Therefore, these banks, like VUB, simply would not be able to compete for deposits with banks unburdened with such low-yielding long term loans unless these low yielding loans were somehow improved.
B. Recognized as nonperforming and written off with assistance Loans, mostly in heavy industry (including armaments), were explicitly recognized as nonperforming and written off with assistance. On November 30, 1992, the NPF announced it would pay VUB Sk 10.9 billion plus interest (at 2.5 percent above the discount rate) over a five-year period to help VUB write off the loans of heavily indebted companies. In December 1993, armament loans of Sk 2.0 billion from VUB and Sk 0.15 billion from Agrobank (AG) were sold to KBB at face value. At the same time, NFP issued to KBB Sk 2.883 billion of bonds, to be repaid over 1994 to 1999 at 14 percent annual interest. In return, KBB wrote off Sk 2.883 of armament loans (the just purchased ones plus Sk 0.733 of the revolving inventory loans it inherited from VUB in July 1991). On April 13, 1993, the NPF contributed bonds valued at Sk 1.55 billion (US$48 million) to IRB, thus allowing IRB to write off Sk 1.2 billion of loans and increase its capital by Sk 0.35 billion.
C. Recognized as especially risky loans partly because they are serviced by the authorities Two loans were recognized not only as especially risky, but have been serviced by the authorities. In 1991, the Ministry of Finance guaranteed Sk 8.9 billion of loans for the Mochovce nuclear power plant. Later, the NPF took over this guarantee and since 1994, has begun servicing the loan. Since 1993, the NPF has paid interest on a Sk 4.236 billion VUB/EBRD loan to the Slovak aluminum company ZSNK. The interest payments are expected to total to Sk 4.236 billion. When that ceiling is reached, ZSNK is liable to repay VUB/EBRD Sk 4.236 billion (the original principal) before it begins to repay NPF Sk 4.236 billion (the accumulated interest payments).
D. Recapitalization financed by the authorities Rather than provide assistance for specific bad debt, the authorities have contributed to the recapitalization of banks, which strengthens banks' ability to write off loans. NPF was responsible for most such transfers: Sk 2.1 billion to VUB, Sk 0.4 billion to CSOB, Sk 1.2 billion to SLSP, Sk 0.35 billion to IRB, and Sk 1.0 billion to KBB. The Ministry of Finance, however, has helped to recapitalize the SZB, Sk 0.21 billion.

Table 3. Continued

E. Loans to the agro-industrial sector Twenty-three percent of VUB's assets — which did not overlap with the above-mentioned revolving inventory credits — were loans to the agro-industrial sector.[4] These loans were likely to become problematic since agriculture had been heavily subsidized in the pre-1990 period[5] and consumer food subsidies were being phased out.[6] The authorities have done little to provide assistance specifically for loans that were made to the agro-industrial sector.
II. Assistance Related to Foreign Liabilities and Export Receivables
A. Foreign Liabilities CSOB as the State's monopoly bank for financing foreign trade operations and for acquiring foreign trade resources, accepted loans in convertible currencies to cover balance of payments deficits; lent money in nonconvertible currencies to CSFR's trading partners within the CMEA; and extended credit to CSFR foreign trade organizations to cover their export claims to countries perceived to be risky. Overall, CSOB accumulated substantial convertible-currency liabilities that needed to be serviced, yet the bulk of its assets, most of which were denominated in nonconvertible currencies, were nonperforming. The Ministry of Finance took over the Slovak share (one third) of CSOB's foreign liabilities.
B. Export receivables 1. At end-1992, Kcs 13.3 billion bonds were issued to IB by the Czech (two thirds) and Slovak (one third) Ministries of Finance. In return, the ministries received an equivalent amount of loans, which previously had been guaranteed by the CSFR Ministry of Finance and mostly represented receivables connected with a government-sponsored construction project in a former CMEA country. 2. In May 1993, the Government directed KBB to purchase from exporters Sk 3.14 billion of "uncollectible export receivables" associated with trade disruptions/embargoes with Iraq, parts of the former Yugoslavia, and the former Soviet Union for Sk 2.2 billion. Later, the Ministry of Finance agreed to pay KBB for these export receivables.[7]

[1]Vojtisek (1993, 70)

[2]For IRB, measured at end-1992 when the bank was established (IRB, *1993 Annual Report*, 1994, 6). For SLSP, measured at end-1991, (SLSP, *1991 Annual Report*, 1992, 21 and *Sporitel'Nfctvo na Slovensku* 1992, 96).

[3]Ten-year housing loans for the construction of family homes or for the repair and modernization of family homes and apartments were granted to members of building cooperatives at 2.7 percent annual interest, while 15-year loans for newly married couples (for purchase of an apartment) were issued, with a state contribution, at 1 percent annual interest (SLSP, *Sporitel'Nfctvo na Slvensku*, 1992, 96).

[4]At end-1991, 16 percent (Kcs 16.6 billion) was lent to agriculture and 7 percent (Kcs 6.6 billion) to the food processing industry (VUB, *1991 Annual Report*, 1992, 28).

[5]Subsidies to the Czechoslovak agro-industrial sector were 6.3 percent of GDP in 1988, higher than in Hungary (4.0 percent) and Poland (5.8 percent) (Marrese 1993, 147).

[6]Losses in agriculture in the early 1990s support this presumption. For instance, in the CSFR in 1991, losses of agricultural enterprises, which faced much higher relative prices for their material inputs and declining domestic demand, totaled Kcs 11.7 billion relative to profit for industry of Kcs 31.6 billion (*Statistical Yearbook of the Slovak Republic 1992*, 1993, 429). Droughts in 1992 and 1993 and the further decline in domestic demand for food led to losses of Sk 8.1 billion in 1992, Sk 6.6 billion in 1993, and Sk 4.2 billion in 1994 (*Slovak Republic: Recent Economic Developments*, 1994, 66; *Statistical Review of the Slovak Republic*, 1994:4, 1995, 32).

[7]Note that KBB's assets rose by Sk 2.2 billion, and the offsetting liabilities were additional deposits by the NPF and SLSP along with an increase in KBB's equity capital of Sk 1.0 billion.

Table 4. Policies Undertaken by the Authorities, 1992–1994

Description	Amount[1]	Method
I. Assistance related to loans to domestic firms and households		
A. Recognized as low-yielding loans		
VUB, revolving credit not yet written off[2]	29.67	Transfer to Kbb
IRB, housing loans[3]	11.25	Ministry of Finance subsidy
SLSP, housing loans[3]	7.31	Ministry of Finance subsidy
SLSP, loans to newlyweds[3]	8.18	Ministry of Finance subsidy
Subtotal	56.41	
B. Recognized as nonperforming loans and written off with assistance		
VUB	10.90	NPF bond
VUB, AB, KBB	2.88	NPF bond
IRB	1.20	NPF bond
Subtotal	14.98	
C. Recognized as especially risky loans partly because they are being serviced by the authorities		
IRB, nuclear power plant	8.90	NPF guarantee
VUB, EBRD, aluminum company	4.24	NPF guarantee
Subtotal	13.14	
D. Recapitalization financed by the authorities		
VUB	2.10	NPF
CSOB	0.40	NPF
SLSP	1.20	NPF
IRB	0.35	NPF
KBB	1.00	NPF
SZB	0.21	Ministry of Finance
Subtotal	5.26	
E. Loans to the agro-industrial sector		
No assistance specificially for loans to agro-industrial sector from authorities other than Sk 2.9 billion transferred from VUB to KBB in 1991 as part of the revolving credit transfer		
Total for category I	89.79	

Table 4. Continued

Description	Amount[1]	Method
II. Assistance related to foreign liabilities and export receivables		
A. Foreign liabilities		
CSOB	24.79	
B. Export receivables		
IB	4.43	
KBB	2.20	
Subtotal	6.63	
Total for category II	31.42	
Overall total	121.21	

[1]In Sk billions. Whenever loans are under consideration, only the principal appears in this column.
[2]In July 1991, Kcs 30.4 billion of the revolving inventory credits held by VUB were transferred to KON, and later to KBB. Subsequently, Sk 0.73 billion were written off.
[3]For IRB, includes the subsidy equivalent of 1993 tax exemptions.

The explicit fiscal cost of these measures (borne by both the State Budget and the NPF, excluding amortization) was 1.3 percent of GDP in 1992 and 1993, and 1.6 percent in 1994 (Table 5).[7] These figures include neither implicit tax deductions related to reserve building from before-tax profits nor the lower NBS profit transfer to the State Budget due to NBS provisioning of its redistribution credits to KBB. Taking into account these less direct costs, the fiscal cost is estimated to have risen from 1.5 percent of GDP in 1992 to 3 percent of GDP in 1994.

Policies to Ensure Prudent Bank Behavior

In order to promote prudential management, the SBCS in 1990 established guidelines for capital/asset ratios, credit/deposit ratios, foreign exchange positions, concentration of assets, and obligatory minimum reserves (9 percent

[7]Total cost (including amortization but excluding the less direct transfers mentioned below) as a share of GDP, equaled 3.5 percent in 1992, 3.6 percent in 1993, and 3.5 percent in 1994.

Table 5. Interest Cost, Amortization, and Debt Service Related to the Authorities' Bank Restructuring Policies *(as a percent of GDP)*

	Interest Cost	Amortization	Debt Service
1992	1.3	2.2	3.5
1993	1.3	2.2	3.6
1994	1.6	1.9	3.5

for short term deposits and 3 percent for longer term deposits introduced on a phased basis). The Central Banking and Commercial Banking Acts of December 1991 established a risk-weighted formula for measuring capital adequacy that meets international standards, and required existing banks to meet a minimum capital adequacy ratio rising from 6.25 percent at the end of 1993 to 8 percent at the end of 1996. Moreover, banks were required to report quarterly on their capital adequacy. In 1992, new regulations on liquidity management, foreign exchange positions and credit risk exposure were issued. These rules were updated once again in early 1994.[8]

In mid 1992, the SBCS directed banks to compile and report monthly data on loans in arrears on the basis of a five-category classification.[9] In addition, the SBCS recommended that banks set aside provisions according to specific guidelines.[10] The SBCS also allowed banks to upgrade collateralized loans on the basis of their judgments about the quality of the collateral. In late 1992, the CSFR Parliament passed Act 610, allowing banks to use before-tax income to increase General Reserves up to 2 percent of all medium and long term loans, plus 10 percent of all doubtful loans, and 2 percent

[8]For example, credit exposure to a single borrower cannot exceed 25 percent of a bank's adjusted capital, and credit exposure to a bank's ten largest borrowers cannot exceed 230 percent of adjusted capital.

[9]Five categories were: standard — assets being repaid on time and a satisfactory financial situation for the debtor; special mention — overdue by 90 days or less and not endangered; substandard-payments overdue for more than 90 days but not considered doubtful or uncollectible; doubtful — payments overdue for more than 90 days but less than 360 days; and loss — payments overdue for at least 360 days.

[10]The SBCS recommended 5 percent provisioning for special mention loans, 20 percent for substandard loans, 50 percent for doubtful loans, and 100 percent for loss loans.

of all guaranteed loans.[11] Banks could also deduct as a cost the total amount of a loan that has been declared as a loss by a court decision. However, banks could create loan-loss provisions from before-tax profits only with the permission of the Ministry of Finance. Such permission has been granted only on rare occasions.

The NBS reintroduced, in February 1993, bank-specific credit ceilings on most banks so as to enhance its control over credit aggregates — in light of heightened pressures on prices and foreign reserves in the aftermath of independence and the dissolution of the monetary union with the Czech Republic — but also for prudential reasons and as a means of promoting competition within the financial sector.[12] These restrictions were inspired partly by a spurt of business lending by SLSP (below). The NBS also informed commercial banks that each bank must undergo an annual audit by external auditors whose selection and terms of reference must be cleared by the NBS. In addition, on-site bank inspections began to take place in late 1993.

Developments in the Financial Position of Commercial Banks

To ascertain the size of bad debt in the banking system, one may rely on information on 'loans in arrears' based on data that are submitted monthly to the NBS and published in an aggregated form. By comparison, a classification according to international accounting standards (IAS) would take into account financial indicators of the debtor to forecast the future debt service capacity of companies and would apply stricter criteria in evaluating the collateral of loans than was permitted under the accounting rules Slovakia inherited from the SBCS.

---

[11]General Reserves may be used when a debtor is being liquidated and the bank's share of liquidation proceeds does not cover the amount owed, or when a judge gives a bank permission to recoup collectable receivables that are several years overdue. Note that any buildup in General Reserves counts as an increase in a bank's liabilities.

[12]The SBCS had bank-specific ceilings in place since 1990, but in 1991–1992 progress was made toward reliance on indirect instruments of monetary policy. In October 1992, the SBCS removed the remaining ceilings on major banks.

Payment Arrears Data

At the end of 1992, 3 percent of all loans were reported as overdue by at least three months (labeled as substandard, doubtful, and loss in Table 6). The proportion of such loans rose to 12 percent by the end of 1993, 30 percent by the end of 1994, and 32 percent by the end of May 1995. Given that this reported sharp deterioration in the servicing of loans occurrs during a period in which the economy is experiencing an economic turnaround and enterprise profitability has improved, it likely reflects an increased willingness of banks to acknowledge problems in their loan portfolios, now that they have built up their general reserves and loan-loss provisions.

Performance of Major Banks Annual Reports Based on IAS

Slovakia's largest commercial banks faced fundamentally different challenges in the early years of their independent existence. VUB needed to focus on improving its loan portfolio by actively pursuing repayments, provisioning, channeling after-tax profit to reserves, and collateralizing its ongoing stock of loans. SLSP needed to gain experience in credit and risk analysis and expand its business services. IRB engaged in little new lending and was primarily responsible for managing its existing portfolio of loans, the majority of which was guaranteed by either the Ministry of Finance or NPF. KBB's sole responsibility was to manage the problematic loans that it had received from other banks. CSOB required recapitalization after the CSFR's foreign trade obligations were lifted from its balance sheet.

As seen below in reviewing the activities of each of the major banks, most challenges have become less worrisome over time. For instance, consider how VUB, Slovakia's largest bank, has repositioned itself. VUB's loan portfolio has shrunk in nominal (15 percent) as well as real terms (59 percent) between the end of 1990 and the end of 1994 (Table 7). The nominal decline is explained by the removal of revolving credits from VUB's portfolio in 1991 (described earlier) and, in subsequent years, its decreasing access to interbank deposits as SLSP, the major source of these deposits, expanded its own lending to enterprises and the Government. VUB's share in total bank credit to enterprises and households thus declined from 48 percent at the end

Table 6. Koruna-Denominated Loans: Standard and Overdue, According to Maturity, 1992–1995 *(in millions of koruny: end-period)*

	1992	1993		1994		1995
	Dec.	June	Dec.	June	Dec.	May
Short-term credits[1]	82.9	92.8	90.7	87.5	95.9	106.1
Standard[2]	64.4	72.8	66.8	57.3	63.4	68.6
Special mention[3]	12.2	11.9	6.5	6.1	5.3	7.3
Substandard[4]	–	0.4	5.8	2.6	2.8	3.6
Doubtful and litigious[5]	5.3	4.8	7.3	9.6	7.8	6.2
Loss[6]	1.0	3.0	4.3	11.9	16.6	20.4
Medium-term credits[7]	50.6	48.9	53.5	50.0	46.9	47.9
Standard[2]	44.5	41.3	41.4	29.7	24.8	23.6
Special mention[3]	5.5	6.0	5.0	6.7	3.3	3.1
Substandard[4]	–	0.1	1.1	1.9	2.9	4.0
Doubtful and litigious[5]	0.6	0.9	4.7	5.8	7.3	6.9
Loss[6]	–	0.5	1.4	5.9	8.8	10.3
Long-term credits[8]	102.5	104.8	116.7	114.4	114.8	115.8
Standard[2]	92.7	93.2	95.8	80.9	76.1	71.1
Special mention[3]	9.0	8.8	14.5	18.8	7.9	8.5
Substandard[4]	–	–	1.5	3.1	11.3	13.1
Doubtful and litigious[5]	0.7	2.6	3.1	5.4	8.5	7.9
Loss[6]	0.1	0.1	6.2	6.2	11.0	15.2
Total koruna-denominated credits	236.0	246.4	260.8	251.8	257.6	269.9
Standard[2]	201.7	207.3	204.0	167.9	164.3	163.2
Special mention[3]	26.7	26.7	26.0	31.6	16.5	19.0
Substandard[4]	–	0.5	8.4	7.6	16.9	20.7
Doubtful and litigious[5]	6.6	8.3	15.1	20.8	23.6	20.9
Loss[6]	1.1	3.7	7.3	24.0	36.3	46.0

Sources: NBS Annual Reports and NBS Banking Statistics Department.

[1]Maturity of up to one year.

[2]Payment have been made on time

[3]Payments are overdue by 90 days or less, but are not endangered.

[4]Payments are overdue by at least 90 days, but not classified as doubtful or loss.

[5]Payments are overdue by more than 90 days, but less than 360 days.

[6]Payments are overdue by at least 360 days.

[7]Maturity of one to four years.

[8]Maturity of over four years.

Table 7. VUB's Profit and Loss Statement, Provisioning, Reserves, 1990–1994[1]

	1990	1991	1992	1993	1994
A. Profit and Loss Statement					
1. Interest income	9.329	19.597	18.036	18.980	19.665
2. Interest expense	–5.784	–13.490	–11.167	–10.871	–11.914
3. Net interest income (1+2)	3.545	6.107	6.869	8.109	7.751
4. Fees and commissions, net	0.172	0.254	1.259	1.243	1.220
5. Foreign exchange profit, net	0.215	0.498	0.692	0.230	0.750
6. Other operating income, net	0.019	0.046	0.176	0.242	1.178
7. Total income (3+4+5+5)	3.951	6.905	8.996	9.824	10.899
8. Provisions for bad loans	–	–2.040	–3.350	–3.944	–5.305
9. Operating expenses	–0.397	–0.664	–1.538	–2.631	–3.274
10. Profit before taxation (7+8+9)	3.554	4.201	4.10	3.249	2.320
11. Taxes	–2.311	–2.672	–1.874	–2.117	–1.719
12. Profits after taxation (10+11)	0.882	1.890	2.234	1.132	0.601
13. Dividends	–	–	–	–0.204	–0.408
14. Appropriations from profit	–0.084	–0.162	–0.098	–	–
15. Retained profit (12+13+14)	0.848	1.727	2.136	0.928	0.193
B. Movements in provisions for bad and doubtful loans					
16. Balance January 1	–	–	2.040	5.292	8.640
17. Provisions made that year	–	2.040	3.350	3.944	5.449
18. Amounts written off	–	–	–0.098	–0.596	–0.142
19. Balance December 31 (16+17+18)	–	2.040	5.292	8.640	13.942
C. Movements in reserves					
20. Balance January 1	–	1.450	5.277	6.746	7.778
21. Retained profit	–	1.727	2.136	0.928	0.193
22. Additional capital	–	2.100	–	–	0.408
23. Capitalized into share capital	–	–	–0.667	–	–
24. Revaluation of fixed assets	–	–	–	0.104	–
25. Balance December 31 (20+21+22+23+24)	–	5.227	6.746	7.778	8.379
<u>Memorandum items</u>:					
PPI growth, in percent, within year	–	50.9	6.0	18.8	9.4
CPI growth, in percent, within year	–	58.3	9.1	25.0	11.7
Outstanding loans[2]	–	117.3	102.0	102.0	100.1
Capital adequacy ratio, in percent[3]	–	6.40	7.23	7.33	8.60

Source: Annual reports of the VUB.

[1]End-year figures, in Kcs billion for 1990–1992, in Sk billions, thereafter.

[2]Includes loans denominated in foreign currencies. Provisions for bad and doubtful loans have not been deducted.

[3]Reported by the VUB in its annual reports. Figure for 1994 is preliminary.

of 1991 to 38 percent two years later, 37 percent at the end of 1994 and 35 percent a year and a half later. Notwithstanding this retrenchment, which implies that good loans have been removed from its portfolio upon repayment, VUB has moved steadily to increase its provisions for bad and doubtful loans and its reserves (lines 19 and 25, Table 7).

Despite VUB's sharp real decline in outstanding loans, VUB's total income (line 7, Table 7) rose in real terms from 1990 to 1992, then dipped slightly during 1993–1994. Early income growth was fueled by the 1991 increase in net interest income and the 1992 increase in non-interest income. VUB's net interest income fell in 1994 in line with the overall steep jump in loans overdue by at least three months (Table 6). VUB's dividends have been modest relative to its provisioning, and retained profit — used to build up reserves — was substantial up to 1994 (lines 13 and 20–25, Table 7). Collateralization and diversification of lending activities have been two other ways by which VUB improved its loan portfolio. For instance, secured loans equaled 69 percent of all loans at the end of 1993, up sharply from 52 percent a year earlier and negligible amounts at the beginning of the reform, (VUB, *1993 Annual Report*, 1994, 7). In addition, the composition of VUB's lending has shifted from state enterprises to private ones, with lending to cooperative farms largely unchanged.[13] Since many of VUB's pre-1991 clients were larger firms that have yet to be privatized, the shift in the composition of clients represents substantial diversification. As a result of all of the above, VUB reported improving capital adequacy ratios, from 6.4 percent at the end of 1991 to 7.3 percent two years later and 8.6 percent three years later.

At the end of 1994, VUB's provisions totaled Sk 13.9 billion, and guarantees plus collateral totaled Sk 17.1 billion. Based on IAS, VUB's international auditors determined that not less than Sk 6.0 billion additional provisioning was needed to cover nonstandard loans (VUB, *1994 Annual Report*, 1995, 1).

[13]From the end of 1990 to that of 1994, the share of VUB's loans going to state enterprises fell from 88 percent to 57 percent; to private enterprises from zero percent to 31 percent; and for cooperatives (mostly cooperative farms) from 11 percent to 10 percent (VUB, *1991 Annual Report*, 1992, 26; VUB, *1992 Annual Report*, 1993, 21; VUB, *1993 Annual Report*, 1993, 11; VUB, *1994 Annual Report*, 1995, 10).

Next, note that SLSP has become less dependent on households. For example, SLSP, which held all household deposits before 1990, controlled 85 percent of those deposits (and 45 percent of total deposits) at the end of 1994. In the pre-1990 period, SLSP lent only 20 percent of its deposits to households, and placed the rest with the central bank. Despite the lack of experience in evaluating credit risk of enterprises, SLSP's loan portfolio grew rapidly in 1991 to 1992 through lending to small- and medium-size enterprises. Since then it has stabilized in light of a tight ceiling on its outstanding loans.[14] In 1993, a department of bad debt was established at SLSP's head office in order to curtail what were perceived to be unwise lending decisions in branches throughout the country.[15]

While consolidating its lending, SLSP's total income was roughly unchanged in real terms (up 31 percent in nominal terms) from 1992 to 1994, with substantial growth in non-interest income in 1993 and in interest income in 1994 (lines 3–10, Table 8). During this period, SLSP almost tripled its loan-loss provisioning and increased its reserves 60 percent (lines 21 and 24, Table 8). In its annual reports based on IAS, SLSP reported capital adequacy of 6.3 percent in 1992 and 1993, then 6.9 percent in 1994.

Third, IRB[16] has made steady progress through 1994, yet recent problems with guaranteed energy loans have caused some concerns. IRB has had two main functions: managing its portfolio of inherited loans and developing into an investment bank. Any new lending has been almost exclusively short term and has fallen to a minuscule level. (Only ½ percent of outstanding loans were short term at the end of 1994.) IRB reduced its loan portfolio

---

[14]SLSP's lending growth was directly related to the privatization process, in which SLSP took the lead in lending to small- and medium-size enterprises. Indeed, lending to the enterprise sector went from Sk 3 billion end-1990 to over Sk 26 billion by end-1992, at which time more than half of all private sector loans were being held by SLSP.

[15]This department's primary responsibilities have included: debt recovery from SLSP's biggest financially troubled borrowers as well as the establishment of more rigorous guidelines for evaluating collateral, especially real estate, and for determining the appropriate instances when bankruptcy procedures should be initiated. Loan recovery from SLSP's other clients have continued to take place at branch offices.

[16]IRB has been operating since March 1, 1992, but inherited the Slovak share of IB's portfolio only at the end of that year.

Table 8. SLSP's Profit and Loss Statement, Provisioning, and Reserves, 1992–1994[1]

	1992	1993	1994
A. Profit and Loss Statement			
1. Interest income	13,432	15,665	18,351
2. Interest expense	–8,543	–10,776	–12,283
3. Net interest income (1+2)	4,889	4,889	6,068
4. Fees and commissions, net	336	443	380
5. Foreign exchange profit, net	132	205	251
6. Gains from investment activities, net	223	477	517
7. Share of profits of associates	–	19	93
8. Losses on disposal of fixed assets	–14	–10	–8
9. Other income	51	33	55
10. Total income (3+4+5+6+7+8+9)	5,617	6,058	7,363
11. Operating expenses	–1,468	–1,705	–2,454
12. Provisions for loan losses from before tax income	–2,382	–2,410	–3,268
13. Profits before taxation (13+14+15)	1,767	1,943	1,641
14. Taxes paid	–1,201	–112	–1,298
15. Other adjustments to before-tax profit	158	–477	87
16. Profit after taxation (13+14+15)	718	1,354	430
B. Movements in Loan-Loss Provisions			
17. Balance January 1	213	2,595	4,263
18. Provisions made that year: General	2,382	1,894	1,230
19. Specific	–	516	2,038
20. Amounts written off	–	-742	–19
21. Balance December 31 (17+18+19+20)	2,595	4,263	7,512
C. Movements in Total Reserves[2]			
22. Balance January 1		1,763	2,299
23. Allocations of profit		536	510
24. Balance December 31 (22+23)	1,763	2,299	2,809
Memorandum items:			
PPI growth, in percent, within year	6.0	18.8	9.4
CPI growth, in percent, within year	9.1	25.0	11.7
Outstanding loans to enterprises and households[3]	47.4	50.5	48.9
Capital adequacy ratio, in percent[4]	6.32	6.33	6.94

Source: Annual reports of the SLSP.

[1]End-year figures, in Sk billions.

[2]Total reserves consist of the legal reserve fund and the risk reserve.

[3]Includes loans denominated in foreign currencies. Provisions for bad and doubtful loans have not been deducted.

[4]Reported by the SLSP in its annual reports.

(with NPF help and by avoiding new lending) from Sk 38 billion at the end of 1992 to Sk 33 billion two years later.[17] At the end of 1994, one third of IRB's loan portfolio consisted of housing loans, subsidized and guaranteed by the state and another third of loans were to the energy sector (most to the Mochovce nuclear power plant, guaranteed by the Ministry of Finance and the NPF).[18] Preliminary data indicate that by the end of 1994, IRB had provisions of Sk 3.7 billion, equivalent to about 11 percent of its outstanding loans, and reserves of Sk 1.7 billion. According to its annual reports based on IAS, IRB's capital adequacy ratio rose from 5.5 percent at the end of 1992, to 6.5 percent a year later, and to 7.8 percent two years later.

Fourth, KBB has been making every effort, amid restrictive circumstances, to encourage servicing of its loans. KBB has no deposit network, has a loan portfolio burdened with items such as uncollectible export receivables, continues to receive the bad loans of other Slovak banks, may not make new loans, and is not subject to normal banking regulations.[19] Although the initial portfolio of KBB was similar in quality to that of other major banks, its loans have tended to be more frequently in arrears: debtors apparently prefer to service debt to other banks, which, unlike KBB, can block their current accounts for late payments or promise new loans. For the same reason, KBB has been unable to collateralize its loans in contrast to other major banks. KBB is thus perceived to be seriously insolvent. As noted above, the NBS has been provisioning for its redistribution credits.

Fifth, CSOB has become a sound universal bank. Earlier, CSOB had the foreign-trade assets and liabilities of the CSFR lifted from its balance sheet. In 1992, it received Kcs 2.2 billion of bonds from the Czech NPF

---

[17]At end-June 1995, IPB's outstanding loans totaled Sk 37.5 billion. Most of the increase (Sk 3.9 billion) since end-1994 was due to an accounting change in March 1995 that categorized the overdue interest payments on IRB's Mochovce (nuclear energy) loans as new lending.

[18]There is no explicit guarantee on the remaining 80 percent of the Mochovce loans, though it is generally believed that either the NPF or the Government will fully back these loans.

[19]Therefore, it does not have to meet the minimum capital adequacy ratios required by the NBS.

to write off nonperforming loans, and Kcs 0.4 billion from the Slovak NPF and another Kcs 1.1 billion from the Czech NPF for recapitalization, (CSOB, *1992 Annual Report*, 1993, 13). A new stock offering in 1993 added Kcs 5.055 billion to CSOB's base capital. More recently, as a result of the reduction in its nonperforming assets facilitated through an agreement between the Ministries of Finance of the Slovak Republic and the Czech Republic, CSOB was able to return to profitability. Its net profit in 1994 was Kc 2.0 billion compared to the net loss of Kc 10.8 billion in 1993, (CSOB, *1994 Brief Report*, 1995, 4).

For all banks, corporatization and privatization (partial though it may be) has positively affected the quality of management.[20] Banks now compete with one another for the best personnel, and compensation among financial organizations is generally higher than in most other areas of the economy. These factors have produced a broad strata of young bank employees who have been anxious and able to absorb technical assistance from abroad to improve the professionalism of banking in Slovakia.

Strategy for Bank Restructuring

The NBS and an international consulting firm completed, in the second half of 1994, a study in accordance with IAS based on an outside audit of the four major banks where most of the bad debt is concentrated. The study emphasized that each of the large banks had different weaknesses, yet all except KBB could, under appropriate conditions, internally generate sufficient resources to cover shortcomings in the levels of provisions and general reserves. In particular, if these three banks were allowed to provision for bad loans with before-tax profit, they should be able to recapitalize themselves without outside resources. The study called for adoption of regulations on loan classification and loan-loss provisioning in line with

[20]SLSP is a state-owned joint stock company, VUB has been partially privatized (less than 50 percent), and IRB has been privatized (yet the NPF and the Restitution Funds still own 37 percent of IRB's shares).

international norms that were introduced in March 1995,[21] and for tax-deductibility of loan-loss provisioning by banks. The Ministry of Finance has delayed introducing the latter measure because of concern over the associated loss in profit-tax revenue and of the possibility that tax-deductible provisioning would encourage banks to be insufficiently prudent in their lending.[22]

With the above concerns in mind, the NBS has created and partially implemented the Program on Bank Restructuring. Effective from July 1, 1995, banks were given three months to prepare internal rules and procedures that will enable them to organize their accounts in accordance with the new classification and provisioning system. However, banks may petition for three additional years to comply with the new provisioning regulations.[23] Another element of the Program on Bank Restructuring is the possibility of some form of assistance from the Ministry of Finance. Most likely this will involve allowing qualifying banks to provision tax-free during 1996–1998 as long as they adopt business plans approved by the NBS, in consultation

---

[21]Mandatory provisioning has replaced the non-mandatory guidelines inherited from the SBCS. Moreover, the new provisioning regulations leave less room for subjective evaluation, and in that sense are stricter than the previous recommended guidelines. Also the new regulations attempt to discourage refinancing of arrears through fresh, unwarranted loans and introduce basic principles related to restructured claims. Loans are now classified in accordance not only with the lateness of debt service (the previous emphasis was on length of arrears), but also on conditions related to the financial situation and reliability of borrowers. The amount of required provisioning is as follows: zero percent for standard loans; 5 percent for special mention loans; 20 percent for substandard claims; 50 percent for doubtful and litigious claims; 100 percent for loss claims; and 100 percent for unpaid interest, fees and commissions which are classified as substandard.

[22]Such an argument pays little attention to the general notion that provisioning allows banks to spread the lumpy costs of bad loans over time, and thus to paint a more stable picture of their financial well-being. Therefore, tax-free provisioning on a permanent basis — though not necessarily 100 percent tax-free — makes good economic sense.

[23]Unless exempted, banks will prepare their accounts for the third quarter of 1995 in accordance with the new system. A bank may seek a three-year exemption from having to create provisions by the end of September by preparing a bank restructuring plan that must be submitted to and approved by the Bank Board of the NBS.

with the Ministry of Finance, and forego distribution of dividends.[24,25] The underlying belief is that, once currently immobilized banks improve their financial base, they will be more willing to take prudent risks on longer-term lending opportunities. In this light, it is natural that KBB, which does not engage in new lending, will waive participation in the program. Any of its financial difficulties will be addressed through financial transfers from the authorities, including the NBS. Privatization of the major state-controlled banks (SLSP and VUB) will be considered only after progress has been made with the restructuring and recapitalization of the banks.

While many of the above changes in the regulatory/supervisory framework represent substantial improvements in the banking environment, little progress has been made with regard to the implementation of an effective bankruptcy law. A bankruptcy law — a revised version to the 1991 CSFR law — took effect fully in June 1993, yet it included conciliation procedures that were flawed in several respects.[26] Implementation of the bankruptcy law has been further hampered by an overburdened and inexperienced judicial system.

Conclusion

Slovakia's eclectic and pragmatic approach to bank restructuring has been effective thus far, though it is far from any theoretical ideal. It has consisted

---

[24]The Government was expected to submit to Parliament, in September 1995, a draft amendment to the Income Tax Law permitting participating banks to claim full tax deductibility for loan-loss provisioning over the period 1996–1998. The amendment was expected to become effective on January 1, 1996.

[25]The business plan is expected to be a tool through which banks will focus on improving management practices and containing administrative costs, including salaries.

[26]The bankruptcy law is technically flawed in the following ways: (1) initiation of bankruptcy triggers a mandatory conciliation process during which time debt-service is automatically suspended for three months; (2) each creditor, regardless of the size of the claim or its seniority, has one vote in the conciliation process; (3) foreign creditors may not initiate conciliation procedures; (4) any creditor may challenge in court a work-out that has been accepted by the majority of creditors during the conciliation procedure; and enterprises considered to be strategic are exempted from the bankruptcy law. (Certain firms in agriculture, forestry, communications, and transportation, plus all state-owned enterprises are exempted.)

of a combination of debt write-offs in exchange for bonds; recapitalization after assets have been transferred to a work-out bank; removal or subsidization of low-yielding loans; self reliance in the form of provisioning, setting aside reserves, and improving collateral; regulatory and supervisory reform; and prudential bank management. However, this success is not likely to have been possible without the sharp upturn in the economy, itself dependent on exogenous events such as the economic revival in Western Europe.

References

Begg, D., and R. Portes (1993). Enterprise Debt and Economic Transformation: Financial Restructuring of the State Sector in Central and Eastern Europe. In C. Mayer and X. Vives, eds., *Capital Markets and Financial Intermediation*, Cambridge University Press, Cambridge.

Brainard, L. J. (1991). Strategies for Economic Transformation in Central and Eastern Europe: Role of Financial Market Reform. In H.J. Blommestein and M. Marrese, eds., *Transformation of Planned Economies: Property Rights Reform and Macroeconomic Stability*, OECD, Paris, 95–118.

Czechoslovak Trade Bank (CSOB). *Annual Report.* Bratislava, various years.

Dittus, P. (1994). Bank Reform and Behavior in Central Europe. *Journal of Comparative Economics* **19**, 335–361.

Investment and Development Bank (IRB). *Annual Report.* Bratislava, various years.

Marrese, M. (1993). Agricultural Price Reform: Effect on Real Incomes and the Inflationary Process. In A. Braverman, K.M. Brooks, and C.S. Csaki, eds., *The Agricultural Transition in Central and Eastern Europe and the Former U.S.S.R.*, World Bank, Washington, 111–132.

Marrese, M. (1994). Banking Sector Reform in Central and Eastern Europe. *East-Central European Economies in Transition*, Joint Economic Committee, U.S. Congress, Washington, 111–132.

Mitchell, J. (1995). *Canceling, Transferring, or Repaying Bad Debt: Cleaning Banks' Balance Sheets in Economies in Transition.* Cornell University, Ithaca.

National Bank of Slovakia (NBS). *Annual Report.* Bratislava, various years.

Slovak State Savings Bank (SLSP). *Annual Report.* Bratislava, various years.

Slovak State Savings Bank. (1992). *Sporitel'Nictvo na Slovensku (Savings Activities in Slovakia).* Bratislava.

Statistical Office of the Slovak Republic. *Statistical Review of the Slovak Republic*. Bratislava, quarterly.

Statistical Office of the Slovak Republic. *Statistical Yearbook of the Slovak Republic*. Bratslava, various years.

Vojtisek, P. (1993). Restructuring of the Banks in the Former Czech and Slovak Federal Republic. In H.J. Blommestein and J.R. Lange, eds., *Transformation of the Banking System: Portfolio Restructuring, Privatization and the Payment System*, OECD, Paris, 69–75.

VUB (General Credit Bank). *Annual Report*. Bratislava, various years.

Part Five

Foreign Capital Flows and Domestic Capital Markets

SHORT TERM CAPITAL INFLOWS AND LONG TERM EXTERNAL EQUILIBRIUM

Andras Uthoff[1]

Introduction

Financial liberalization in Latin America has challenged economic authorities with the need to cope with capital surges (CEPAL 1995, Chapter XI; Ffrench Davis and Griffith-Jones 1995). This paper suggests that careful macroeconomic management is required to produce long term external equilibrium. In the long term, the growth rate of imports, which are needed to expand production, has been positively and strongly correlated to export growth rates.[2] In addition, fixed capital formation is in the long term largely financed from national saving.[3] Accordingly, the objective of macroeconomic policy should be to avoid unnecessary fluctuations in imports and saving in order to promote economic growth. Macroeconomic policy management would benefit from prior identification of changes in international capital flows. If net capital

[1]This paper has not been submitted to editing by CEPAL; responsibility for its content rests solely with the author.

[2]In other words, growth should be led by exports. There are important exceptions to this rule; some less developed countries have traditionally depended on official transfers from abroad.

[3]One of the currently most controversial issues observed within the recent capital surge episode is the large short term substitution between foreign and national saving (CEPAL 1996, Chapter IV).

inflows are permanent, authorities can appreciate the currency, increase the current account deficit, and allow for increases in consumption. If, on the other hand, net capital inflows are transitory or volatile (as has usually been the case in Latin America), these same measures could be distorting and sources of future imbalances with large social costs.

This paper suggests that market forces where the capital account is open will always react to capital import as though they were permanent and induce immediate adjustments in prices and resource allocation. However, there are economic policies that can smoothly guide market forces while authorities assess the probable duration of the capital flows (Ffrench-Davis, Agosin and Uthoff 1995; Zahler 1992, 1995).

The paper is divided into three sections: in the first, the volume, origin and composition of capital inflows are analyzed; in the second, six selected countries are grouped according to the policy mix they use to deal with capital surges; lastly, the paper concludes with policy recommendations.

Volume, Nature and Composition of Net Capital Inflows

International financial markets have changed dramatically in recent years, and these changes have produced an increase in capital flows toward Latin America. What concerns policy makers is the extent to which these capital flows have increased as the result of changes in the recipients' macroeconomic policies and prudential regulation rather than as the result of changes in the industrialized countries. From the perspective of the recipient country, the former responds to domestic policy, while the latter are exogenous in nature.

As shown in Tables 1 and 2, net capital inflows into Latin America reached an absolute record of US$60 billion annually for the period 1992 to 1994, representing 4.3 percent of the recipient countries' GDP and just short of the 5.3 percent of GDP reached in 1977 to 1981. Rapid increases in capital inflows have been particularly impressive in countries such as Mexico, and to a lesser extent in Argentina and Peru, all of which received little external capital during the years of the debt crisis. In other countries such as Chile and Costa Rica, the increase was less impressive because these countries had access to capital imports during the debt crisis.

Table 1. Capital Account: Total for Latin America *(values at current prices as a percentage of GDP)*

	1977–1981	1983–1989	1990–1991	1992–1994
Direct investment	0.89	0.71	0.79	1.00[1]
Portfolio investment	0.25	0.04	1.36	2.66[1]
Short and long term loans	4.15	0.49	0.09	0.02[1]
Long term loans	4.08	0.97	–0.33	–0.02
Short term loans	0.07	–0.48	0.42	0.04
Capital account balance[2]	5.28	1.26	2.59	4.30

Source: Derived from IMF and ECLAC data bases (Szalachman and Held 1996).
[1]These shares exclude capital inflows to countries included in the sample during 1994. Therefore, the total balance does not add to the sum of the components.
[2]Components do not sum to total due to errors and omissions.

Table 2. Net Capital Inflows into Latin America[1] *(annual averages)*

	Total net flows (US$ billions)					Percentage of GDP[2]			
	1977–1981	1983–1990	1990–1991	1992–1994[3]	1995[4]	1977–1981	1983–1990	1990–1991	1992–1994[3]
Latin America	28.9	9.4	28.2	62.0	22.4	4.5	1.3	2.6	5.1
Argentina	1.9	1.4	1.1	10.6	–0.4	2.0	2.1	0.6	5.1
Chile	2.6	1.5	2.3	3.5	0.3	12.7	7.0	7.3	8.8
Mexico	8.2	0.8	17.0	27.0	–16.9	5.1	0.2	6.3	9.1

Source: ECLAC 1995.
[1]Includes long and short term capital, official unilateral transfers and errors and omissions.
[2]These are approximate estimates highly sensitive to the exchange rate used when converting GDP from national currency into U.S. dollars; for 1990–1994 an average was used from two alternative estimates: one with the exchange rate derived from real parity in 1990 and another based on current exchange rates from each year.
[3]Figures for Mexico include those up to October 1994.
[4]Preliminary figures

In order to warn macroeconomic policy makers of the dangers of capital surges, two questions are relevant to the analysis. First, what are the sources of these surges? Second, are the recent surges less volatile than in previous episodes in Latin America?

What is Happening in Countries that are Sources of Capital Surges?

Four characteristics of international capital inflows show that, to a large extent, recent capital surges are not responding exclusively to domestic factors:

- Capital inflows have largely changed their sources as well as their composition. Between 1983 to 1989 and 1992 to 1994, foreign investment increased, denoting stronger confidence in the region's economies. However, only a quarter of this capital inflow was foreign direct investment (FDI). The largest share was securities, especially bonds, which have largely replaced commercial bank loans (except short term loans). This change from commercial loans to bonds and other securities is a worldwide trend, and reflects international market conditions rather than any particular characteristics of Latin American economies.
- Capital inflows coming from the United States were especially important from the early 1990s to 1994. Investments originating in the United States to Brazil, Argentina and especially Mexico are concentrated in securities. Capital inflows also reflected the supply in the United States stock markets of both primary and secondary American Depository Receipts (ADRs), particularly during 1993 and 1994. External factors that have attracted U.S. investors into Latin America are geographic proximity, improvement of political linkages, knowledge of the region, hemispheric integration, and looser production regulation. The fact that a large share of bonds have been denominated in U.S. dollars is also an indicator that U.S. investors are behind them. It is most likely that much of the capital import from the United States represents the return of flight capital (Culpeper 1995).
- Capital inflows from Europe, though less important than those from the United States, have also increased. However, they are countercyclical with those from Japan and the United States and are concentrated in FDI in the manufacturing sector while capital flows from Japan and USA are largely focused on the primary sectors (Griffith-Jones 1995).
- Institutional investors in all regions of origin (the United States, Japan, and Europe), especially pension funds and insurance companies, have significantly increased their total assets (Chuhan and Jun 1995) and have at the same time increased the share of their assets invested abroad (Griffith-

Jones 1995). Furthermore, countries in all three regions of origin have changed their rules and regulations so as to improve developing countries' access to their capital markets and to increase the ability of investment institutions to directly invest abroad, especially in the United States and, to a minor degree, in Europe (Culpeper 1995).

Are These Capital Flows Volatile?

There are two characteristics of the recent surge in capital inflows that have tended to make these flows volatile. First, the new capital inflows have important exogenous but changeable sources. These result from loose monetary policies and low interest rates in countries that belong to the Organisation for Economic Co-operation and Development (OECD), and their effect on international capital movements. This has been particularly true in the United States from the beginning of the 1990s (Calvo, Leiderman, and Rienhart 1993). The improved returns in Latin America attract foreign investors who had been benefiting during the 1980s from relatively high interest rates in low-risk OECD countries. Second, volatility has also increased due to the nature of new financial instruments that are more complex and not well understood by all participants, including financial intermediaries. Volatility may also potentially increase due to the importance that derivatives are acquiring in financial activities. These instruments are not regulated and have no capital requirements. Their trade is largely promoted by intermediaries receiving initial commissions without bearing any risk. Finally, information on securitization and derivatives is extremely poor.

In short, macroeconomic policy makers are being challenged by the increase in capital inflows, their concentration on securities and bonds and their potential volatility. Three lessons seem to be important in achieving long term foreign equilibrium, stable capital inflows, macroeconomic stability, and sustainable growth. First, authorities should avoid losing control over exchange rate policy. In particular the nominal exchange rate should not be used to achieve one rigid or extreme objective such as price stabilization.[4] Second, it is necessary to be cautious about the destination of capital inflows,

[4]Policy makers often try to stop inflation by means of a currency appreciation. Doing so may well distort other variables that, in turn, affect capital inflows.

especially in trying to direct them toward productive investment. Excessive portfolio investment in emerging capital markets and imported consumption goods may very well lead to financial bubbles and unsustainable disequilibria. Third, growth of imports in excess of exports should be of concern, and monitored carefully. Failure to do so may end in a current account deficit that is unsustainable in the long term.

Some Countries' Recent Experiences

Between 1990 and 1994, financial liberalization and capital surges produced a short term substitution (not reinforcement) between national and foreign saving. The data show that the long term trend between import and export growth, as well as that between national saving and fixed capital formation are at stake. This can be formalized with two simple models presented in the following section.

Long Term Trends Between Import and Export Growth Rates

A two gap model developed by Solimano (1984, 1987) is used to group countries according to their deviation from long term trends of exports and imports in the presence of large net capital inflows. The model assumes the economy is dependent on imports, and that feasible levels of employment and output are the result of import capacity. It assumes that there is a set of relative prices that is consistent with this equilibrium.

Two prices become relevant in this context: the interest rate and the exchange rate. If the domestic interest rate that is consistent with stabilization objectives is larger than the international interest rate adjusted for devaluation expectations and risk, then capital inflows will be encouraged, reinforcing currency appreciation and affecting the tradable sector. If, on the contrary, the domestic interest rate is lower, then stability is threatened, inflation is stimulated and the current account deficit grows, thus producing an unsustainable macroeconomic equilibrium.

Three sets of equations are used to find an indicator upon which countries can be grouped. The first is the balance of payment equilibrium conditions in foreign currency:

$$B = P_x X - P_m M + F - (iD + TR) \qquad (1)$$

where B is the rate of reserve accumulation; P_x is the nominal price of exports; X is the volume of exports; P_m is the nominal price of imports; M is the volume of imports; F is the flow of foreign capital (net of amortization payments); i is the relevant international interest rate (adjusted for risk); D is the stock of external debt denominated at a floating rate; and TR is net transfers.

A second equation is a short term imports function:

$$\hat{M} = G\hat{y} \qquad (2)$$

where G is the short term import elasticity with respect to output.

A third equation is a short-term production function:

$$Y = L^{1/d} \qquad (3)$$

where L is the level of employment and d is the short term employment elasticity with respect to output.

Solving (1) for M, then differentiating and using both short term functions (2) and (3), we obtain[5]:

$$\hat{L} = (d/G)[Q(\hat{p} + \hat{x}) + W(\hat{f}) - Z(\hat{z})] \qquad (4)$$

where employment growth will result in a weighted average of real export growth $\hat{x}$, terms of trade growth $\hat{p}$, real foreign exchange flow net of reserve accumulations growth $\hat{f}$, and real financial service payments abroad net of transfers growth. The respective weights are the ratios of exports (Q), net capital inflows less reserve accumulation (W), and financial services net of transfers (Z) divided by imports. This weighted average is finally multiplied by (d/G).

According to this model, sustainable growth with external equilibrium requires: (a) sustainable growth of real exports and relatively stable terms of trade; (b) complementarity between alternative sources of import finance; and (c) avoidance of a large share of volatile financial inflows.

---

[5]For purposes of the arithmetic, the following identities have been used, $p = P_x/P_m$; $f = (F - B)/P_m$, and $z = (iD + TR)/P_m$. Also, in general, $\hat{x}$ refers to the rate of growth of X.

Long Term Equilibrium between Fixed Capital Formation and National Saving Effort

Domestic saving, foreign saving and gross domestic investment as a share of GDP, all at current prices, indicate a country's "accumulation effort." The indicator that shows the result of this effort is gross domestic investment as a share of GDP, at constant prices as shown in (5).[6] Two sources of investment finance can be identified, the national and external saving effort and the change in relative prices that affects the purchasing power of such effort. It will be shown later that currency appreciation is, in the 1990s, the most important factor in changing the price of investment. In fact, the relatively larger imported component of investment ensures that the response of investment prices to currency appreciation is greater than the price of total GDP.

$$gdi^{o} = gdi / (pgdi / pgdp) \tag{5}$$

In the above equation, 'gdi' is gross domestic investment, equal to gross national saving plus foreign saving, both at current prices; 'gdi^{o}' is gross domestic investment at *constant prices* as a proportion of gdp at these prices; 'pgdi' is a price deflator for gross domestic investment; 'pgdp' is a price deflator for gdp.

This relation by no means excludes behavioral functions. Real disposable income and other saving determinants explain national saving rates derived from variables at current prices. They must be envisaged as variables explaining the behavior of the saving effort by nationals and not necessarily leading to a "quantum" definition of national saving in a system of accounts at constant prices.

The absence of a proper deflator for national saving raises questions about the relation between saving and investment. While the total saving rate (national plus foreign) and gross domestic investment at current prices are included in identity (5) and equal by definition, it is only "assumed" that they are equal at constant prices.[7] This assumption excludes the relation

---

[6]For a discussion of concepts and definitions of saving in systems of national accounts, see Held and Uthoff 1995.

[7]The complication is derived from the treatment of the terms of trade (Held and Uthoff, 1995).

between investment at current and constant prices shown in (that same relation). If, for instance, the relative price of gross domestic investment were to fall, accounts of capital accumulation at constant prices would ignore its effect on real domestic investment and allocate the larger quantum of investment to more national saving (at constant prices), and not to the real saving effort (at current prices).

Equation (5) is very crucial. It distinguishes three nonadditive *ex post* sources to finance increases in gross domestic investment at constant prices: (a) increases in national saving efforts; (b) increases in foreign saving efforts; and (c) changes in the relative price of gross domestic investment.

Recent Regional Performances

The increase in net foreign capital inflows into Latin America after 1990 had Keynesian-type positive effects. The increasing availability of imported capital released the foreign exchange constraint under which most countries were operating. The larger supply of imports allowed a better utilization of existing production capacity. The purchase of foreign reserves by the Central Banks, increased money supply, which — in addition to rising income — reactivated aggregate demand. Output expansion was quite generalized and especially strong in Argentina, Chile, Peru, and Venezuela. Mexico was an exception. As shown in Table 3, despite the large increase in private foreign capital inflows, Mexican output did not expand very much because the economy was already operating at close to production capacity.

Table 3. Gross Domestic Product *(annual growth rates)*

	1970–1980	1980–1990	1990–1994	1995	1996	1997
Argentina	2.8	–0.9	7.7	–5.0	3.5	5.3
Brazil	8.6	1.6	2.3	4.2	2.8	3.0
Chile	2.5	2.8	6.8	10.1	7.3	6.9
Colombia	5.4	3.7	4.0	6.2	2.2	3.2
Costa Rica	5.5	2.3	4.9	2.2	–0.5	3.1
Mexico	6.7	1.7	2.6	–6.6	5.3	7.3
Peru	3.9	–1.2	4.9	7.7	2.4	7.7
Latin America	5.6	1.2	3.6	0.5	3.5	5.3

Source: ECLAC, on the basis of official statistics.

All countries did not change the composition of import finance in the same way. Those economies that successfully reactivated their economies after the debt crisis via export expansion (Colombia, Costa Rica and Chile — see Table 4), accumulated reserves instead of adjusting their economies. Those economies less successful in increasing their exports in this period adjusted their economies to the new international financial conditions. The larger increase in the share of imports financed with foreign capital made the latter economies more vulnerable to foreign capital volatility. Furthermore, they operated within a set of relative prices that limited a rapid response of output and employment to changing conditions. When this happened at the end of 1994 (the *tequilazo* in Mexico), these countries experienced a larger decline in output and employment.

Table 4. Export Growth Rates

	1986–1990	1991–1993	1994	1995	1996	1997
Argentina	6.1%	–1.0%	18.4%	20.3%	5.6%	17.7%
Colombia	12.7	8.5	0.7	0.7	3.4	8.0
Costa Rica	10.4	11.4	–0.3	6.2	11.2	3.5
Chile	11.5	10.2	8.6	11.4	18.7	10.7
Mexico	5.8	3.9	11.8	27.0	17.1	18.6
Peru	–4.9	8.8	15.4	7.9	5.1	12.8

There were also important differences in the size and structure of the finance of gross domestic investment at constant prices. As shown in Table 5, regional averages between 1983–1989 and 1992–1994 show that while foreign saving "efforts" increased by more than two percentage points of GDP, gross domestic investment "results" increased by only 1.4 percentage points of GDP. The difference is explained by a fall of national saving "efforts" by 2.2 percentage points of GDP, which, in turn, was only slightly compensated by declines in the relative price of gross domestic investment. This pattern is particularly important in Argentina, Mexico and Peru and to a minor extent in Colombia, where increases in gross domestic investment were financed largely by additions to foreign saving and declines in the relative price of gross domestic investment due to currency appreciation. Both of these sources are reversible. In addition, a relative large substitution between foreign and national saving took place in these countries. In Chile and Costa Rica, in contrast, gross domestic investment was largely funded from additional national saving efforts and only to a minor extent from currency appreciation.

Table 5. Saving "Efforts" and Gross Domestic Investment "Results" *(% of GDP)*

Country	1983–1989	1992–1994	Change	1995	1996
Argentina					
National saving "effort"[1]	16.4	15.5	–0.9	16.2	17.2
Foreign saving "effort"[1]	2.2	2.9	0.7	0.9	1.4
Gross domestic investment[2]	16.9	20.2	3.3	19.4	20.3
Brazil					
National saving "effort"[1]	20.9	19.6	–1.3	16.8	17.3
Foreign saving "effort"[1]	0.7	-0.4	–1.1	2.5	3.0
Gross domestic investment[2]	16.5	13.8	–2.7	15.9	15.3
Chile					
National saving "effort"[1]	13.6	24.7	11.1	27.6	23.3
Foreign saving "effort"[1]	5.8	2.8	–3.0	–0.2	4.4
Gross domestic investment[2]	15.1	22.1	7.0	22.9	23.8
Colombia					
National saving "effort"[1]	19.1	19.0	–0.1	16.9	14.3
Foreign saving "effort"[1]	0.6	1.5	0.9	5.9	5.0
Gross domestic investment[2]	17.6	21.9	4.3	25.5	23.3
Costa Rica					
National saving "effort"[1]	17.6	22.7	5.1	22.3	21.8
Foreign saving "effort"[1]	7.6	5.8	–1.8	1.1	1.2
Gross domestic investment[2]	21.1	24.0	2.9	23.2	22.5
Mexico					
National saving "effort"[1]	21.6	15.5	–6.1	19.3	22.7
Foreign saving "effort"[1]	–0.9	6.5	7.4	0.5	0.5
Gross domestic investment[2]	16.9	21.6	4.7	16.6	18.4
Peru					
National saving "effort"[1]	20.2	16.9	–3.3	18.2	19.6
Foreign saving "effort"[1]	2.5	5.0	2.5	6.7	5.3
Gross domestic investment[2]	18.9	21.9	3.0	27.8	25.6
Latin America					
National saving "effort"[1]	19.9	17.5	–2.4	17.9	18.5
Foreign saving "effort"[1]	0.6	2.8	2.2	1.9	1.9
Gross domestic investment[2]	16.8	18.2	1.4	17.5	17.7

Source: ECLAC with IMF data and official estimates.
[1]At current prices.
[2]At constant prices.

Policy Lessons

In Latin America, when governments undertake the liberalization of foreign trade and domestic capital markets, trends in currency markets are only one of the many factors that should be monitored before advocating real currency appreciation. Of equal or greater importance is the governments' assessments of productivity gains and external competitiveness. Governments should constantly monitor, in addition to real exchange rates, export growth and the size of the current account deficit. In addition, special concern should also be given to national saving effort.

In Argentina, Mexico and Peru, the currency appreciated much more than in Chile, Colombia and Costa Rica. The first three countries faced increasing current account deficits. Consequently, their gross domestic investment was increasingly financed by external saving. Furthermore, declines in the relative price of gross domestic investment due to currency appreciation also became an important source of investment finance.

If real exchange rate appreciation is not to undermine long term external equilibria, it should reflect medium and long term market forces. Otherwise authorities should make efforts to maintain the power and right to intervene in the foreign exchange market whenever they judge that it departs from medium and long term fundamentals. This has proven feasible in Chile since 1991 (Zahler 1995), and in Colombia during the 1970s and the early 1990s (Urrutia 1995; ECLAC 1995, Chapter XI).

Tables 4 and 5 group our six countries according to their performance in changing both the structure of finance of their imports as well as the share of their increase in gross domestic investment that was financed with external saving and currency appreciation. One can see that those countries that have experienced a sudden release of their foreign exchange constraint have also generated an excess supply of foreign exchange and an appreciation in the real exchange rate. This increased the domestic demand for tradables, and at the same time produced a wealth effect on consumption due to the important appreciation of financial and real assets.

As a consequence, aggregate demand expanded, imports increased, existing commercial surpluses fell, current account deficits increased, and thus capital imports increased (ECLAC 1995, Chapter XI). Consequently, domestic expenditure rose more than domestic output, reducing national saving efforts.

The nonfinancial current account surpluses at constant prices were reduced, and a trade deficit at current prices appeared in 1992 for the first time since 1981.

In such a radical process of rapid relative price changes, it should not come as a surprise that trends in basic macroeconomic variables depart from those consistent with medium and long term natural forces. In order to avoid unsustainable movements in sensitive variables such as export growth and national saving, authorities cannot rely exclusively on liberalizing markets. There is an important place for active public policies. These should focus on the regulation of the composition of capital inflows, the exchange rate and money supply, as well as in the promotion of a stimulating environment for saving, investment, and productivity gains.

Three levels of intervention are available to create the adequate policy mix in cases where capital surges produce currency appreciation and affect the sustainability of external equilibrium.

- The first level is in the foreign exchange market with the aim of moderating the effect on the nominal exchange rate. Central banks can purchase foreign exchange and accumulate reserves to this end. Monetary authorities can pursue different levels of intervention. The most popular at present is a dirty float of the currency.
- The second level is in the money market where authorities must be certain to sterilize the monetary effects of reserve accumulation. Conditions to do so are not the same across countries. The most popular mechanism is open market operations. In tight financial markets, this procedure can be very distorting whereas in deep domestic markets, the effect on interest rates and economic activities might be smaller. Fiscal discipline is a crucial element at this level.
- The third level is in the capital account. Authorities can adopt different policies including incentives to capital outflows and capital requirements and quantitative controls on capital flows. The purpose is to stimulate those flows that are consistent with domestic absorption capacity and redirect them toward productive investment and, at the same time, to discourage short term speculative inflows.

When confronted with pressures for currency appreciation, authorities can also design policy measures to increase foreign currency outflows.

Measures to do so include incentives to capital outflows by relaxing regulations that constrain either domestic capital investments abroad or the repatriation of FDI. They can also change the amortization schedule of foreign loans. Measures have also been taken to stimulate investment with large import components. On the supply side, measures to stimulate increases in productivity and reduce local costs by complementing foreign exchange policy with social pacts related to wage and price dynamics can be pursued in order to encourage the competitiveness of domestic firms faced with currency appreciation.

Correct pricing at the macroeconomic level and sustainability of external equilibrium have to be complemented by an appropriate institutional environment. The latter would facilitate the intermediation of capital imports into real investment needs. Three developments have proven to be important. First, the government can improve public finance solvency by giving the central bank greater autonomy, addressing pension system deficits, and reducing all sources of quasi-fiscal deficits. Second, authorities can adopt severe reforms in the banking sector to insure prudential regulation and supervision, improvement of organizational regulation and supervision, and development of financial markets in the sense of completing those segments where long term funding is intermediated and improving access of small firms to capital markets. Third, the government can foster the development of securities and insurance markets. Stock markets should be competitive, with access regulated by norms concerning open corporations and information requirements. Institutional investors should be prudentially regulated through regulations concerning the diversifications of their portfolio, establishing reserve requirements and capital requirements. Independent risk classification institutions should be developed, and custody of financial assets should be protected. Finally, these markets should be permanently developed through incentives for the creation of new corporations, new financial intermediaries, and new financial instruments.

The third area of intervention is oriented to the diversification of foreign capital flows. These measures overlap with the other two areas already discussed. Increasing uncertainty about exchange rate determination may radically change short term incentives for arbitrage. Nevertheless, measures can be adopted to directly impose restrictions on capital inflows. These include reserve requirements without interest payments in order to balance interest rate differential between domestic and international financial markets adjusted for currency risks, and also quantitative controls (maturity periods, minimum volumes for bond emission and rules for the participation of foreign capital).

References

Calvo, G., E. Leiderman, and C. Reinhart (1993). Capital Inflows and Real Exchange Rate Appreciation in Latin America: The Role of External Factors. *IMF Staff Papers* **40** (1), 108–151.

CEPAL Comisión Económica para América Latina (1995). *Balance Preliminar de la Economía de América Latina y el Caribe 1995.* United Nations, Santiago, December.

CEPAL (1996). *Fortalecer el Desarrollo. Interacciones entre Macro y Microeconomía.* United Nations, Santiago.

CEPAL (1995). *América Latina y el Caribe: Políticas para Mejorar la Inserción en la Economía Mundial.* LC/G. 1800(SES.25/3), Santiago, April.

Chuhan, P., and K. Jun (1995). El Financiamiento Latinoamericano en los Mercados de Capital de Japón. In R. Ffrench-Davis and S. Griffith-Jones, eds., *Las Nuevas Corrientes Financieras hacia la América Latina. Fuentes, Efectos y Políticas*, Serie de Lecturas No. 81 de El Trimestre Económico, Fondo de Cultura Económica, Santiago-Mexico City.

Culpeper, R. (1995). La Reanudación de las Corrientes Privadas de Capital hacia América Latina: El Papel de los Inversionistas Norteamericanos. In R. Ffrench-Davis and S. Griffith-Jones, eds., *Las Nuevas Corrientes Financieras hacia la América Latina. Fuentes, Efectos y Políticas*, Serie de Lecturas No. 81 de El Trimestre Económico. Fondo de Cultura Económica, Santiago-Mexico City.

Ffrench-Davis, R., M. Agosin, and A. Uthoff (1995). Movimiento de Capitales, Estrategia Exportadora y Estabilidad Macroeconómica en Chile. In R. Ffrench-Davis and S. Griffith-Jones, eds., *Las Nuevas Corrientes Financieras hacia la América Latina. Fuentes, Efectos y políticas*, Serie de Lecturas No. 81 de El Trimestre Económico, Fondo de Cultura Económica, Santiago-Mexico City.

Griffith-Jones, S. (1995). Corrientes de fondos Europeos hacia América Latina: Hechos y Planteamientos. In R. Ffrench-Davis and S. Griffith-Jones, eds., *Las Nuevas Corrientes Financieras hacia la América Latina. Fuentes, Efectos y Políticas*, Serie de Lecturas No. 81 de El Trimestre Económico, Fondo de Cultura Económica, Santiago-Mexico City.

Held, G., and A. Uthoff (1995) Indicators and Determinants of Savings for Latin American and the Caribbean. Working Paper No 25, CEPAL, Santiago, April.

Held, G., and R. Szalchman (1997). Flujos de Capital Externa en América Latina y el Caribe: Experiencias y Politicas en los Noventa. Serie de Financiamiento No. 40, CEPAL, Santiago.

Solimano, A. (1984) Devaluation, Employment and Inflation: Essays on Macroeconomic Adjustment. Ph.D. Dissertation, Massachusetts Institute of Technology.

Solimano A. (1987) Restricción Externa, Nivel de Actividad y Política Salarial en Guatemala, 1979–1984. Programa Regional de Empleo para América Latina y el Caribe, *Política Salarial, Inflación y Restricción Externa*, Santiago.

Urrutia, M. (1995). La Cuenta de Capital Durante un Proceso de Liberalización Económica. Presented to the Conference, "Setenta Años del Banco Central de Chile", Santiago, August.

Zahler, R. (1992). Política Monetaria con Apertura de la Cuenta de Capitales, *Revista de la CEPAL*, No. 48, Santiago.

Zahler, R. (1995). Conferencia Inaugural del 70th Aniversario del Banco Central de Chile. *Boletín Mensual del Banco Central de Chile*, No. 810, Santiago, August.

THE MACROECONOMIC CONSEQUENCES OF INVESTMENT LIBERALIZATION FOR DEVELOPING COUNTRIES

Stephen Guisinger[1]

Introduction

The Uruguay Round of the General Agreement on Tariffs and Trade (GATT) paid only limited attention to investment, but the Tokyo Round that preceded it paid even less attention to the subject. As an issue for multilateral negotiation, investment has had a U-shaped trajectory. The Havana negotiations that were the precursor to the GATT gave investment a fairly high status. The negotiators exhibited a rather curious foresight because foreign direct investment (FDI) was still in its infancy. After Havana, the ranking of investment, either portfolio or direct, on the agenda of various GATT rounds fell precipitously. Only with the Uruguay Round has investment begun to climb its way back from obscurity.

The reasons for the heightened interest in investment are not hard to uncover. Total sales of overseas subsidiaries now exceed the value of world exports by a factor greater than two. If one excludes minerals and unprocessed agricultural products from exports (to compare like kinds of value-added

[1]This study draws extensively on the author's study on the same topic prepared for, and presented to, the OECD Workshop on the Multilateral Agreement on Investment, Hong Kong, March 26–27, 1996.

activities), the ratio of subsidiary sales to export sales grows even larger. Data on export versus subsidiary profits suggests an even larger ratio. The evidence seems clear: FDI simply cannot be pushed under the carpet of trade-related issues. It requires prompt and comprehensive multilateral treatment.

The Organisation for Economic Co-operation and Development (OECD) has launched negotiations among its members on the Multilateral Agreement on Investment (MAI). The MAI would consolidate and extend the disciplines on investment that have been in force among its members for the past three decades. The MAI is built on the same principle as the World Trade Organization (WTO) — non-discrimination. The MAI would ensure signatories pre-and-post establishment national treatment and most-favored-nation treatment. It would contain a section on investment protection — expropriation, convertibility, repatriation. Presently, it does not include sections dealing with performance requirements and investment incentives, but suggestions to include these issues have been made.

The purpose of this paper is not to analyze the MAI itself but to examine some of the macroeconomic consequences for developing countries of investment liberalization that would follow the adoption of a worldwide instrument on investment. Many governments seem reluctant to continue reforms, in part because of the uncertain impact on important economic variables, such as inflation and employment, but also because the long term benefits of further liberalization are not clear.

This study reviews the limited research that has been carried out on the effects of investment reform on developing countries. The paucity of research in this area can be explained to some extent by the absence of a credible measure of the restrictiveness of investment regimes. There is no measure of the quantitative importance of investment restrictions comparable to the concept of effective protection that is used to measure trade protection. The multitude of empirical studies of effective protection now available have allowed statistical testing of hypotheses relating trade policy to economic activity. No similar quantitative measures of investment restrictions exist to test similar hypotheses about the macroeconomic effects of investment regimes.

The absence of credible measures of investment restrictions leave only two avenues open for the study of linkages between investment regimes and economic activity. The first is to draw inferences from the experience of trade policy reforms, which produce results that are in many ways similar to investment reforms. Investment liberalization and trade liberalization cannot be treated as independent processes. Trade liberalization creates opportunities for foreign investors by expanding possibilities for exports. Investment liberalization creates opportunities to expand exports by bringing in new investment. The recent experiences of countries undergoing trade liberalization suggest that investment regimes are likely to be sustained over a period of years and are unlikely to have adverse effects on important economic variables such as the level of employment, income distribution and investment.

Recent developments in the theory of economic growth suggest an important place for both trade and investment liberalization. One of the major catalysts in the new theory of growth is the diffusion of research and development through the medium of foreign investment. The more open economies are to both trade and investment, the greater the possibilities of permanently raising their long term rate of growth due to the increased opportunities for technology diffusion.

The second method for exploring links between investment regimes and economic performance is to trace the effects of investment liberalization on the economy using large-scale economic models that capture multiple interactions between economic sectors and factors of production. To explore these interactions, simulations of investment liberalization were undertaken using the SALTER model. However, the SALTER model, like other large-scale models, does not capture technology diffusion and export externalities that many believe to have important impacts on the rate of economic growth.

The study concludes with what might be described as optimistic agnosticism about the effects of investment liberalization on the macroeconomies of developing countries. We cannot be certain about the issue because of critical gaps in the data, but what little we do know suggests that investment liberalization probably does not need to have adverse macroeconomic impacts and, under certain conditions, the impact may be quite favorable. Two types of research are needed. The first is large-scale comparative empirical study of the liberalization process in developing countries similar in scope and depth to the OECD, National Bureau of Economic Research (NBER) and World Bank studies of trade liberalization. The second is a more extensive scenario generation using large-scale simulation models.

It should be emphasized at the outset that this study is not about the benefits and costs of FDI. There have been numerous attempts to assess the impact of FDI on developing countries. Most of these studies have been done on the assumption of continuity in existing systems of trade and investment protection. This study makes no attempt to assess benefits and costs of changes in FDI with or without protection. This study is about the macroeconomic consequences of liberalization. On the basis of these consequences, one could draw judgements about net benefits or costs, but that is a topic for another study.

Investment Liberalization and Developing Countries

Over the past two decades, governments in developing and developed countries have liberalized rules and regulations regarding FDI. No two governments have liberalized to the same degree or at the same pace, so it is hard to draw simple generalizations about these liberalizations. It appears that liberalization has proceeded at a faster pace among developed countries. While almost all developing countries have liberalized to some degree, only a handful have approached levels of liberalization achieved by developed countries. Full liberalization would entail an essentially "free investment" climate comparable to free trade, including, among other factors, most-favored-nation and national treatment, right of establishment, and full convertibility of the principal and earnings on foreign investments.

Liberalization efforts in some developing countries have been only tentative. In part, this hesitancy is due to fears that liberalization could have adverse repercussions on their economies, especially if the reforms were not properly designed and carefully coordinated with other policies. For example, liberalization of investment regimes before liberalization of trade could lead to large rents in protected industries accruing to foreigners. Not only would this produce a real welfare loss for the country, but the political repercussions could be severe. Governments also fear that comprehensive and rapid liberalization could destabilize the economy.

The principal focus of this study will be on relatively short term (between one and five years) effects of liberalization, although long term effects are also discussed. The analysis will proceed on the assumption that liberalizations are across-the-board and swiftly implemented. Partial liberalization and liberalization phased in over a number of years are much harder to assess even though they are more typical.

The task of reviewing the literature on investment liberalization in developing countries is both simple and depressing. Simple because there is almost no literature, depressing for the same reason. There is a rich literature on the effects of trade liberalization on macroeconomic variables, and considerable scholarly work has been done on the impact of FDI on host economies under existing investment regimes. However, for a variety of reasons discussed below, the link between investment liberalization and macroeconomic performance has received scant attention from researchers.

In the absence of a literature on the topic, the paper adopts some devious means for creating a pool of evidence on which some tentative observations can be based. "Grasping at straws" would not be too vivid a metaphor to describe this process. This exercise has, however, a noble goal: the generation of some hypotheses that could be investigated when serious research begins on this topic.

For the purposes of this paper, an investment regime will refer to the array of policies that directly affect the profitability of investments. These policies fall into one of three categories: 1) fiscal incentives and disincentives; 2) investment restrictions; and 3) trade policies. Fiscal incentives refer to the cash grants, subsidized loans, accelerated depreciation allowances, tax holidays and other inducements that governments use to encourage investment. Fiscal disincentives include taxes on corporate profits and income remittances abroad. Investment restrictions are the limitations that governments impose on investment. Some of these are explicit and automatic: investment in certain industrial sectors is allowed or forbidden. Some are subjective and discretionary: investment proposals must be approved by government agencies whose criteria may not be transparent. Trade policies include import duties, quotas and export subsidies that affect the price of traded goods. While many other policies influence the investment climate, these policy groups have the most direct bearing on investment profitability.

One critical lacuna in the literature is a comprehensive measure of the restrictiveness of investment regimes. Edwards notes in his survey of the effects of trade liberalization on developing countries that the emergence of the concept of the effective rate of protection in the early 1960s made possible large-scale studies of the protective effects of trade policies both across countries and over time (Edwards 1993, 1362). Without a comprehensive measure of the impact that all trade policies have on the profitability of investment, economists had to rely on partial and very imperfect measures of the restrictiveness of trade regimes. The emergence of the effective rate of protection concept represented a kind of mini-paradigm shift in the way that economists, and then policy makers, viewed trade policy and, more importantly, the reforms that were needed.

Investment regimes lack an analogous measure. Of the three policy components that make up an investment regimes, only one — trade policy — has a widely accepted quantitative measure, namely the effective rate of protection. Theorists have made progress in providing an analogous measure for fiscal incentives. Eric Bond and Stephen Guisinger (1985) incorporated fiscal incentives in an expanded version of the effective rate of protection to show that Ireland's accession to the EEC was accompanied by a substitution of investment incentives for tariffs in order to maintain the country's attractiveness to foreign investors. Guisinger (1989) showed that the effective rate of protection, the user cost of capital, and the ratio of the financial to the economic rate of return are all logically related. Any one of these three indices could be used to measure the net incentive (fiscal incentives less fiscal disincentives) provided by a host government to investors.

The greatest need is the quantification of investment restrictions. It does not appear to be an insuperable problem from the standpoint of theory. A host government's denial of right of establishment is analogous to a prohibitive tariff or a zero import quota. A host government's non-national treatment of foreigners imposes costs on the inward flow of capital in much the same way a tariff raises the cost of imported goods. Lack of convertibility (or the risk that a currency might become inconvertible) raises costs to investors. There is no fundamental reason why researchers could not devise tariff equivalents for these policy-induced costs. Perhaps the greatest challenge to theory is the representation of the deterrent effect of an investment approval agency using subjective criteria.

The real problems lie in empirical estimation. Estimates of investment restriction costs are much more difficult to collect than costs imposed by trade policies because of differences in the way that restrictive policies are applied. Within the same industry, tariffs and quotas apply uniformly to all importers, so that only one piece of information is needed for each imported product. For example, all quota holders reap the same benefit from the quota-constrained supply of imports and each holder raises the domestic selling price above the C.I.F. price by the same amount. In contrast, investment restrictions are often imposed on a project-by-project basis even within the same industry or product category. No two investors in the same narrowly defined industrial category face exactly the same set of restrictions or incentives. Amassing reliable data on each project, identifying the dozen or more restrictions and incentives that apply to the typical investment in developing countries is a daunting task. The author knows of no study where this detailed data have been collected even for a restrictive sample. While it would be incorrect to say that we know nothing about the degree of restrictiveness, our knowledge is largely qualitative and subjective. As a result, comparisons of the degree of restrictiveness across countries and across time are difficult. It is easy to understand why so few studies have attempted to examine the effects of investment liberalization on macroeconomic variables.

What Can We Learn from Trade Liberalization?

If there are no studies of the macroeconomic repercussions of investment liberalization, we can look to other policy liberalization experiences for lessons they might provide. Of the liberalizations that developing countries undertake, trade liberalization comes closest to resembling investment liberalization, since both bring about increases in imports and exports. One could argue that investment liberalization and trade liberalization are mirror images of one another: investment liberalizations free capital inflow, which gives rise to new imports and exports, while trade liberalizations free imports and exports, which give rise to new capital inflows. In both liberalizations, imports, exports and capital investment rise more or less simultaneously. In reality, the magnitude of these changes may be quite different with trade liberalizations having a greater impact on all three variables. However, the ways in which these liberalizations affect the economy are the same.

The link between trade, capital and growth has been made in a number of other research studies. Robert E. Baldwin (1992) has emphasized, for example, that capital accumulation from both domestic and foreign sources contributes significantly to the effects of trade liberalization on output. Brad De Long and Lawrence Summers (1993) found a very strong link between investment in equipment and economic growth. Although perhaps of smaller significance in developing countries than in developed countries because of the vast range of experience with growth rates, the link is nonetheless evident from the data, and the line of causation runs from equipment investment to growth and not vice versa. Since little equipment is produced in developing countries, equipment investment can only arise if the country's trade policy permits equipment imports. This is another way in which trade liberalization and investment liberalization are tied together. De Long and Summers find net social rates of return to capital investment averaging in the neighborhood of 25 percent. Although De Long and Summers do not examine FDI directly, it is evident that to the extent lower investment restrictions permit greater amounts of FDI, their data support a strongly positive link between FDI and economic growth.

The literature on trade liberalization is vast. This paper will survey just three studies that have been selected for two principal reasons. The first and most important reason is that these are all prominent studies in the field of trade liberalization. All three were large-scale, multi-country studies of trade liberalization, involving more than 50 economists who spent several years examining interrelationships between trade, protection and economic performance. The second reason is that I was the only economist of the 50 involved to work on all three — as research assistant in the first and as principal author of country studies (Pakistan in both instances) for the other two. The first study, sponsored by the OECD and directed by Ian Little and Maurice Scott, took more than four years to complete, produced seven book-length studies of developing countries and culminated in the landmark summary volume, *Trade and Industry in Some Developing Countries* (Little *et al.* 1970). The second study, sponsored by the NBER, was directed by Anne Krueger and Jagdish Bhagwati. It took more than three years to complete and included more than a dozen country studies. Krueger (1978) prepared the summary volume, *Foreign Trade Regimes and Economic*

Development: Liberalization Attempts and Consequences. The last of the three, and perhaps most ambitious of all, was sponsored by the World Bank and appeared in five volumes under the generic heading, *Liberalizing Foreign Trade*. The study took more than five years to complete and covered eighteen developing countries. A summary was prepared by the three study directors, Demetris Papageorgiou, Armeane Choksi and Michael Michaely, under the title, *Liberalizing Foreign Trade in Developing Countries: The Lessons of Experience* (1990). It is interesting to note that while the principal theme of these studies was trade policy, they did examine other related reforms, including capital markets and foreign investment regulations. All three studies are surveyed by Edwards (1993).

It is unfair to try to capture the richness of these studies in just a few paragraphs. However, while the three covered much the same ground, each focused on a different aspect of the liberalization process. The OECD study took a snapshot picture of the trade protection system and explored the consequences of observed differences in inter-country and inter-industry rates of effective protection for the growth of industry, trade and the overall economy. The NBER study studied changes in trade policy regimes over time. The authors posited a five-step evolutionary process. In Phase 1, countries impose across-the-board quantitative controls. In Phase 2, the uniformity disappears as the system becomes more complex and discriminatory. In Phase 3, liberalization begins with a few tentative measures. In Phase 4, liberalization proceeds in earnest. Phase 5 culminates with complete liberalization from quota restrictions (although not tariff protection).

The World Bank study concentrated on the consequences of liberalization episodes on various macroeconomic variables and for that reason has the greatest relevance for the present study. The Bank project had several objectives within this concentration. First, were the effects of liberalization different in the short and long term — for employment levels, growth, the balance of payments and income distribution? Second, were the costs in any time frame — short or long — so great in relation to benefits that liberalization should not have been undertaken? Other study objectives included suggestions about the appropriate types of investment trade reforms. For example, is there an optimal sequencing of policies in the liberalization process, that is, should quota liberalization be first before all others? Was fiscal contraction a necessary adjunct to trade liberalization? A last objective was to determine if there were there common factors that explained liberalization failures? Each of these is examined below, relying heavily on Papageorgiou *et al.* (1990), after a general review of the findings of the study.

The Bank study covered nineteen countries that together had 36 different episodes of liberalization. Episodes were classified according to whether they were "weak" (for example, small reductions in tariffs or only a small number of sectors liberalized) or "strong." The authors measured performance outcome according to whether liberalization was sustained, partially sustained or completely reversed. Of the 36 episodes, 24 were either fully or partially sustained and only 12 ended in failure. These episodes were divided about evenly between weak and strong. One interesting finding was that both weak and strong liberalizations produced sustained liberalizations. However, strong liberalizations had a slightly higher probability of success — 75 percent compared to 58 percent for weak liberalizations. Interestingly, a country's failure in one episode was not a good predictor of failure in subsequent episodes. Of 13 countries that experienced an initial failure, 11 made a subsequent attempt, of which ten were successful to some degree (sustained fully or partially).

One of the unique contributions of the study was to examine the sequencing of trade policy reforms. Was it better, for example, to relax quantitative restrictions before reducing tariffs? The answer revealed by the study was an unambiguous "yes." The failure rate for liberalizations that did not first relax quantitative restrictions was almost 90 percent, the same as the success rate of those that did. Thus, care in planning the sequencing of policy liberalizations appears important.

Another finding was that the macroeconomic policy adopted by liberalizing countries mattered. The study found that "expansionary fiscal and monetary policies are the single most important cause of a reversal of trade reforms" (Papageorgiou *et al.* 1990, 22). In other words, governments that liberalized their trade regime experienced, in many cases, short term reductions in revenues as tariffs were lowered. The rush to import worsened the current account of the balance of payments and in general added to inflationary pressures in the economy. A restrictive monetary and fiscal policy was necessary to offset these initial shocks, but, later on, could be gradually relaxed. The study also looked at the reverse effect: what impact does fiscal policy have on trade reforms? The authors concluded that an expansionary fiscal policy made it difficult for countries to launch trade reforms. In other words, a precondition for trade reform was a sound fiscal and monetary policy.

The broad results can be summed up this way:

- There are no systematic adverse effects from trade liberalization and the costs of any required adjustments are small.
- If anything, trade reforms promote competition, stable prices and employment in the long term.
- Stronger reforms implemented quickly appear to be more sustainable than weak ones.
- One of the surest guarantors of the smooth implementation of trade liberalization is a politically stable regime pursuing sound monetary and fiscal policies.

Table 1 summarizes these points and offers conjectures on their implications for reforms of investment policy.

One small part of the study was devoted to the study of the sequencing of trade and capital market reforms, including liberalization of foreign direct investment. The authors begin by asserting that "Liberalizing the capital market typically means removing all or most restrictions on external capital flows" (Papageorgiou *et al.* 1990, 30). This assumption seems clearly at odds with the experience of most developing countries over the past two decades when governments liberalized restrictions in a piecemeal fashion. Indonesia, for example, only gradually reformed its investment laws, beginning in the 1970s and not yet reaching completion. The authors argue that trade should be liberalized before capital markets for three principal reasons: first, the turbulence created by capital market reforms might delay trade reforms; second, if capital markets are reformed first, capital may flow to the most highly distorted and least efficient industries; finally, if capital reforms are implemented first, then trade reforms might be endangered by a large and sudden influx of foreign capital. This influx would drive up the exchange rate, hurting exports and increasing the demand for imports.

In only four of the 36 episodes studied were trade reforms accompanied by capital market reforms. These episodes included the reforms in Argentina,

Table 1. Characteristics of Trade Reforms and Implications for Investment Reforms

Issue	Implication for Trade Reforms	Possible Implication for Investment Reforms
Does the strength of the reform matter?	Stronger reforms work better	Perhaps slower introduction better for investment reforms
Does an initial failure produce more failures?	No	No
Is the proper sequencing of policies important?	Yes: end quantitative restrictions first	Possibly yes: reform investment restrictions before investment incentives; trade policies before investment regimes
Does the accompanying macroeconomic policy matter?	Yes	Yes
What effect does reform have on the budgetary position?	Ambiguous	Possibly positive
Is a sound macroeconomic climate important before launch?	Yes	Yes
Do disagreements with outsiders play a role?	No effect	Possible yes to initiate and sustain the reforms
Is political stability important?	Yes	Yes

Chile, Uruguay and Israel. In all four cases, trade reforms resulted in large inflows of capital, and in the three Latin American cases, these inflows led to strong currency appreciations. Once the capital inflows stopped, sharp depreciations of the currency followed.

One final part of the study worth noting relates to income distribution. Because of the many factors that affect the income distribution, the authors found it difficult to devise a theoretical case that would explain why trade reforms would necessarily improve income distribution. Trade reforms would unleash many forces, some of which would operate in opposite directions on wages and incomes of the lower income groups. The empirical evidence from the 36 episodes was also mixed. The authors note that since devaluations accompanying trade reforms normally raise incomes of workers in the manufacturing and traded goods sectors relative to incomes in the service sectors, some improvement in income distribution should occur. This assumes that the prior trade policies resulted in an overvalued exchange rate, depressing incomes in the tradeable goods sectors.

Liberalization of Trade and Capital: A Case Study of Turkey

One recent evaluation by Aricanli and Rodrik (1990) of the 1980–1984 Turkish liberalization confirmed a number of the conclusions emphasized in the World Bank study, but at the same time went further in underscoring the need for policy credibility. In the late 1970s, Turkey faced, as did many other developing countries, a debt crisis of major proportions. In January 1980, Turkey initiated a new exchange rate policy that produced a real devaluation of the lira of over 50 percent by 1987. In line with the World Bank's findings on the characteristics of successful liberalizations, the government introduced austerity measures that dried up the home market, leaving manufacturers no alternative but to export. The government launched an export promotion campaign, backed by tax rebates and other subsidies. The government reformed public enterprises and announced a plan to privatize public holdings throughout the economy. It introduced various financial liberalizations, in particular the deregulation of interest rates, resulting in positive real interest rates for the first time in many years. In 1984, the government liberalized imports by replacing the positive list (goods that could be imported) with a negative list (goods that could not be imported), although tariffs were later increased several times to provide new revenues.

At the same time as the general financial liberalization, the government began to unwind restrictions that had severely limited FDI: the approval process was simplified and other bureaucratic impediments were removed. Liberalization efforts were intensified in 1985 to 1986 when, according to Aricanli and Rodrik (1990), all "conceivable disincentives" to foreign investment were eliminated. The result of these reforms was marked success in achieving greater exports and almost total failure in attracting foreign investment. One reason lay in the danger identified by the World Bank study: simultaneous liberalizations can spell trouble. However, in the case of Turkey, investment reform did not result in exchange-rate-appreciating inflows of capital. No capital flowed in. Why?

As Aricanli and Rodrik emphasize, "Foreign investors continue[d] to doubt the durability of reforms and the stability of the financial system" (1990, 1348). In other words, policy credibility was not achieved. While the reforms were sustained in the World Bank's terminology, they were not viewed as stable by investors. The government tinkered constantly with tariffs, tax rates, controls and other measures trying to fine tune the reforms. The constant tinkering planted seeds of doubt in the minds of foreign investors that no amount of success in other areas, such as exports, could overcome.

Investment Reforms and Long Term Economic Growth

The focus of the research reviewed above was on the liberalization process and its impact on prices, employment and growth in the short term. All of the studies concluded that liberalization would improve the allocation of resources and increase the prospects for sustained economic growth, but none demonstrated it. It would be difficult in empirical research to separate out the many factors that contribute to economic growth and show that liberalization was linked to one or more of these factors. As noted earlier in this paper, no good empirical measures of investment regimes and investment liberalization exist, so linking a very qualitative concept to quantitative data on growth is an act of statistical desperation.

Since a direct attack on this question is ruled out, two indirect approaches can be pursued. First, since liberalization of foreign investment has a high probability of increasing exports, how does long term economic growth benefit from exports? Second, what does modern growth theory have to say on the issue of capital accumulation and especially foreign investment?

The first question is addressed by Edwards (1993). He concludes that while substantial evidence exists to link export growth to economic growth, the issue is far from settled. In particular, Edwards finds that most studies have specified regression equations without the benefit of an underlying model theoretically linking exports to growth. Plainly, exports are a component of demand. Increases in this, or any other, component will produce higher rates of growth. But the authors surveyed by Edwards feel that exports provide an additional impetus to growth, perhaps stemming from positive externalities. Edwards finds the evidence on the externalities issue mixed and a fruitful area for further research.

The second question relates directly to modern economic growth theory. Paul Romer (1989) has provided a theoretical basis for establishing a long-run equilibrium relationship between openness and growth (Edwards 1993, 1389). Romer argues that where firms use capital, labor and a large number of specialized inputs, firms can either engage in production of final goods or devote resources to research and development (R&D). R&D efforts will result in a larger availability of intermediate products and a higher marginal product for capital. Freer trade allows firms to specialize in the intermediate products in which they have comparative advantage. Other authors, such as Edwards (1993) and Grossman and Helpman (1991) have devised models, showing that free trade permits greater transfers of technology from developed to developing countries. Very recently, Coe *et al.* (1995) have shown that even though governments in developing countries do not support R&D themselves, they can still enjoy the benefits of R&D done in industrial countries through the medium of inter-affiliate transfers from parent to subsidiaries. They found that "a developing country's total factor productivity is larger the greater is its foreign R&D capital stock, the more open it is to trade with industrial countries, and the more educated is its labor force. The foreign R&D capital stock only affects productivity when interacted with the import share. The estimated elasticities suggest that R&D spillovers from the North to the South are significant and substantial."

Although growth models do not directly address the issue of foreign investment, it is not difficult to see how liberalization of investment regimes can produce results parallel to those of trade liberalization. All of these models depend to some degree on indigenous production of R&D in developing countries. If one adds the assumption that foreign investment carries a greater initial capacity to generate R&D and that innovations are diffused throughout developing countries at a greater rate in the presence of foreign firms, then foreign investment is bound to accelerate the process of attaining higher long-run equilibrium growth rates.

What remains to be done, of course, is to put these theories to rigorous empirical test. As Edwards (1993) so correctly points out, most empirical testing of theories about growth are based on cross-section data have inherent limitations when it comes to drawing inferences about behavior over time. Some analysis of the effects of foreign investment over prolonged periods of time has begun, but is still in its infancy. Bajo-Rubio and Sosvilla-Rivero found, for example, that FDI "[was] one of the main factors underlying the strong growth rates experienced by the Spanish economy for the last thirty years" (1993, 104). Although they do not explore in detail the investment regimes under which FDI entered Spain during the period studied, it is clear from their narrative that Spain underwent several liberalizations that made increasing levels of FDI possible.

What We Learn From Simulations

The second major method available to examine the macroeconomic effects of investment liberalization is simulation through large-scale models. One such simulation model is SALTER, a multi-region multi-sector model of the world economy designed to examine the short-run and long-run effects of economic policies. (The following description borrows extensively from McDougall (1993).) The SALTER model had long been run without any equations describing the capital accumulation process and international capital movements. McDougall's contribution was to add equations that enabled simulations to be run, permitting capital to accumulate out of increased household saving and corporate profits.

All simulation models have their strengths and weaknesses that follow from the way they are structured. For example, the SALTER model does not track the economy through time. Instead, it compares alternative states of the economy at a single point in time. SALTER is a system of non-linear equations that describe the interactions between major regions of the world. SALTER does not permit national exchange rates within each region to vary. Instead the region's exchange rate moves against an international standard (such as Special Drawing Rights).

Adding capital accumulation and international capital mobility to the SALTER model involved one important change in the way the model is conceived. As noted, SALTER has been a comparative statics model with no time dimension. The essence of capital accumulation is, of course, a change in wealth over time. The McDougall extension involves an artificial step of solving the capital accumulation and mobility equations outside of the model, using certain assumptions about the time paths of the explanatory variables inside the model. The model assumes a representative international financial intermediary. One important limitation should be mentioned. There is no taxation on foreign income recipients. To incorporate withholding taxes would require an additional equation that explained the timing and rate of income repatriation. The SALTER model includes taxes on land, domestic capital and households.

Bijit Bora and Guisinger (1996) used the McDougall extension of the SALTER model to examine the long term general equilibrium aspects of liberalization. What we have found is not surprising. Investment liberalization produces an initial "shock" to the system, in this case represented by FDI raising the stock of host country capital. This larger capital stock produces higher real wages and higher returns to land. The real values of exports and imports increase, though for exports at a faster rate, sometime significantly so. Because of the closed nature of the model, there are no balance of payments effects — adverse or otherwise — because any trade surplus is offset by changes in net foreign income and net capital inflows.

Consumer prices fall or remain unchanged in most countries, though in a few countries inflation increases. The SALTER model does not allow for lax monetary or fiscal policies — government expenditures are always met by revenues, for example. There is a terms-of-trade effect associated with the capital transfer, as prices in the capital-importing countries fall, but rise in capital-exporting countries.

When the size of the capital shocks — the transfers of funds between host and home — increases, these features become more pronounced. Importantly, there seem to be no scenarios in which macroeconomic indicators take on alarming magnitudes. In short, foreign investment in the SALTER model is not a painless procedure, but the pain seems limited and small in relation to benefits.

Conclusion

This survey of the effects of investment liberalization on the macroeconomies of developing countries can be summed up fairly succinctly. Investment liberalization and trade liberalization cannot be treated as independent entities. Trade liberalization creates opportunities for foreign investors by expanding possibilities for goods exports. Investment liberalization creates opportunities to expand exports by bringing in new investment. Lessons can be learned from trade liberalization that have relevance for governments contemplating investment liberalization. The experience of developing countries in launching trade liberalization has been favorable. Based on studies by the World Bank and others, successful forms of liberalization tend to share some common characteristics. Reforms that are comprehensive and deep are likely to be more successful than those that are tentative. A sound fiscal and monetary policy is an important prerequisite. Trade reforms should generally be implemented before investment reforms. The research on long term growth suggests that foreign investment pays a positive and significant role, largely thorough the diffusion of technology from developed to developing countries.

Simulation models provide an independent source of information about the effects of investment liberalizations. Some very preliminary runs of the SALTER model suggest that the effects of investment are positive. No adverse effects in terms of inflation, deteriorating terms of trade, unemployment or balance of payments deterioration were observed in the various runs of the model.

In summary, optimistic agnosticism about the macroeconomic consequences of investment liberalization in developing countries seems warranted. The optimism arises from the fact that investment reforms, properly sequenced and coordinated with trade policy reforms and undertaken under conditions of sound monetary and fiscal policies, are likely to improve rather than worsen macroeconomic conditions in developing countries. The agnosticism is due to the fact that we cannot measure investment restrictiveness. Confirmation of this optimism must await better data and improved conceptual tools. While trade policy researchers possess good measures of the restrictive effects of trade protection and have moved far along toward generating convincing statistical evidence on the link between trade policies and various measures of economic activity, investment policy researchers are, metaphorically speaking, still reading tea leaves and animal entrails in trying to figure out how changes in investment policies affect economic performance.

Perhaps the time has finally come for a research effort on investment that parallels the large-scale comprehensive research projects on trade policy reviewed in this paper. Sales of overseas subsidiaries of multinational firms are more than double export sales. How far does this ratio have to rise before the World Bank, the OECD and other organizations that have traditionally funded research on international economic policy issues decide that investment policy deserves the same treatment as trade policy? Investment is still subject to heavy regulations and taxation. Policy makers will be making important decisions in the next few years concerning investment policy, not only with regard to initiatives, such as the Multilateral Agreement on Investment, but also on other important topics. Some in-depth longitudinal and comparative studies of the experience of both developed and developing countries with investment liberalization would be a valuable source of information for these officials.

References

Aricanli, T., and D. Rodrik (1990). An Overview of Turkey's Experience with Economic Liberalization and Structural Adjustment. *World Development* **18** (10), 1343–1350.

Bajo-Rubio, O., and S. Sosvilla-Rivero (1994). An Econometric Analysis of Foreign Direct Investment in Spain, 1964–1989. *Southern Economic Journal* **61**, 104–120.

Baldwin, R. (1992). Measurable Dynamic Grains from Trade. *Journal of Political Economy* **100** (1), 162–174.

Bond, E., and S. Guisinger (1985). Investment Incentives as Tariff Substitutes: A Comprehensive Measure of Protection. *Review of Economics and Statistics* **67** (1), 67–90.

Bora, B., and S. Guisinger (1996). *Impact of Investment Liberalization in APEC.* Working Paper, Department of Economics, Flinders University, Adelaide.

Coe, D., E. Helpman, and A. Hoffmaister (1995). *North-South R&D Spillovers.* Discussion Paper, Centre for Economic Policy Research, London.

Dee, P., C. Geisler, and G. Watts (1996). *The Impact of APEC's Free Trade Commitment.* Industry Commission, Canberra.

De Long, B., and L. H. Summers (1993). How Strongly Do Developing Economies Benefit from Equipment Investment? *Journal of Monetary Economics*, **32** (3), 395–415.

Edwards, S. (1993). Openness, Trade Liberalization, and Growth in Developing Countries. *Journal of Economic Literature* **31**, 1358–1393.

Grossman, G. M., and E. Helpman (1991). Trade, Knowledge Spillovers and Growth. *European Economic Review (Papers and Proceedings)* **35** (3), 201–223.

Guisinger, S. (1989). Total Protection: A New Measure of the Impact of Government Interventions. *Journal of International Business Studies* **20** (2), 280–295.

Jomini, P., R. McDougall, R. Watts, and P. Dee (1994). *The SALTER Model of the World Economy: Model Structure, Database and Parameters*. Industry Commission, Canberra.

Krueger, A. O. (1978). *Foreign Trade Regimes and Economic Development: Liberalization Attempts and Consequences*. Balinger, Cambridge.

Little, I., T. Scitovsky, and M. Scott (1970). *Industry and Trade in Some Developing Countries*. Oxford University Press, New York.

McDougall, R. (1993). *Incorporating International Capital Mobility in SALTER*. SALTER Working Paper No. 21, Industry Commission, Canberra, June.

Papagergiou, D., A. Choksi, and M. Michaely (1990). *Liberalizing Foreign Trade in Developing Countries: The Lessons of Experience*. The World Bank, Washington.

Romer, P. (1987). Growth Based on Increasing Returns Due to Specialization. *American Economic Review* **77**, 56–62.

IS THERE COMPETITION FOR FOREIGN DIRECT INVESTMENT?

Joel Bergsman[1]

A revolution has occurred in attitudes toward incoming foreign direct investment (FDI). Especially in the developing world, the fear and loathing of FDI that prevailed during the 1960s and 1970s have been transformed almost universally into a desire to get more of it: *dependistas* have lost out to *entregistas.* In Western Europe, few policymakers would now pay much attention to the pleas for restricting inward FDI first advanced in 1968 by Jean Jacques Servan-Schreiber in *Le Defi Americain* (*The American Challenge*, 1993). Korea and India, two strong holdouts against this trend, have also reversed to a significant extent. Canada has moved from regulation to promotion. Among the industrialized countries, perhaps only Japan retains its *de facto* unwelcoming stance.

This shift in attitude among many less developed countries (LDCs) is due in part to scarcity of other sources of capital. Concessional aid funds have expanded a bit in absolute terms, but are harder and harder to find for many countries, and commercial lending — the recycling of the Organization of the Petroleum Exporting Countries (OPEC) surplus — dried up after its "bubble" in the 1970s and early 1980s. Among all countries, FDI is sought not only, or even mainly, as a source of financial capital. FDI is almost always associated with other things that all countries, especially

[1]Contributions from Sanjaya Lall, Charles-Albert Michalet and Neda Pirnia are gratefully acknowledged. All views expressed in this paper are those of the author alone and do not necessarily reflect the positions or policies of the IFC or the World Bank.

developing countries, need as much or more — management skills, technology, and access to export markets. Neither aid, commercial lending nor Eurodollar loans bring these inputs with them, so the appeal of FDI is multi-dimensional.

While this about face has been taking place in country attitudes, the nature of international business has been changing too. In the 1950s and 1960s, "multinational" corporations (MNCs), regardless of the label chosen, tended to have more or less independent operations in the several countries in which they were located. As described by a friend who was for a while head of Brazilian operations of a large manufacturing MNC, headquarters gave him almost complete latitude in running operations in Brazil, and cared only about his bottom line. Today, in that same MNC as in most others, operations in Brazil, Scotland, China, and a dozen other countries are designed interdependently. Production of various parts and components, assembly, licensing, and similar activities are located in various countries according to something that approximates a coherent world-wide strategy.

Although this strategy may not be fully worldwide or even fully coherent, increasingly MNCs have become truly "inter-" or even "trans-" national, rather than simply "multi" — that is, they optimize, or strategize, or at least think, in terms of one integrated world-wide system involving all or most of their subsidiaries. Such a strategy includes not only subsidiaries or other companies linked by common ownership, but also quite a few other companies with whom they have more or less formal alliances. These MNCs locate different operations in different countries according to how well their entire system works together. Even within a single product line, engineering may be in one or two places, for example, production in different ones, and financing in yet another. [Michael Porter (1990, 1993) is a leading explicator of this phenomenon.] Their home is the world.

Part of this phenomenon, which is usually called "globalization," is that fewer and fewer production facilities will be located where there is no chance to produce at nearly world-competitive standards of quality, reliability and cost. MNCs may not choose to export from every single factory they run, but they tend to want any new factory they build to be at (or at least near) international standards, and they want the country to have a policy framework and physical environment that is friendly to exports. These and other changes in international production have made it much more costly for countries that do not offer such conditions. The MNCs themselves are in a much more competitive environment today. Their own choices of sites are constrained: they cannot afford to pick a non-competitive location. Countries that are not able to attract MNCs find it much more difficult than it used to be to acquire or develop up-to-date technology or to break into export markets. From the viewpoint of world trade and industrial competitiveness, the distribution of nations is tending to become dichotomous: either a country offers conditions that attract MNCs and thus can compete, or does not and cannot.

In their quest for more FDI in this environment, country after country has established its investment promotion agency. These agencies are vying to attract the most investment — often engaging in bidding wars, especially for large and/or technologically sophisticated investments. Ireland and Singapore, two of the leaders in this game, have become sources of consultants who go all over the world to tell other countries how to do it. The Foreign Investment Advisory Service (FIAS), where I work, counts advice on this topic as one of its core business products and our colleagues at the Multilateral Investment Guarantee Agency of the World Bank Group (MIGA) have a unit devoted to nothing else.

Officials of these promotion agencies seem to be in no doubt that they are in a fiercely competitive business. They see the product that they sell — their country as a site for foreign investments — in competition with sites in other countries, and they are inventing and using all the marketing devices they can think of (or can afford) to convince the potential buyers — executives of multinational companies — to buy from them and not from the competition.

But is it so? In what senses are these countries actually competing with each other? If Indonesia gets a motorcycle plant, does that mean that Thailand or the Czech Republic or Mali does not get one? Do MNC executives start with an idea for an investment project and analyze alternate sites for it, or do they look at sites, one by one, and in each case decide what kind of investment, if any, they should put there?

Some Suggestive Macro Evidence

A corresponding revolution — I argue, a response — to the opening of countries to FDI has occurred in the amounts of such investment, to developed and developing countries alike. This revolution is the explosion in FDI since the late 1980s. The total amounts are much larger than was thought possible just a decade ago.[2] Total FDI flows worldwide increased from around $80 billion per year throughout the 1980s to $360 billion in 1997 — tripling in the last ten years. Flows of FDI to developed countries doubled while flows to developing countries grew even faster, increasing by a factor of twelve from their 1980s plateau of around $10 billion annually to the astonishing levels of over $100 billion annually in 1995, 1996, and 1997.[3]

These increases in FDI are the result of a combination of three mutually reinforcing factors. Huge improvements in transportation, communication, and automation have played a major part. The second factor is the opening up of countries to FDI, the deregulation of their markets, and the greater economic stability of at least a few important host countries — in a phrase, the increase in the number of good places to do business. A third factor is the response of the MNCs, which are seizing those increased opportunities by increasing their investments.

Even at the current high levels, FDI flows are still only a small proportion of total available investable resources. Worldwide FDI is less than 5 percent of total gross saving. This fact, and the recent explosion in amounts of FDI, suggest that there may be no significant supply constraint on FDI. And if there is no supply constraint, in what sense can there be competition?

Interview Results Regarding Eastern Europe

Macroeconomic data and reasoning do not always convince individuals whose day-to-day experiences seem different. (Indeed, such data and reasoning,

---

[2]It is important to distinguish FDI from portfolio investment. The latter is purely financial; the investors have no intent (or ability) to exercise any control over the running of the company in which they invest. As seen many times during the last fifteen years, portfolio investment can be dangerously volatile. Direct investors have longer term interests, and often hold assets that are far less liquid.

[3]The developed–developing country division is that of the World Bank, which puts Korea, Singapore, Hong Kong (China) and Taiwan (China) into the developed category. UNCTAD classifies these as developing, and hence shows even bigger increases in FDI inflows to developing countries.

by themselves, probably *should not* convince anyone.) The business of attracting FDI to any particular place feels extremely competitive and developing country governments often fear that increases in FDI to one country are at the expense of others. That fear multiplied around ten years ago when Central and Eastern European countries abandoned socialism, began to create market economies, and opened their economies to FDI. There was a fear that these reforming countries, with their cumulatively huge market, unsatisfied consumer demands, significant scientific and engineering skills, low labor costs in relation to the European Union, and a large array of state-owned enterprises to be privatized, might well divert a substantial amount of FDI that otherwise would have gone to developing countries.

Partly in response to those concerns, FIAS formed a team to investigate the strategies of foreign investors in relation to the opening of the formerly socialist economies of Europe. Team members who are experts on FDI interviewed executives of more than 120 MNCs in seven sectors (including some in the service sector) in the United States, Canada, Japan, and Western Europe. We asked why they had, or had not, invested in this newly opened region, whether or not their investments there were alternatives to investments in other regions, and the extent to which specific developing countries were live options in competing for investments that did go, or might have gone, to Central or Eastern Europe. The developing countries about which we asked were several "Mediterranean Rim" countries, for example, Egypt, Morocco, Tunisia and Turkey, as well as some major FDI destinations in Asia, such as Indonesia, Malaysia, and Thailand.

The responses showed little or no competition for FDI between Central and Eastern Europe and the developing world. Virtually all of the companies that had invested in Central and Eastern Europe did not seriously consider alternatives in other regions. Typically the Mediterranean Rim countries were considered to lack strong advantages. The Asian countries, although seen as attractive, were either complementary parts of the multinational's global strategy or else not relevant to the more localized strategies being pursued through investments in Europe. Sub-Sahara Africa was *a fortiori* not interesting to these investors, regardless of whether Central and Eastern Europe had opened up or not. There was, however, somewhat more competition *among* the countries within Central and Eastern Europe (Michalet 1997).

Actual flows of FDI mirror these responses of the company executives. Through 1994, no more than about $6 billion per year of FDI flowed into Central and Eastern Europe. Since 1995 the flows increased to between $13 billion and $15 billion, as Hungary, Poland and (for a time) Russia attracted more than they had earlier. These increases (from almost zero earlier) occurred simultaneously with much larger increases into other regions. Brazil received more FDI in *one month* recently than the Russian Federation has received in the *five years* from 1992 to 1996! China gets three or four times as much as Brazil. The simultaneity of these increases again suggests (although it does not prove) that there has not been any supply constraint in operation. The lion's share of the explosion in FDI to the Third World has gone to Asian and Latin American countries, most notably China, as well as Argentina, Brazil, Mexico, Malaysia and a few others. China alone receives more than three times the amount going to all Central and Eastern European countries combined, and Argentina, Brazil, and Mexico each receive as much.

The following statement by Merrill Lynch about China confirms this assertion that there is no significant constraint on the supply of FDI.

> Foreign investments in Asia have always been analyzed from the angle of competition between Southeast Asia and the newcomers, particularly China. Interestingly, IMF figures reveal that the surge of foreign investments in China over the last few years was accompanied by a concurrent increase in foreign investments in Southeast Asia, in terms of both absolute values and as a percentage share of the global total. While this is not meant to say that competition does not exist, the statistics do highlight that the available pool of foreign investment for Asia is not a fixed sum. One country's gain thus may not be another country's loss (Merrill Lynch 1995).

Incentives: One of the Main Instruments of Competition

Since incentives are one of the main instruments of competition, experience in that field should shed some light. FIAS is often asked to advise governments on their corporate tax systems and, in particular, on how to fashion fiscal incentives for investors. FIAS has made comparisons of corporate tax burdens for the Visegrad countries in Central Europe, Russia, a group of Mediterranean

Rim countries, the Maghreb Union in North Africa, and the Association of South East Asian Nations (ASEAN) group in Asia. FIAS has also worked on business tax systems in Hungary, Jordan, Bulgaria, Thailand, Romania, Malaysia, Namibia, Nepal, Senegal, and Trinidad and Tobago.

In this work, especially at a recent seminar for Asian countries FIAS conducted in Bangkok, we found a striking difference of perception between foreign investors on the one hand and governments on the other concerning the influence of investment incentives on FDI location choices. Governments seem to like giving incentives. According to a study conducted by the United Nations Conference on Trade and Development (UNCTAD) (1995), out of 103 countries reviewed, only four did not offer any kind of incentive to foreign investors during the early 1990s, and the number and range of incentives of all types seems to have increased in all regions. This wide use of incentives is in contradiction to the great majority of studies of industrial location. Both interview surveys and econometric analyses conclude that incentives do not seem to have much impact on the decisions of most investors.

There is a voluminous literature on locational incentives. For our purposes, a look at a few of the landmarks will suffice. More than 35 years ago, Robinson (1961) published the results of a survey of 205 companies involving 365 investments in 67 countries. The pattern that Robinson's research found is essentially the same as dozens of other studies published since then: Government officials rated incentives high on the list while executives of MNCs did not (see Table 1).

Reuber (1973) argued that all MNCs are not the same and that they respond differently to different types of incentives, depending on their motivations. Reuber studied 80 investment projects. Among export-oriented projects, fiscal incentives (including tax holidays, duty remission, and accelerated depreciation) were said to have been important in 48 percent of the investment decisions, whereas among investments aimed at the domestic market, 56 percent of responses named protection as the important factor. In a major study conducted in 1985, Guisinger and Associates (1985) reached the same conclusion. This latter study also added an important dimension to the question: investors generally do not consider incentives as a determining factor in their investment if the incentives are more or less matched by

Table 1. Importance[1] Attached to Incentives: Governments versus Investors

Government		Investors	
Tax concessions	41%	Effective development planning and execution	79%
Equal treatment of domestic and foreign investors	37	Liberal capital and profit repatriation rules	79
Positive business climate	31	No restriction on foreign ownership and control	67
Liberal capital and profit repatriation rules	30	Equal treatment of domestic and foreign investors	66
		Minimum red tape	54

Source: Robinson (1961)

[1]Frequency that item was mentioned as important.

competitor countries. Less sophisticated surveys had simply asked whether incentives had influenced an investment decision; in the context of similar incentives being available from many countries, most investors responded, "no." Guisinger asked a different question: would it have made a difference if the country offered no incentives while competing countries did offer them, and a significant number of investors answered, "yes."

More recently, Rolfe *et al.* (1993) noted that preferences are also a function of factors such as the timing of investment (initial or expansion) and the type of process (manufacturing or services). Start-up firms prefer incentives that reduce their initial expenses while expanding firms that are already generating profits will also be pleased with tax-related incentives that affect after-tax profit. Manufacturing firms, requiring larger investment in fixed assets, are more likely to value incentives related to depreciable assets than are service industries. My colleague Wayne Edisis and myself, in a study of the effectiveness of debt-equity swaps as incentives to investors in Latin America in the 1980s, confirmed the importance of reducing initial expenses: the swap discount reduced the cost of the initial investment and did not depend upon future profits. This immediate, certain incentive not only increased the expected return but reduced the amount at risk. It affected the investment decision in more than half of the cases studied (Bergsman and Edisis 1988). This result is consistent with the success of Ireland and a few other countries and regions that seem to have attracted substantial quantities of investments with generous incentive packages including up-front grants.

In sum, understanding where incentives are effective shows us where there is competition for FDI. Basically, competition exists:

- for foot-loose, export-oriented investments;
- among countries or regions that are similar to neighboring countries or regions, and;
- among places where the other aspects of the business climate are also favorable.

There is competition, at least potentially, for *every* footloose investment. In fact, that could be the operational definition of "footloose." There is also some competition for some other investments, among similar, usually neighboring countries that have acceptable investment climates. This competition is particularly keen when the competing locations are parts of the same large market, such as one state within the United States, or one country within the European Union. (Guisinger's research highlights this point.) But such competition is effectively limited to countries with *good and similar* investment climates, and to products with significant economies of scale. Hungary and Poland are not competitors for a Coca Cola plant, but they might be for an auto assembly plant. Belarus is not in the competition with Hungary or Poland for that auto assembly plant since it is so different from either country. The likelihood is that at most the company is considering Poland, Hungary and the Czech Republic.

Many of the investors interviewed about Central and Eastern Europe had considered, or were considering, options among countries in that region for some investments. There is some competition among those countries, but there is almost none among regions. This competition comes not primarily from any scarcity of resources, whether financial or even the time of MNC executives. It comes simply from the fact that for *some* investments and some MNC strategies, there is more than one country with an appropriate location. Competition exists for those investments, among the (usually) few, (usually) neighboring countries that offer similar (and satisfactory) investment climates.

Conclusion

FDI is not limited by the availability of capital, time of MNC executives, or any other supply constraint. Rather, it responds to good opportunities — if there are more opportunities, then there will be more FDI. It is not a zero-sum game. The bulk of FDI that goes to a country that improves its investment environment is not being diverted from other host countries. The main exception is low-tech, cheap-labor-intensive, light manufacturing. FDI in these activities is still important but growing less so as technology changes. Individual countries that want more FDI should not worry about how much other countries are getting. Instead, they should put their own houses in order. How?

The basics of the policy environment continue to be:

- security of persons and property from criminal threats;
- stable politics, decent governance, and stable and sensible economic policies;
- a convertible currency or access to it;
- avoidance of excessive restrictions and regulations;
- a decent and functioning legal system — not only the laws but also the courts and the processes for enforcement.

Only a handful of countries have inherent attractions that are strong enough to draw any significant amount of FDI without these basics. Even Russia, for example, has not attracted much FDI. In the age of globalization, requirements are getting more rigorous. Corporations are increasingly unwilling to produce at less than international cost and quality standards, even if they can make a profit in a protected market. Moreover, the MNCs themselves are under ever greater competitive pressures and cannot afford to settle for less. Increasingly, countries must offer potential investors the facilities needed to be internationally competitive. These facilities vary greatly from one activity to the other, but among the *sine qua non* for the higher-value-added parts of most production chains are the following:

- an environment that facilitates exports. This includes a stable and appropriately valued currency, access to needed imported inputs at world quality and prices, financing, good international transport infrastructure, reasonable taxes, and no quotas or other restrictions on exports;

- good international communications facilities and reliable infrastructure services in general;
- decent business support services;
- a labor force that is educated, trainable, and working under laws and rules that permit flexibility;
- a businesslike government that delivers what it promises and facilitates rather than hassles the operation of privately-owned companies in an open market environment.

By definition, every locality has a comparative advantage in something, but not all such activities are attractive to foreign investors. Countries that do not have large and rich markets, minerals or hydrocarbons, or convenient locations have to work harder. Success is possible, as Korea, Mauritius, and Switzerland attest. Estonia has created a niche for itself by simply having a more honest, businesslike, and facilitating government than its competitors. Within the Russian Federation, several regions such as Novgorod, Nizhny Novgorod, Vladimir, Samara and others are doing the same. As far as FDI is concerned, there seems to be no supply constraint. It will come if an attractive environment in which to do business exists.

References

Bergsman, J., and W. Edisis (1988). *Debt-Equity Swaps and Foreign Investment in Latin America.* IFC Discussion Paper No. 2, October.

Bergsman, J., and S. Lall (1995). How to Get More Foreign Investment. *Financial Times*, July 18.

Guisinger, S. & Associates (1985). *Investment Incentives and Performance Requirements.* Praeger, New York.

Merrill Lynch (1995). Direct Foreign Investments in Southeast Asia Revive. *Asian Economic Commentary*, April 2.

Michalet, C. A. (1977). *Strategies of Multinationals and Competition for Foreign Direct Investment.* Foreign Investment Advisory Service, Occasional Paper No. 10, December.

Pirnia, N. (1995). *The Role of Investment Incentives In Influencing Investors' Locational Choices: A Literature Survey.* Foreign Investment Advisory Service.

Porter, M. E. (1990). *The Competitive Advantage of Nations*. Free Press, New York.

Porter, M. E. (1993). Changing Patterns of International Competition. *California Management Review,* Winter 1986, 9–40; reprinted in United Nations, *Library on Transnational Corporations*, Vol. 4, 138–169.

Reuber, G., H. Crookell, M. Emerson, and G. Gallais-Hamonno, (1973). *Private Foreign Investment in Development*. Clarendon Press, Oxford.

Robinson,. H. J. (1961). *The Motivation and Flow of Private Foreign Investment*. Stanford Research Institute, Menlo Park, California.

Rolfe, R. J., D. Ricks, M. Pointer, and M. McCarthy (1993). Determinants of FDI Incentive Preferences of MNEs. *Journal of International Business Studies* **24** (2), 335–355.

Servan-Schreiber, J. Jacques (1993). Excerpts from *The American Challenge*. In United Nations, *Library on Transnational Corporations*, Volume 7, 51–67.

United Nations Center on Transnational Corporations (1992). *The Determinants of Foreign Direct Investment: A Survey of Evidence*. United Nations, New York.

United Nations Conference on Trade and Development (1995). *Incentives and Foreign Direct Investment: Background Report by the UNCTAD Secretariat*. Geneva.

Wells, L. T. (1986). Investment Incentives: An Unnecessary Debate. *CTC Reporter*, Autumn, 58–60.

INDEX